LOVE AS A WAY OF LIFE

Love
AS A WAY OF LIFE

SEVEN KEYS TO TRANSFORMING
EVERY ASPECT OF YOUR LIFE

GARY CHAPMAN

DOUBLEDAY

New York London Toronto Sydney Auckland

DOUBLEDAY

Copyright © 2008 by Gary Chapman

All Rights Reserved

Published in the United States by Doubleday, an imprint of The Doubleday Publishing Group, a division of Random House, Inc., New York.

www.doubleday.com

DOUBLEDAY is a registered trademark and the DD colophon is a trademark of Random House, Inc.

LIBRARY OF CONGRESS CATALOGING-IN-PUBLICATION DATA
Chapman, Gary D., 1938–
    Love as a way of life : 7 keys to transforming every aspect of your life / Gary Chapman.
        p.   cm.
    1. Love—Religious aspects—Christianity. 2. Interpersonal relations—Religious aspects—Christianity. I. Title.
    BV4639.C424 2008
    241'.4—dc22

                                                        2007050546

ISBN 978-0-385-51858-1

PRINTED IN THE UNITED STATES OF AMERICA

10 9 8 7 6 5 4 3 2 1

FIRST EDITION

To Davy Grace and Elliott Isaac and the

children of their generation, with the prayer

that they may succeed in creating a world

in which love will be a way of life.

Contents

ACKNOWLEDGMENTS ix

INTRODUCTION xi

PART ONE: WHY WE WANT TO LOVE

CHAPTER ONE *The Satisfaction of a Loving Life* 3

PART TWO: THE SEVEN SECRETS TO LOVE

CHAPTER TWO *Kindness* 15
Discovering the Joy of Helping Others

CHAPTER THREE *Patience* 40
Accepting the Imperfections of Others

CHAPTER FOUR *Forgiveness* 65
Finding Freedom from the Grip of Anger

CHAPTER FIVE *Courtesy* 86
Treating Others as Friends

CHAPTER SIX *Humility* 111
Stepping Down So Someone Else Can Step Up

CHAPTER SEVEN *Generosity* 133
Giving Yourself to Others

CHAPTER EIGHT   *Honesty* 159
Revealing Who You Really Are

PART THREE: MAKING LOVE A WAY OF LIFE

CHAPTER NINE   *Making Love a Way of Life in Marriage* 187

CHAPTER TEN   *Making Love a Way of Life in Parenting* 200

CHAPTER ELEVEN   *Making Love a Way of Life in the Workplace* 210

CHAPTER TWELVE   *The Motivation to Love* 220

EPILOGUE **229**

NOTES **231**

READERS' GUIDE **237**

Acknowledgments

This book would not have been written without the scores of individuals who have modeled love for me as a way of life. My first taste of love came from my parents, Sam and Grace. While Dad is deceased, I'm still trying to return to Mom some of the love that she gave to me. Karolyn, my wife for more than four decades, has been my most intimate source of love. She speaks my love languages and does so without prodding. My two grown children, Shelley and Derek, bring me great joy as I see their lifestyle of love. Nothing could be more satisfying to a parent.

I am indebted to Jim Bell, who not only shared the idea for this book but also persistently encouraged me at each turn of the road. Tricia Kube has been my administrative assistant for twenty-six years. She not only computerized the manuscript but, as always, handled office details so that I could give attention to writing. Kay Tatum was of immense help in technical support.

In the process of writing, Elisa Fryling Stanford shared her editorial and writing skills to bring cohesiveness to the manuscript. Trace Murphy and the editorial team at Doubleday did an exceptional job in molding the finished product.

I must also thank the scores of individuals who have shared their observations of love along the road of life. In my seminars and on the Internet, I have solicited stories from people who have "caught" others expressing love as a way of life. After all, it is "real life" examples that touch the heart and motivate us to aspire to love. Without their help, this book would have been lifeless. I hope that they will be rewarded when they see their stories encouraging others to pursue love as a way of life.

Introduction

My daughter, Shelley, and I boarded the plane in Phoenix feeling fortunate that we had been bumped to first class. I was assigned 4A, however, and she was seated in 7A, both window seats. All twenty-eight seats in first class were full, so we were hoping that someone would be willing to change seats so that we could be together for the four-hour flight.

Shelley said to the man seated in the aisle seat beside 7A, "Would you be willing to change seats so that I can sit with my father?"

"Is it an aisle seat?" the man asked.

"No, it's a window seat."

"Can't do that," he said. "Don't like crawling over people to get out."

"I can understand that," Shelley responded as she took her seat.

A bit later the man who had been assigned the aisle seat beside me arrived. I said, "Would you be interested in sitting in Seven A so that my daughter and I could sit together?"

He glanced back at 7A and said, "I'd be happy to."

"I really appreciate that," I said.

"Not a problem," he replied with a smile as he picked up his paper and moved to 7A.

Later I reflected on that incident. What accounted for the two different responses? The men were about the same age; late fifties or early sixties was my guess. Both were dressed in business attire. Yet one held to his aisle seat with tenacity, while the other freely gave up the aisle to accommodate our desire.

Could it be that one man had a daughter and the other did not?

Could it be that the man who freely gave up the aisle seat really preferred a window seat? Or was it just that they had gone to different kindergartens and had different mothers? Had one been taught to share and help people, while the other to "look out for number one"? Did one have a loving gene that the other did not get?

For decades I have observed similar events, both large and small, and have asked myself, *What makes the difference between "lovers" and those people who seldom show an attitude of concern and care for others? What are the characteristics of loving people? How were these character traits developed?*

In the past year, trying to answer these questions, I have traveled the country observing behavior, interviewing people, reading available research, and examining religious teachings and practices. I have also drawn upon my thirty-five years of experience as a marriage and family counselor.

In the course of this study of love, I've named what I believe are the seven characteristics of a loving person:

- Kindness
- Patience
- Forgiveness
- Courtesy
- Humility
- Generosity
- Honesty

These seven traits are not vague feelings or good intentions. They are habits we learn to practice when we decide to become authentically loving people. They are basic, practical traits that are doable in everyday life. Yet the result of making these traits a habit is remarkable: satisfaction in relationships.

Love is multifaceted. It is like a diamond with many surfaces yet one display of beauty. In a similar way, when put together, the seven key characteristics of love form a loving person. Each trait is critical. If you are missing one in your relationships, you are missing something significant.

I believe these traits are the keys not only to successful relationships but to success in all of life. That's because the only way to find true satisfaction in life is to love others well.

How to Use This Book

In *Love as a Way of Life* you will find many stories from people across the country who have discovered, or are trying to discover, the joys of living out the seven traits of a loving person. You will also find practical ideas on how to develop these characteristics in your own life. Let me suggest that you not rush through the book but instead take the time to explore each facet of love in every type of relationship in your life. With that in mind, please note that each chapter in Part Two includes the following elements:

- *Questionnaire.* This simple self-test will challenge you to think through how one of the seven loving traits is shown in your life. I encourage you to take this test before you read the chapter in order to alert your mind to your strengths and weaknesses in relationships as you read about the character trait.

- *A new definition.* Early in each chapter I provide my definition of what a certain character trait looks like in the context of authentic love.

- *Habits to acquire.* Because each of the seven traits of a loving person is a habit, acting them out in daily life is built on smaller habits. The boxes throughout a chapter give you ideas about how to make the concept of loving authentically a reality in your life.

- *Competitors.* We wouldn't need any book on love if we didn't have emotions, personal weaknesses, and circumstances to overcome in our relationships. Each of the seven character traits has many competitors, or enemies, but usually one competitor stands out. In this section of each chapter, I'll briefly look at one thing that might be working against developing a particular character trait in daily life. When we are alert to the competitors to love, we are better able to overcome them.

- ***"What would your relationship be like if . . ."*** I've found in my own life that it helps to dream about how things could be and then try to make those dreams real. This section, at the end of each chapter, encourages you to realize how different your relationships could be if you made some changes, even small ones, in how you relate to others.

- ***Making it personal.*** Whether you are reading this book alone or sharing the journey with a group, the questions at the end of each chapter will help you reflect on how the subject of the chapter relates to your life in specific ways. Since the goal of this book is that you not only will learn about love but will also become a better lover, at the end of this section I offer suggestions for personal growth.

Love as a Way of Life is for anyone who wants to have better relationships and succeed in life. Nothing has more potential for changing the world for good than loving actions that flow from people who value relationships. And as we'll discover, nothing brings more joy than genuinely loving others.

I have written this book not in the technical language of psychology or sociology but in the language of the man and woman who live down the street. I believe it is the common person like you or me who holds the key to creating a world in which relationships are valued above all else, in which serving others is normal and expected, in which children grow up to respect each other—yes, even love each other. This is not an impossible dream. It is in fact a dream within reach of each of us.

LOVE AS A WAY OF LIFE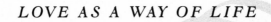

Part One

WHY WE WANT TO LOVE

CHAPTER ONE

The Satisfaction of a Loving Life

It is one of the beautiful compensations of life, that no man can sincerely try to help another without helping himself.

—RALPH WALDO EMERSON

You are a person with multiple relationships. Those relationships may include neighbors, coworkers, children, a spouse, parents, siblings, and friends. They undoubtedly include the clerk at the grocery store, the guy who just came to fix your plumbing, and even the woman who called you during dinner last night to ask you to take a "quick survey" although she wasn't "selling anything." In fact you have some kind of relationship with every person you interact with every day.

If you are like most people, you want to have the best possible relationships. However, it's likely that you've discovered how difficult relationships can be. We have misunderstandings over who gets the car, who washes the dishes, and even why someone left the coffeemaker on overnight in the break room.

When your close relationships are strained, you wonder if you're missing something, maybe something that other people have found. If love is so important, and you know that you love someone, why is the relationship still painful?

True Success

In my counseling office I have listened to hundreds of people share their stories of broken relationships and shattered dreams. Just last week a man told me, "I never thought this is where I would be at the age of forty-two. I have two broken marriages, seldom see my children, and have no purpose for living."

Most of us begin our adult journey with high aspirations. We expect to work hard, make money, accumulate things, have loving families, and enjoy life. For many people, these dreams turn to nightmares before the midpoint of life. The message of hope that I have sought to share in my office through the years is that life is not over until it is over. Today is the day to turn your life in a positive direction.

I believe the key to success is discovering the power of loving others. What does true success look like? Everyone seems to have a different answer: money, promotion, fame, tenure, winning the game. All these are legitimate pursuits, but what is the one thing that gives a true sense of accomplishment? My own definition of *success* is "leaving your corner of the world better than you found it." Your "corner" may be focused on a single town or a neighborhood within a city, or it may carry you to dozens of countries. Whatever your sphere of influence, when you are seeking to enrich the lives of others through relationships, you will find the most satisfying form of success.

The truth is, you are *made* for relationships. To experience the richness of loving relationships is better than anything money, fame, or professional acclaim could bring. If the word *love* sounds nebulous right now, my hope is that this book will help you see what love looks like in daily life. When we love others because we value them as individuals, we experience a joy unlike any other.

> **When you seek to enrich the lives of others,**
> **you find the most satisfying form of success.**

Why Another Book on Love?

The key to finding joy in loving others is to focus on *giving* love, not on getting it. That reality is my primary motivation for adding another book on love to the thousands of articles and hundreds of books that have been written on this topic in the last fifty years. Most of what has been written focuses on "getting the love you want." Receiving love is a beautiful result of loving others, but the pure joy of love comes first from having a loving attitude, no matter what we get in return.

AN ATTITUDE OF LOVE

More than a decade ago I wrote a book on how to express love effectively in our relationships. *The Five Love Languages* has now sold more than four million copies in the United States and has been translated into thirty-five languages around the world.[1] In *The Five Love Languages*, I looked at five primary ways we give and receive love:

- Words of affirmation
- Quality time
- Gifts
- Acts of service
- Physical touch

Each of us speaks some languages more naturally than others. If we speak the love language of someone else, she will feel loved. If we fail to speak her language, she will feel unloved even though we are speaking some of the other love languages.

The feedback from readers has been extremely encouraging. Thousands have written to say in effect, "Thank you for helping me do what I have always wanted to do: love others well."

What has been disturbing is the number of people who have indicated that they understand the concept of the five love languages but are not willing to learn to speak the love language of family members. One husband told me with great defiance, "If it is going to take washing dishes, vacuuming floors, and doing the laundry for my wife to feel loved, you can forget it." He had the knowledge of love but not the attitude of love.

I had made the assumption that if people knew how to express love effectively, they would be eager to do it. I now realize that assumption was wrong. Love languages are important ways to communicate love, but without a basis for the love languages, our words and actions are empty.

The seven traits of a loving person are not an add-on to the five love languages; they are the *foundation* for every language of love. In order to love effectively in any relationship, we need to use these seven habits to cultivate an attitude of love in the most ordinary of interactions.

THE ROAD TO GREATNESS

I am convinced that most of us have a desire to be better lovers. We want not only to care for others but also to love authentically in all our interactions. We feel good about ourselves when we expend energy to help others; it seems right and noble. We feel bad when we reflect upon our selfish actions.

When all is said and done, the most satisfied older adults are those who have invested their lives in giving love away. They may be people who have accumulated great wealth or they may live on meager incomes. They may hold positions of renown or they may be unknown to the larger world. But if they have invested in making the world a better place in which to live, a smile of contentment can be found on their faces. I don't know the details of your life, but I know that when the seven characteristics of a loving person become a natural part of the way you relate to others, you will find that kind of joy.

My desire is that *Love as a Way of Life* will help the husband who said "Forget it" to loving his wife realize that love is the road to greatness. I hope it will help you make the same discovery. As someone once said, everyone loves a lover. Self-centered living leaves us alone and empty. Love as a way of life leads to the deepest satisfaction possible.

The Meaning of Authentic Love

The meaning of the word *love* is often confusing because the word is used in so many different ways. Every day we hear people say things like, "I love the beach. I love the mountains. I love New York. I love my dog. I love my new car. I love my mother." On a romantic evening, they will say, "I love you." People even talk about "falling in love." Imagine that! I sometimes want to ask, "How far do you fall, and what does it feel like when you hit the ground?"

Love is not an emotion that comes over us or an elusive goal dependent on the actions of others. *Authentic* love is something within our capabilities, originating in our attitudes and culminating in our actions. If we think of love as a feeling, we shall be frustrated when we can't always work up that feeling. When we realize love is primarily an action, we are ready to use the tools we have to love better.

Authentic love brings out our authentic selves,
the people we want to become.

THE BEAUTY OF AUTHENTIC LOVE

Authentic love is as simple and real as the kind of love it takes to listen to an employee who is having a difficult day, to take your kids out for a back-to-school dinner in August, to donate money to the local fire department, to compliment a friend, to give your spouse a back rub before bed, or to clean the kitchen for your roommate when you are already tired from a long day of work.

Authentic love might be as bold as the kind of love that motivates people like Ruby Jones of New Orleans. This sixty-seven-year-old nurse chose to ride out Hurricane Katrina with her eight dying patients in the hospice unit at the Lindy Boggs Medical Center when the storm hit the shores of her city. "Don't try to be Superwoman," her children told her. Ruby was just trying to do her duty. She reported to work on Sunday and did not leave until Thursday, when her patients were evacuated. As the storm broke windows and blew open doors, she told her patients, "We are here with you, and we aren't going to leave." When the medical center lost power and drinking water and began flooding, Jones continued to bathe and feed her charges and dress their wounds. When she left on Thursday after her patients had been evacuated, she was hungry and thirsty, but she had kept her promise to stay with her patients until the end. During the most harrowing moments, love for her patients sustained her.[2]

Recently I visited a fifty-two-year-old mother of five who was dying of cancer. I had observed her life for a number of years and found her to be one of the most loving people I had ever met. She faced death with realism yet with a positive spirit. I won't forget what she told me: "I have taught my children how to live. Now I want to teach them how to die." Authentic love sees even death as an opportunity to love others.

CHOOSING TO LOVE

It's true that those who live lives of love are not exempt from the difficulties of life. If you have been told that love will alleviate all your problems, you were misinformed. History shows us that many people, even the most loving, not only have suffered earthquakes, floods, tornadoes, hurricanes, automobile accidents, sickness, and other afflictions but have even been persecuted for advocating a life of love.

How can a person endure such pain and still desire to pursue a love-filled life? Sometimes it is in the midst of difficulty that we find our greatest opportunities to experience and share love. One of the beautiful things about living a love-filled life is that we are not dependent on circumstances for our satisfaction. We find joy in our choice to love others, whether or not they love us in return and whether or not circumstances go the way we want them to.

Love might be accompanied by feelings of compassion for those we are helping. But first, love is an attitude that says "I choose to focus my life on helping others."

RADICAL LOVE

When we love authentically, we realize how radical true love can be. Love is enough to change a superpower. For example, by taking care of the poor and loving even their enemies, Christians in the first few centuries overcame a decaying, self-centered culture. They began by loving one another in small ways, sharing possessions and food and showing compassion to women, children, and other marginalized people of the time. The power-hungry, decadent culture of the Roman Empire accepted the new sect largely because observers said, "See how they love one another."

Serving others goes against the cultural norm of giving so we can get. We might not fit into the world around us when we set out to love others, but authentic love gives us the opportunity to discover a deeper joy than ordinary ways of the world can give.

A Matter of Survival

All this may sound good, but in a world of constant conflict, does love stand a chance? Our newspapers and television screens are filled daily with reports of our inhumanity toward one another, much of it perpetrated in the name of religion or out of personal greed. Watch any talk show and you will see that we have lost the art of meaningful dialogue. Any news program will remind us that we have little respect for those who disagree with us. Politicians and religious leaders seem to be in attack mode most of the time and rarely are willing to listen to one another.

I believe that not only does love stand a chance in this world, but in fact it is our *only* chance. If we can come to respect one another as fellow humans who need one another and choose to look out for one another's well-being, the potential for good is unlimited. If we fail to do so, we shall lose our dignity and we shall use the technological advances of the last fifty years to destroy one another. If we are going to solve the problems in our global society, we need the respect and meaningful dialogue that flow from love.

Is buying a homeless woman a bowl of soup or taking your daughter to the park or driving a coworker to the mechanic when his car breaks down really going to make a difference in the world? The answer is an overwhelming yes. We might have loftier ideas of what it means to love, such as making a grand sacrifice of time or money or even giving our lives, but why should we be willing to die for someone when we won't fill up the gas tank for her? Every trait of authentic love begins with small things.

If all of us become authentic lovers, we can make a difference in a world of turmoil. Love is not only realistic but our only hope of survival.

If you truly want to love someone,
begin in small ways.

How Can I Grow in Love?

No matter what our backgrounds are, being a loving person does not come without work. Something in our makeup as humans fights against our desire to love authentically.

The part of our nature that puts our own well-being above that of others could be considered our false self. The ego-centered pull of this false self is so pervasive that it has become a way of life for many. That is why when great lovers, such as some of the people we will meet in this book, appear on the stage, we are drawn to them. These authentic lovers are acting out the part of our nature that pushes us to love others. This true self serves others because only in serving do we find satisfaction in relationships. Whether we are conscious of it or not, when we act without love, we are not being true to our core identities. Because we are made for relationships, when we offer authentic love to someone, we are being who we really are.

Cultivating the seven characteristics of love helps us build the strongest possible relationships through our attitudes, lifestyles, and actions. When we fail to value relationships through these seven characteristics, we are negative toward others, restless, and ready to attack or defend.

When we make a decision to love authentically, our desire to grow in love and show our true selves begins to flow more naturally from our transformed hearts. Our role is to open our hearts and minds daily to receive love and to look for opportunities to share it with others. The more we do this, the more easily we love others.

THE POWER OF AUTHENTIC LOVE

The politician Lee Atwater is an example of a person who learned to live out of his true self. In the 1980s he was a successful consultant for the national Republican Party. His approach was to ruin the reputations of his political enemies by planting demeaning stories in the media. In the middle of his political career he was diagnosed with a life-threatening disease. Before his death he made telephone calls and wrote letters to those whom he had attacked, asking for forgiveness and expressing his sorrow over what he had done.

One of the recipients of these letters was a Democratic politician whose political life had been nearly destroyed when Atwater revealed an episode in the man's past. In Atwater's letter to this man he said, "It is very important to me that I let you know that out of everything that has happened in my career, one of the low points remains [that] episode."

The Democratic politician was deeply moved by Atwater's apology. He later attended Atwater's funeral and said, "I hope those young political consultants who would emulate Atwater's tactics of driving up the negatives of their opponents with the politics of fear will realize that Lee Atwater, confronting death, became . . . an advocate of the politics of love and reconciliation."[3] Atwater reminds us of the joy and rich relationships that come when we choose to act out of our true selves and express authentic love.

My hope is that as you go farther on the path of true love, you will enjoy seeing your attitudes and behaviors change. The journey toward a new level of loving will not end at the final page of this book, but reading stories about the seven traits of a loving person will allow you to taste the fruit of love and never again be satisfied with the dullness of a self-centered lifestyle. If you are successful, building genuine relationships will become such a habit of your days that the greatest joy you know will be in making love a way of life.

Making It Personal

Are you ready for the journey? If so, then perhaps you would like to sign the following commitment:

"I commit myself to reading and discovering the seven characteristics of love discussed in this book. I will seek to cultivate my heart with love for others. I want to love others as I in turn deserve to be loved."

Name _____ Date _____

1. How would you define success? How does your life today reflect the fact that you view success in that way?
2. How much of your life right now would you say is spent in expressing love to others?

3. Can you recall a specific act of love you have performed in the past week? How do you feel about what you did?

4. Of the seven characteristics of a loving person—kindness, patience, forgiveness, courtesy, humility, generosity, and honesty—which one comes most naturally to you right now? Which one is the most challenging?

Part Two

THE SEVEN SECRETS TO LOVE

CHAPTER TWO

Kindness

DISCOVERING THE JOY OF HELPING OTHERS

No act of kindness, no matter how small, is ever wasted.

— AESOP

"I've got this thing for people who are left out," Sylvia says. "When I saw him come in that first day, I made a special effort to say hello. He was scruffy, so I was drawn to him."

In his mid-fifties, James spent much of his time sleeping and drinking. He was homeless, but the local shelter wouldn't take in people who drank. So James, with a small group of his friends, slept in the city park. He started working at Sylvia's office after a couple who reached out to the homeless community had helped him find a job.

Sylvia, an energetic grandmother and part-time receptionist, made it a point to look for James every time she was at the office. He told her about his family and his past. They got to know each other.

When James told Sylvia he was going to New Mexico for a while, she wasn't sure she would see him again. Four months later he returned with news: He had cancer. He had gone to say good-bye to his mother, but she had turned him away. Now, scared and alone, he was back in town.

"He lived in a shoddy motel for a while because he wasn't sick enough to be in the hospital," Sylvia remembers, "but within a few months he was in a nursing home with government assistance."

Since James received no visits from his family, Sylvia started visiting him regularly as his health declined. They talked about his memories from childhood and the dreams he had about heaven. They talked freely of his fears and hopes about death. Over the months, Sylvia watched his body deteriorate as his pain increased. When James was too weak to talk, she held his hand and sang to him. When he died, Sylvia was the only person there.

"I don't remember thinking I was being kind," she says now. "It was just the thing to do. I talked to him. Paid attention to him. So many people are alone in this world; James didn't have to be."

Kindness means noticing someone else and recognizing his needs. It means seeing the value in every person we meet. And like every trait of a loving person, kindness can be much simpler, and more powerful, than we realize.

～ *Is It My Habit to Be Kind?*

As you take the following self-test, consider your most common words and actions. You'll quickly see that the goal as authentically loving people is for *c* to be the most natural answer to every question. But it's important to be aware of where you are *now* as you take steps to loving more authentically.

1. When I am in a public place, such as a clothing store, I . . .
a. Find myself snapping at people who get in my way.
b. Try to engage with as few people as possible.
c. Enjoy any opportunity to smile at someone.

2. When doing good for someone involves a sacrifice of time, money, or convenience on my part, I . . .
a. Dismiss the idea without seriously considering it.
b. Am willing to sacrifice if I know I'll get something in return.
c. Consider whether the sacrifice is worth it and try to make it work.

3. When someone is unkind to me, I . . .
a. React in anger.
b. Try to avoid that person as much as possible.
c. Look for a way to be kind to her.

4. When I hear of other people doing charitable activities on a Saturday afternoon, I . . .
a. Hope they don't ask me to participate, because they obviously have freer schedules than I do.

b. Feel guilty for not participating.

c. Consider how I could do something similar in my neighborhood.

5. When I see someone who dresses or acts very differently from me,
   I . . .

a. Feel superior to him.

b. Try to avoid him because he makes me uncomfortable.

c. Try to engage him in some way because he might be able to teach
   me something.

The Key to Love

When I was growing up, my childhood friends and I were taught from the Bible to be kind to one another, but not every child in my Sunday school class was kind. Some of the children were kind until someone stole their toys, messed up their artwork, or pushed them at the water fountain. When provoked, they forgot about kindness and went back to being ego-centered children. Their behavior said, "Don't mess with me or my stuff." A few of the children were almost never kind. On the whole, the children with whom I grew up seemed to be kind to the children who were kind to them and unkind to those who treated them unkindly.

My observation is that adults are not much different from children in this respect. A husband is kind to his wife when she is kind to him. He willingly takes out the garbage when she has cooked a good meal. He speaks kindly to her when she speaks kindly to him. He volunteers to wash her car after she has given him a pleasurable sexual experience.

But what does it look like to be kind in the face of injustice and ill-treatment? One husband shared his experience. "I had been harsh with my wife by cutting down her ideas and telling her that what she said was not logical. I raised my voice and told her exactly what I thought. She walked out of the room, and I returned to the ball game on television. Thirty minutes later she walked in with a sandwich, chips, and a Coke, all neatly arranged on a tray. She placed the tray on my lap and said, 'I love you.' Then she kissed me on the cheek and walked out. I sat there thinking: *This is not right. This is not supposed to happen.*

I felt like a jerk. Her kindness overwhelmed me. I put the tray down, went into the kitchen, and apologized." This wife demonstrated the kindness of authentic love, and it changed her husband's heart.

The irony is that making kindness a way of life brings great joy not only to others but also to ourselves. When we are kind no matter what, we see what a difference everyday choices make.

KINDNESS: the joy of meeting someone else's needs before your own simply for the sake of the relationship.

The Big Impact of Small Kindnesses

The four women at the corner table at Starbucks were laughing and talking. They also kept their eyes focused on the area where the cash register was located. Earlier that day they had pooled their money and bought a Starbucks gift card. "Please use this to ring up all the people placing orders until the card is empty," they had told the clerk. Then they had sat down to enjoy one another's company and the looks on the faces of patrons discovering that their coffee was free that day.

This same group of women spent a cold Saturday morning giving away hot chocolate to kids and parents at a junior high soccer game. They potted dozens of pansies and distributed them to residents in the local nursing home. When their friend Marcy was diagnosed with rheumatoid arthritis, they hired someone to clean her house once a month so she would have more energy to spend with her teenagers.

What strikes me most about this group of women is not just their commitment to acting kindly in the least expected places but their sheer delight in being kind. They love others because they know that love for the sake of love is worthwhile.

HABITS TO ACQUIRE
Be alert to the ways people around you are kind to you and others. Notice how kindness changes that encounter or relationship.

One of the steps in learning to express acts of kindness is to *observe* acts of kindness. Often, especially in the family, we take acts of kindness for granted. Someone cooks a meal, and someone washes the dishes after the meal, but no one acknowledges these simple but major acts of kindness. Someone washes towels, mops floors, cleans mirrors, and mows grass. These may be more than utilitarian acts; they may be a spouse's way of expressing love. But does anyone acknowledge these actions as ways of loving?

I sometimes challenge people to record every act of kindness they observe throughout the day. Here is one man's list of kindnesses he observed in one day:

- When I failed to respond to the alarm clock, my wife awakened me so I would not be late to work.
- When I drove out of my development, a man paused and waved me into the flow of traffic.
- When I got to the office, my administrative assistant had already booted up my computer.
- When I went for a break and did not have a dollar for the drink machine, a fellow employee loaned me a dollar.
- I went to lunch alone and was invited to sit with two men from another department. I enjoyed our conversation.
- In the afternoon, I received an e-mail from one of our customers, thanking me for the timely way in which I had processed his order. (I don't get many e-mails like that.)
- When I left the office building, a security man opened the door for me.
- As I pulled my car from the parking lot into the street, a woman in another car allowed me to merge into her lane.
- When I arrived home, Weasels (our dog) met me at the car, wagging his tail.
- When I walked inside, my wife greeted me with a hug and kiss.
- My wife had dinner under way. I washed my hands and helped her—my act of kindness. After we had eaten, I put the dishes in the dishwasher.
- After dinner, my wife volunteered to walk the dog while I took one final look at my e-mails.

- My wife joined me in watching the news.
- Later she went with me to the mall to look for a backpack.
- Before going to sleep, she kissed me and told me she loved me. It was a good day.

Many times people are surprised at the large number of kind acts they observe in a short amount of time. When we become aware of those acts and learn to express appreciation for them, our desire to show kindness grows as well. Once we desire to become a kind person, it becomes easier to recognize opportunities for kindness throughout the day. Such opportunities abound at home, in the workplace, in the grocery store, and anywhere else we encounter people.

I remember a day I dropped my shirts off at the laundry. When I returned to my car, I found myself sandwiched between two window-less vans. There was no way I could see approaching traffic from either side. A middle-aged man walking across the parking lot saw my plight. He looked both ways and motioned for me to pull out of my cave. I gave a friendly wave and said, "Thank you." As I left the parking lot, I thought, *What a kind man! He didn't have to do that. He could have looked the other way, but he saw my situation and chose to respond with an act of kindness.*

I still remember this act of kindness though it happened almost two years ago. This man's simple decision to stop and help me has inspired me to do the same for others. That's the beauty of acting kindly in our relationships and encounters: One act of kindness provokes another.

Why am I including such "small" examples of love under this crucial trait of a loving person? Because kind acts, whether small or large, reflect a desire to serve others, and *service* is at the heart of any loving person. Kindness means serving someone else even if it involves sacrifice. The women at Starbucks sacrificed money to bring joy to others. The man who helped me out of that parking spot sacrificed a few moments of his time that day. Large or small, acts of kindness communicate, "You are a person of value."

**We cannot love authentically if we are not willing
to sacrifice.**

A Matter of Survival

A number of years ago George H. W. Bush, then the president of the
United States, emphasized the value of community volunteers and pictured them as being a "thousand points of light" in the nation.[1] His im-
agery and lofty challenge received considerable media attention. The
Points of Light Foundation grew out of that challenge and continues
to coordinate volunteer efforts throughout the country.[2]

Kindness is not a political issue. It is a matter of human survival.
In a dog-eat-dog world, eventually there's only one dog left. Without
acts of kindness, the world becomes a dark and lonely prison for each
of us. With acts of kindness, we can help one another survive.

**In a dog-eat-dog world, eventually there's only
one dog left.**

CORPORATE KINDNESS

We all know stories of groups of people banding together to show love
to others. The popularity of the television series *Extreme Makeover:
Home Edition* demonstrates the strong attraction people have for acts
of kindness. Numerous people have told me that they cannot watch
the program without shedding tears of joy for the families that are
helped by Ty Pennington and his crew.

On the local scene, we have opportunities to volunteer in many
ways. For instance, every year the town of Longview, Washington, has
a Servant Week. Churches and organizations in Longview call up civic
organizations and ask, "What can we do to serve you?" For a full week
hundreds of volunteers take time out of their schedules to help with
everything from painting the fence at the golf course to organizing files

at city hall to spreading new mulch at city parks. People of all ages and backgrounds participate. They ask for nothing in return.

Such acts of kindness are displays of authentic love. Global catastrophes such as terrorist attacks, Hurricane Katrina, the Indian Ocean tsunami, and the AIDS epidemic of Africa often provoke generous displays of corporate kindness as well. Yet ask any aid worker or volunteer and she will say, "I'm the one who was privileged to help someone in need."

INDIVIDUAL KINDNESS

Soon after Renee moved with her family into a townhouse complex in Iowa City, she noticed that several of the elementary schoolchildren in her neighborhood had to walk to school; their homes fell just within two miles of the school, so they were not eligible to take the school bus. Most of the children lived in low-income households. Many of their parents either didn't have cars or didn't have driver's licenses. Some of the parents had to get to work early or worked the night shift and were sleeping when the kids left in the morning.

Renee knew it would be almost impossible to ride bikes on the snowy Iowa mornings that were soon to come, so she talked to the school principal about what could be done to help these kids get to school in the morning. Over the next year the principal passed Renee's phone number on to any family in the neighborhood that needed a ride. Renee picked up and dropped off her neighbors in her minivan on her way to and from school with her son. It was a simple act of kindness that came from noticing a need and doing something about it. As a result, she formed friendships with many of her neighbors and was able to show her son how easy it can be to help others.

Although corporate kindness is extremely important, especially in times of disaster, the more important need is for individual acts of kindness that are expressed as a way of life. Almost anyone can respond to a crisis situation because the need is so glaring. It takes a truly caring person to identify opportunities of kindness in the flow of daily life.

Kindness is at its best when we don't have to stop to think about it.

We often become so involved in our own concerns that we fail to see the needs of those around us. Once we see the needs, we must take the giant step from seeing to responding. That will probably mean sacrificing one or both of two prized possessions, money and time.

We might think we have too little of either of these resources to help others. We often reason, *I would get involved if I could, but since I can't, I'll make a contribution to charity.* Making a contribution to charity is indeed an act of kindness, and sometimes this may be the best thing we can do, but most of us have room for growth when it comes to personally offering expressions of kindness in everyday life.

More than two thousand years ago (that's two thousand years before the rush of faxes, iPods, and cell phones), the Greek philosopher Socrates warned, "Beware of the barrenness of a busy life." We might not think we have time to compliment the receptionist or to let the person at the front desk of the movie theater know that someone's car lights are on in the parking lot. Or we may be so preoccupied with the next thing on our agendas that we don't even make the choice whether to take the time to be kind or not. But how much more fulfilling our lives could be if people were more important to us than the clock!

When kindness becomes a natural part of our lives, we don't need to stop and think about whether it is worth it. All of us have different abilities and opportunities. The challenge is to use the knowledge and skills we have to meet the needs of those around us.

⌒ The Beauty of Kindness

One of the joys of writing this book was hearing stories from people across the country about how they have experienced kindness in their lives. Here are just a few examples of how we love one another:

- Karen from Ithaca, New York, told me about her friend Kathy who "spent six months taking a coworker friend to chemotherapy treatments. She also picked up prescriptions and spent time with her, helping her around the house."
- Spencer always sneaks a note of encouragement into his wife's suitcase before she leaves on a business trip.

- Debbie had a surprise celebration for the office janitor's anniversary with the company.
- Lauren brought Chris a cheeseburger, fries, and a milk shake, his favorite, when Chris couldn't leave the house after back surgery.
- Thirty years later Robert still remembers the neighbor who brought him a twenty-nine-cent head of lettuce because it was on sale.
- When Kyle arrived at work one morning, he discovered that his assistant had bought him a space heater for his office simply because she'd noticed the room got cold.
- Joseph writes, "I love you!" in the margins of the checkbook when he corrects an addition mistake his wife has made.
- When Helene and Alex returned from vacation, they found that their neighbor had mowed their lawn.
- An older friend told me, "I grew up with an alcoholic father and an overworked mother. Life was hard. But I had a loving grandmother who cared for me every afternoon when I got home from school. She always had cookies and milk and hugs for me. I shudder to think where I would be today if my grandmother had not been in my life."
- Kim took care of Dorothy's baby free of charge when Dorothy went back to work a few days a week.
- Mary brought in a pot of stew for her department on a snowy day.
- "No matter how many questions I asked as we watched a ball game," Nate remembers, "my dad always took the time to answer me and explain the rules."
- The day before Jasmine's in-laws arrived to meet their new grandson, a group of her friends descended on her house with scrub brushes, vacuums, and mops, and spent the afternoon cleaning for her.

A Change of Attitude

Most of us will admit that if we are going to become truly kind people, we need to experience a change of attitude. The false self of self-centered living says, "I'll be kind to you if you will be kind to me." The true self of authentic love says, "I'll be kind to you regardless of how you treat me." How do we feed the true self? How do we experience a change of attitude so that we are inclined to be kind to others even when they are strangers or (more difficult still) when we know them well and they treat us harshly?

KINDNESS CHANGES PEOPLE

Jake and Connie had a rocky marriage. Jake traveled extensively for his job and was rarely available to help with the kids. Connie complained, and Jake got defensive. Meanwhile, Connie's ongoing struggle with mental illness grew worse. At times she couldn't get to work in the morning or get the kids to school. As Connie grew weaker and needed Jake around the house more and more, his attitude toward his family gradually began to change. He stepped down in his company so he could be home more often, and he decided to see what kindness rather than selfishness could accomplish.

"I've realized," he says, "that I'm the best thing they've got going. I'm going to do everything I can to serve them and stop worrying about whether or not they're satisfying me. This is the kind of relationship some people leave, but I don't spend time thinking about that. I want to do the laundry, do the dishes, help the kids with their homework. I don't sit around thinking about what they're not doing or being for me."

Without a change in attitude, Jake might be tempted to give up. But he is choosing to express authentic love in the most difficult circumstances, believing that kindness brings healing. And he is beginning to see his kindness change the whole household. Connie laughs more and has more energy to be involved in others' lives. Their kids are thriving on structure at home and less hostility between their parents. Jake didn't know if he would see any change in his family when he chose kindness over anger, but he knew that only steady love had potential to bring his family together.

Our goal is never to use kindness to manipulate people. But when we see how a kind act can change a person—make a tired car mechanic smile or ease the stress of a demanding boss—we become more eager to be kind.

On a global level, history teaches us how kindness, more than hostility, can strengthen nations. Over the last few years, for example, the Guantánamo Bay detention camp has been a lightning rod for debate. Controversy reigns about the methods used to interrogate foreign detainees suspected of Taliban or al-Qaeda involvement. After several years of harsher methods of interrogation, however, officials are finding that "most of the productivity we see over time [in terms of collecting intelligence] comes from the milk of human kindness." When interrogators take time to earn the respect of a prisoner and "approach the subject in a friendly and businesslike manner," they are most likely to gather needed information.[3] We can never underestimate the influence of human kindness.

PUTTING ON KINDNESS

A second step in changing our attitude is realizing that each one of us has the potential to express kindness as a way of life. One of the kindest men I've ever met once told me, "Every morning I put on my glasses, my pants and shirt, my jacket, and my cap. Then I picture myself putting on the overcoat of kindness. I wrap it all around me and pray I will touch people through my kindness today." This man did touch the lives of hundreds of people. He mowed lawns for sick neighbors, raked leaves for the elderly, gave away recorded lectures and books to those he thought would listen or read, and paid camp fees for needy children. When he died, his funeral lasted more than three hours as people from all walks of life stood to share their encounters with his kindness.

When we wear kindness as part of our clothing, we don't stop to think about whether we should be kind in a certain situation. Wherever we go, kindness is our constant companion.

I once saw a television interview with a woman who had emerged from a horribly abusive marriage. When the interviewer asked her how she had survived, she said that sometimes all it took was a person smiling at her in the grocery store to help her get through the day.

No matter what our personalities, habits, or pasts, each of us has countless opportunities every day to be kind to people on the phone, at the office, and in the home. When we visualize ourselves wrapped in kindness each day, who knows what lives we might change?

WHEN KINDNESS IS REJECTED

The third aspect of a changed attitude is realizing that it is not our responsibility to make people respond positively to our expressions of kindness. We each have the capacity to receive and reciprocate love—

or to reject the love offered to us. When a person rejects our kindness, it's easy to pull back or get angry. But people are free to accept kindness with gratitude, to turn it away, to accuse us of selfish motives, or to reciprocate with expressions of kindness. Their response is out of our control.

Blake got hooked on drugs when he was ten years old. He went through his first drug program when he was thirteen and four more treatments before he turned twenty. Even after he had become a successful artist, he continually returned to drugs. Through years of this abuse, his mother, Marilyn, showed love to him. When doctors told Blake the drugs were damaging his heart, she loved him. When the drugs caused him to say horrible things to her, she loved him. "This is not my son," she said, always believing in the person she knew him to be.

At times love meant saying no to Blake when he needed money or refusing to let him stay with her because he would steal things from her home and sell them for drug money. But she always reminded him that she loved him. She felt called to be a presence of hope and acceptance in his life.

After two heart valve transplants, Blake was given two years to live. His mother didn't want him to die alone or in a care facility. She committed herself to taking care of him in her home until the end.

At the time of Blake's death he had not apologized for his actions, but his attitude was beginning to soften. He started to make eye contact with his mom, although he would not express gratitude for her care.

The title of the homily at Blake's funeral was "Love Is Enough," a tribute to the hope we have that kindness is always worth it. In a broken world, relationships do not always work the way we want them to. We might never see the influence of our acts of kindness. But when we love authentically, we are faithful even when loving is difficult.

True love always involves a choice. If someone reciprocates with kindness, we can have a meaningful relationship. If he rejects our expressions of kindness we can continue to hope that in time he will turn and walk toward us instead of away from us. In the meantime, our attitude is one of love: We desire his best and seek to express that desire with kindness. And we believe even in the darkest times that love will be enough.

 *Getting Started*

Here are some simple ways to show kindness in everyday life. I'm sure you can think of many more.

- Give a store clerk a compliment.
- Hold the door open for someone.
- Smile at a child. If he initiates conversation with you, listen.
- Host a free car wash in your community.
- Let the person behind you in line at the grocery store check out first.
- Share your umbrella with someone when it's raining.
- When going through a toll booth, pay the toll of the car behind you as well as your own.
- Mow your neighbor's grass, rake her leaves, or shovel her walk.
- Visit an elderly person.
- Tip people well.
- When someone is going through a difficult time, suggest things you might do to help, such as get groceries, watch the children, and clean the house, rather than say, "Let me know if I can help."
- Get several people together and go door-to-door in a neighborhood, asking if you can do yard work at no charge.
- Take your assistant out to lunch on her birthday.
- Be aware of what makes a friend or family member feel loved, and strive to communicate love in that way.
- If you notice someone excelling at his job, look for an opportunity to tell his boss.
- Call someone who has experienced a death in the family, even if the loss is not recent.
- Stop at a child's lemonade stand and buy yourself a drink.

Sticks and Stones

Many of us as children learned maxims that contain more falsehood than truth. One of these is "Sticks and stones can break my bones, but words can never harm me." The fact is, negative, condemning words can hurt for a lifetime.

When Molly was just out of college, she had little money to set up her first apartment. In her search for furniture, she raided her parents' attic and found her grandmother's antique desk. It needed work, but it would be a beautiful addition to her home.

Molly spent a weekend carefully repairing and polishing the desk. When her father saw it, instead of affirming her work or making helpful suggestions, he grunted and shook his head in disapproval. Molly moved the desk into her living room but did not forget her father's silent criticism.

Ten years later the refinished desk sat in the home Molly shared with her husband and two daughters.

"Would have been better with Danish oil finish," her father said one day, gesturing toward the desk.

"What I heard," Molly says, "was that my life would have been better with a different finish. I just couldn't please him."

Some of us received an unfair share of unwholesome words as we were growing up. The challenge for all of us as adults is to replace unkind words with loving words in our vocabulary. Our natural tendency is to give to others what we received. But when we love intentionally, we can learn to speak words of kindness.

POSITIVE WORDS

Do the words you speak in your home and job build up others? Or do they make life more difficult for others?

If we live a life of authentic love, we will tie acts of kindness to words of kindness. The father who says to his teenager in exasperation, "Okay, you can go out. Now get off my back," has made a positive statement, but he has spoken unkindly. The teenager leaves feeling estranged from her father.

The loving father might say, "You can go out, and I hope you have a good time. I love you, so be careful." His tone of voice and facial expression are as important as his words.

It can be easy to slip into habits of teasing and putting down others, especially when the other person is a family member. That's why I love overhearing couples speaking kindly to each other. The other day I heard a husband chiding himself for the time he'd locked his family out of the house. "That was just once, honey, and it worked out," his wife said easily. She took an opportunity for criticism and turned it into a chance to affirm.

Some time ago I was counseling with a middle-aged daughter whose father had died. She told me, "Mom and Dad put each other down for forty-seven years. I could never understand why they stayed married."

"Do you think they would have spoken differently if they had been married to someone else?" I asked.

"Probably not," she said, "because they both gave me negative words also. And I think I was a pretty good daughter. I think they were just two negative people who happened to marry each other."

How tragic that some people choose to have a negative attitude toward life and unwholesome words flow from their mouths daily!

> Never underestimate the power of kind words to change someone's life.

AFFIRMING WORDS

Years ago Nicky Cruz, a drug-addicted gang leader on the streets of New York City, confronted David Wilkerson, a young man committed to helping people like Nicky. "You come near me and I'll kill you," Nicky warned.

"You could do that. You could cut me in a thousand pieces and lay them out in the street and every piece would love you," Wilkerson responded.[4] Is anyone surprised that in time Nicky Cruz left his life on the streets and is now making a positive impact in the world?

The kind person looks for ways to verbally affirm others.

- What wife would not like to hear, "You look nice in that outfit"?
- What husband would not feel encouraged by the words "I appreciate all you do to make my life easier"?
- What coworker would not feel built up by hearing a boss say, "Thanks for your hard work on this project. I know you went beyond the call of duty"?

Kind words affirm who people are and what they do.

HOPEFUL WORDS

I recently attended a meeting at which the psychologist John Trent was speaking. He told his own story of growing up in a single-parent home. His dad was an alcoholic and left his mom when John was young. John and his siblings harbored a lot of hurt and anger, which showed up in their behavior. He and his brother were expelled from elementary school for their misconduct.

When he was a senior in high school, John received a failing grade on his term paper. John said, "I thought it was good. I worked hard on it. Of course, I didn't start on it until the night before it was due, but I worked hard."

His mother looked at his paper with the failing grade and said, "Well, you didn't include any footnotes, and you left out the table of contents, but this is so well written. I would not be surprised if someday you used your words to help people."[5] John grew into that encouragement; today he is a prolific and popular writer.

Kind words see the best in the individual and call it forth.

TRUTHFUL WORDS

Kind words are not always positive words. Genuine love confronts people when their behavior is destructive. Sonya, speaking about her maternal grandmother, tells me, "She loves me unconditionally even when she tells me something I need to do better. Through my ups and downs, she's always supported me. She lets me know when I am wrong but never withholds her love from me."

When we confront someone for the benefit of the other person in a spirit of meekness, then even confrontation can hold words of kindness. The challenge is to speak the truth and to speak it in love.

SPEAKING IN KINDNESS

How do we learn to speak words of kindness?

- *Become aware of the importance of words.* Your words are powerful enough to give life or death. One way to heighten your own awareness of this truth is to listen to the words of others. You might even write down the kind words you hear from others throughout the day as well as record any unkind words you hear. This can be an eye-opening experience.

- *Listen to yourself speaking.* To make this a habit, ask yourself after each verbal interaction with another person, *What kind words did I say and what unwholesome words did I say?* Then go back and apologize for the unwholesome words spoken. Because apologizing can be difficult, it often provides a good reminder to change our patterns of speech.

- *Replace unwholesome words with wholesome words.* A good place to begin is in private. When you find yourself saying nasty things to other drivers, why not change your words? Instead of saying, "You fool, you're going to kill somebody," maybe you can say, "May you get home safely and not kill yourself or someone else first." When you rephrase negative statements into positive statements in private, you are far more likely to do it in public.

- *Remember the value of every person you meet.* Each one of us has a unique role in life. Receiving and giving love are part of fulfilling that role, even if someone seems unlovable at times. If you have in mind how important each person is, you are far more likely to speak words of kindness.

HABITS TO ACQUIRE

Catch yourself when you are thinking negatively about yourself or someone else. Replace those words in your mind with something positive about you or the other person.

Competitor to Kindness: Bad Habits

If acting kindly does not come naturally to you, it's not because you are an unkind person. I wrote this book because every one of us has the potential to love others. Often our failure to love others authentically comes from a simple lack of practice.

We usually think of bad habits as vices like biting nails or eating chocolate before bed. But habits can also relate to things we *don't* do. If it's not our habit to look a waiter in the eye when we order, it won't occur to us to do so. If we're used to leaving the refrigerated creamer on the kitchen counter at the office for someone else to put away, most days we probably won't even realize we're doing it.

Have you heard the old joke "How many psychiatrists does it take to change a lightbulb?" The answer is: "One. But the lightbulb has to want to change." The first step in changing a habit of unkindness is to want to be kind.

One young woman told me, "I knew my roommate liked a clean bathroom, but somewhere along the line I'd gotten into the habit of leaving the wet towel on the floor. It was always hung up the next time I took a shower, and I didn't think much about it. Then one morning that towel glared at me from the floor. I realized I'd gotten into a pattern of unkindness without even realizing it. I made it a habit to pick up my towel every day. Then I started noticing other ways I could be kind to my roommate, like keeping the television volume low when she was trying to sleep. I was amazed at all the bad habits I'd gotten into! It became a game to think of ways to be kind to her by recognizing what made her feel loved."

Kindness generates kindness. That's why it's helpful to read about acts of kindness other people are performing. Not only does it give us specific ideas, but it also makes our minds more alert to opportunities to be kind. (Several newspapers, such as the *Chicago Sun-Times*, have recently started running stories of "random acts of kindness" in the community.)

When we make kindness an intentional habit, we are more likely to see the worth of each person. As our new vision of people clarifies, we *want* to be kind simply because every person we meet is worthy of affirmation.

Developing Kindness

A middle-aged businessman came to me restless and dissatisfied with his life. Richard often bickered with his wife, and his kids seemed to avoid him. He knew he was critical of his family and employees, but he didn't know how to change.

The first thing I suggested was that Richard keep a record of words he spoke or things he did at work or home that he would consider unkind.

He came back the next week and told me, "When I looked back over my day and listed my unkind words and actions, I realized I needed to change."

Just realizing how unkind he could be was a major step in Richard's becoming a kind person. Then it was time for him to deal with past failures. Each night he reflected on ways he might have hurt people that day. The next day he returned to the people to whom he had been unkind and apologized.

"It was one of the most life-changing weeks in my life," he said. "By the end of the week I felt like I had broken a negative pattern." He smiled. "There's nothing like apologizing to motivate a person to change his behavior."

The rubble of past failures had been cleared. He was now ready to begin building a new lifestyle of kindness. I suggested he start with his family. He said, "I think it would be easier to start at work."

"Much of what people call kindness," I said, "is simply human manipulation to get someone to buy our product or treat us with kindness. That's not the kindness to which we aspire. We are talking about acts and words of kindness designed to benefit the other person. We're not talking about the mere niceties of good manners; we're talking about kindness flowing from true love."

"Okay," Richard said, "then I'll start at home. I think I've got it."

I nodded, but I knew it was a lesson that would have to be repeated, primarily because I know my own heart and how many times I have become discouraged at my own tendency toward unkindness. I encouraged Richard to dedicate himself each morning to seeing opportunities for kindness both in his family and at work.

Months later Richard said to me, "It was the beginning of the best chapter in my life. My wife and children are into kindness big time, and my work atmosphere has become much more pleasant." As a counselor I was thrilled to see Richard experiencing the fruit of being kind.

No one wakes up one morning and decides, *From now on, I will be a kind person.* Kindness, like every characteristic of love, develops over time as we open our hearts and minds to becoming more loving people. We begin by agreeing with this purpose: Yes, I want to have a life characterized by kindness. Knowing that the false self is egocentric, we must consciously learn how to keep kindness on our agendas every day.

~ *Body and Soul*

One of the great things about loving authentically is that it brings healing to our own souls *and* bodies! Several scientific studies have shown that acting kindly has physical and mental health benefits. For example:

- Acts of kindness release the body's natural painkillers, the endorphins.
- The feeling of euphoria and subsequent peacefulness after performing an act of kindness is so common that it's called a helper's high.
- Helping others can minimize the effects of disease and other physical disorders.
- Acts of kindness have been proved to reverse feelings of depression, hostility, and isolation. As a result, stress-related health problems often improve after you help someone else.
- The health benefits and sense of calm from an act of kindness return for hours or days after the event, whenever the act of kindness is remembered.
- Caring for other people in a positive relationship has been shown to improve the immune system.
- Acting kindly toward other people increases one's sense of self-worth, optimism, and overall satisfaction in life.[6]

Pay It Forward

After Erin's son was born, Jessie offered to watch him whenever Erin and her husband needed a date. She also passed on books and games that her kids weren't using anymore, and always seemed to have a little gift for the baby when she saw him. One evening, as Erin strapped her son into his car seat after Jessie had spent the day babysitting, Erin asked if there was something she could do for Jessie. She asked cautiously because she wasn't sure if she would have the time or energy to help with much.

"Oh, no," Jessie said. "So many people have helped us over the years. It's nice to be able to pass it on."

Although Jessie didn't use the term, she was showing the value of paying it forward. When someone does something kind for us, we want to pass that kindness on to others.

Many of us are familiar with the phrase *pay it forward* from Catherine Ryan Hyde's novel *Pay It Forward* and the Warner Brothers film adaptation of the same name. In fact writers and philosophers have explored this aspect of kindness for decades, even centuries. Consider this letter from Benjamin Franklin, written on April 22, 1784:

> *Dear Sir,*
>
> *I received yours of the 15th Instant, and the Memorial it inclosed. The account they give of your situation grieves me. I send you herewith a Bill for Ten Louis d'ors. I do not pretend to give such a Sum; I only lend it to you. When you shall return to your Country with a good Character, you cannot fail of getting into some Business, that will in time enable you to pay all your Debts. In that Case, when you meet with another honest Man in similar Distress, you must pay me by lending this Sum to him; enjoining him to discharge the Debt by a like operation, when he shall be able, and shall meet with another opportunity. I hope it may thus go thro' many hands, before it meets with a Knave that will stop its Progress. This is a trick of mine for doing a deal of good with a little money. I am not rich enough to afford much in good works, and so am obliged to be cunning and make the most of a little. With best wishes for the success of your Memorial, and your future prosperity, I am, dear Sir, your most obedient servant,*
>
> *B. Franklin.*[7]

Franklin was acknowledging that the most powerful way to return someone's kindness is to pass that kindness along to someone else. In this way, he could take the little he had to give and let it multiply.

One of the beautiful things about loving authentically is that it energizes us. When we are kind to others, we look for other ways to be kind, and when others are kind to us, we are motivated to pass that kindness on.

HABITS TO ACQUIRE
When someone acts kindly toward you, make it a point to perform a similar act of kindness to someone else.

One Boy's Sacrifice

Fifteen years ago Jeff and Kristi Leeland's baby boy, Michael, had weeks to live. The only thing that might save him was a bone marrow transplant, costing $200,000. The Leelands' insurance company refused to pay for the transplant, and on Jeff's teacher's salary, the couple could not afford to pay for it themselves.

That's when Dameon, one of the most picked-on kids in the junior high where Jeff worked in Kirkland, Washington, handed Jeff twelve $5 bills, the entirety of the bank account he'd just emptied. When he heard of Dameon's donation, the principal of the school started an account with Dameon's $60, inspiring the students at Kamiakin Junior High to add their own contributions to Dameon's effort. Soon the community rallied behind the students. In less than four weeks Dameon's act of kindness had sparked a citywide drive that raised $227,000 for Michael's lifesaving transplant.

Seeing the influence of one child's act of service, the Leelands launched Sparrow Clubs USA, a nonprofit organization of school-based clubs that provide opportunities for kids to help other kids in medical crises. Since 1995, Sparrow Clubs have raised more than $2.5 million to help more than four hundred seriously ill or disabled children. Children inspired to volunteer on behalf of their "adopted Sparrow" have collectively contributed more than one hundred thousand hours of community service across the country.

Jeff says one of the added benefits of Sparrow Clubs is the "subtle but very positive and effective influence that can disarm the negative culture of an entire school" when children work together to show kindness. "A greater sense of unity and grace permeates the school culture as kids serve the community in the common cause of helping their adopted Sparrow."[8]

We may not ever see the results of our sacrifice when we act kindly, but authentic love calls us to serve others simply because we know that one act of service can change lives. Whether we are serving a homeless man, a child, or the person across the dining room table from us, when we act kindly, we acknowledge the value of another person. Kindness can be remarkably simple. Its effects can last a lifetime.

What Would Your Relationships Be Like If You . . .
- Saw every encounter with another person as an opportunity to express kindness?
- Decided to be kind not only on pleasant days but also on difficult days?
- Donated one week each year to joining others in a project of kindness to those in need?
- Spoke words that benefited others and apologized for any unkind words and actions?
- Always looked for opportunities to affirm the value of another person?

Making It Personal

QUESTIONS FOR DISCUSSION AND REFLECTION

1. Describe a time when you felt the helper's high of being kind to someone.
2. What is one of your favorite ways to be kind?
3. When has an act or word of kindness inspired you to pass that kindness on to someone else?
4. As you look at the self-test on page 41, what stands out to you about how naturally kindness is a part of your life?
5. When do you find it most difficult to be kind?

OPTIONS FOR APPLICATION

1. Try to visualize every person you meet as:
   - Valuable beyond measure

- Gifted
- Born for a unique role in life
- Capable of receiving and reciprocating true love

Try to visualize yourself as:

- A transformed person who is in the process of developing attitudes of true love
- Someone who has the potential of being clothed with kindness
- Someone empowered to express kindness in the face of rejection or unkind treatment
- Someone able to give people freedom to receive, reject, or reciprocate acts of kindness
- Someone who sees every individual as an opportunity to express kindness

You may want to print these points on an index card and put the card in a place you will see every day, such as the bathroom mirror.

2. Choose a day this week, and record all acts and words of kindness that you observe throughout the day. Simply list what was done or said and who did it or said it.

3. At least two mornings this week think of five opportunities you might have in the day ahead to express kindness to someone in words or actions. At the end of the day record the acts of service you did.

4. Practice hearing yourself talk. After each verbal encounter, ask yourself, *What did I say that was kind?* and *What did I say that was unkind?* Then apologize for each of your unwholesome statements.

CHAPTER THREE

Patience

ACCEPTING THE IMPERFECTIONS OF OTHERS

They also serve who only stand and wait.
—JOHN MILTON

It always strikes me as a reflection on human nature that as we walk to our cars in a parking lot, we get impatient with the drivers barreling through the lanes around us. *Why can't they wait a few seconds while we get out of the way?* Then as soon as we get in our cars, we become impatient with the pedestrians walking so slowly in front of us.

It's not hard to find stories of impatience on the road. In July 2007 the California Department of Transportation temporarily shut down Highway 138 because drivers were getting so annoyed with construction along that route. The forty-four-million-dollar road-widening project was meant to alleviate accidents on the well-traveled thoroughfare, but apparently the inconvenience to drivers on tight schedules was too much. Frustrated with slow-moving traffic, drivers abused construction workers with death threats, BB guns, and even, in one instance, a flying burrito. The results of the road rage only heightened drivers' impatience; all drivers had to take a half hour detour until the construction was completed.[1]

In Western culture we are not trained to be patient. When a supervisor gives an assignment and we ask. "When would you like this completed?" the answer is often "Yesterday." The message is clear: There is no time to waste. Get it done, and get it done quickly.

In our personal lives we expect instant gratification. Just waiting for the computer to boot up in the morning is annoying. In order to purchase things we cannot afford today, we use charge cards even if we have to pay more later. We pay extra to get products delivered overnight. We use interstate highways that keep us from the slowed pace of local traffic. Once we get off the interstate, we pound the steering wheel if the car in front of us does not move immediately when the light turns green.

If we get so impatient with technology, cars, and possessions, is it a surprise that we get impatient with people? In fact the very idea of being patient with people is countercultural. Yet patience is one of the seven traits of a loving person. Only an intentional choice to love will allow us to develop patience in today's world.

～ How Patient Am I?

Take the following self-test to see how often you respond in patience— choice *c*—to people and difficult situations.

1. When someone cuts in front of me on the road or in line, I . . .
a. Honk my horn, snap at the person, or do something else to show my annoyance.
b. Figure I probably did something wrong.
c. Take a deep breath.

2. The last time someone got angry with me, I . . .
a. Got defensive and yelled.
b. Retreated.
c. Listened.

3. When someone fails to meet my expectations, I . . .
a. Get angry at him.
b. Give up.
c. Figure out how to encourage him.

4. When someone I love messes up—*again*—I . . .
a. Tell her I'm not sure if she'll ever get her life together.
b. Look the other way.
c. Offer support of who she is even if I don't agree with what she did.

5. When I do something wrong, I . . .
a. Get so annoyed with myself that it's hard to concentrate on anything else.
b. Feel I am a bad person.
c. Apologize.

Everyone Is in Process

When Craig and Lauren signed up to write letters to inmates at the local prison, they never imagined their care for a prisoner would extend to opening their own home to her. As they got to know Rebecca through her letters, they realized that she was a woman trying to make the best of life. And she was alone.

In her late thirties, Rebecca was in her fourth year of an eight-year prison sentence for embezzling money from a construction company. Craig and Lauren started visiting Rebecca in prison, and she grew to depend on them for support. When she moved to a halfway house thirty minutes from their home, they committed themselves to helping her transition to life with a job and financial responsibilities again.

It was not an easy transition. More than once, distraught at what she'd just done, Rebecca called Craig in tears from the halfway house. She failed to report tips from her housecleaning job, then left her waitressing job early one day without telling anyone, then bought a cell phone even though she wasn't allowed to have one. After finally securing a job as a receptionist—with the help of Craig and Lauren—she had such an outburst of anger at her employer one day that he fired her.

At the halfway house she stretched nearly every rule she could, despite warnings that the next time she could be sent back to prison for the remaining years of her sentence. However, each time she failed at something, Craig and Lauren talked with her, admonished her, and let her know that they still wanted to be in her life.

"To be honest, most of the time it's frustrating," Lauren says. "We love her with a very tough love. We invest in her not knowing if she will continue lying or not, if she will keep this job or not."

When Rebecca was granted parole more than a year after they first met her, Craig and Lauren welcomed her into their home until she found a place of her own.

"We see that she wants to do what is right," Lauren says, "and she's made some big improvements. The fact that she is trying keeps us all in the game. As a parolee she lives in a fishbowl. One wrong move and everyone knows about it. I ask myself, *What if all my wrong moves were exposed?* Her weaknesses might be more noticeable than mine, but we need to identify her mistakes and help her correct them, not reject her as a person."

Craig and Lauren demonstrate the key to developing a patient attitude: They know that each one of us is still in process. Life is a slow journey of becoming the people we choose to be. In fact this book is written with the premise that people are in process and that many people desire to be more loving than they presently are. Though none of us *deserves* the patience of others, when we are patient in our relationships, we remind ourselves and others that each of us can be on the way to becoming better people.

Patience: allowing someone to be imperfect.

All in the Attitude

Patience takes on different forms in different relationships. The patience we use to forgive the waitress who brought the wrong order is different from the patience we use when waiting for a prodigal daughter to pull in the driveway. But being patient in one area of our lives helps us be patient in all areas.

One of my favorite examples of this is the life of Florence Nightingale. Nightingale was born into a wealthy family and could have had a carefree existence. Instead, as she grew into a young woman, she devoted her time to visiting the sick in local villages and became an advocate for better medical care in London. In 1845 she announced her decision to become a nurse despite the protests of her family. Nursing had a bad reputation in the mid-nineteenth century and was not a desirable profession for young ladies in the upper classes. Nightingale believed she was called to the nursing profession, however, and dutifully pursued nursing studies as her interests in the social issues of her time increased.

In 1854 Nightingale organized a party of thirty-eight nurses and arrived in Turkey to help the wounded of the Crimean War. She faced rejection again when the British doctors told her that she and her nurses were not welcome there. When Nightingale insisted, she was given permission to scrub blood from the floor. Ten days later new casualties arriving from battle overwhelmed the hospital, and Nightingale and her nurses were finally able to put their skills to work.

Nightingale's patience with those who put down her vocation translated into patience with those she helped. The soldiers loved her, calling her the Lady with the Lamp because of how she cared for them at night. She sent letters and wages home for the men and established hospital reading rooms. Most important, she steadily improved sanitary conditions in the hospital despite the initial disapproval of the doctors. Her diligent research and steady belief in the importance of hygiene saved thousands of lives. In later years she wrote her best-known book, *Notes on Nursing,* which encouraged observation and sensitivity when relating to patients, a radical approach to nursing at the time.

Nightingale's work over a lifetime changed the nursing profession and led to the founding of the Red Cross. She was able to love others, and save lives, because she was patient with those who went against what she believed to be right. She could not change medical conditions immediately, but she knew that over time her hard work and care for her patients would influence others.

> **Being patient in one area of our lives helps us be patient in all areas.**

Only an attitude of patience can maintain that level of diligence over years. Whether we are fighting for improved social conditions or interacting with a stranger at the bank, if we have developed an attitude of patience, we will be more fully able to love everyone we meet. Let's look at two keys to developing this attitude in everyday life.

HAVE REALISTIC EXPECTATIONS

Patience requires us to see others as we want to be seen ourselves. People are not machines from which we can expect to get a perfect product. In the heat of everyday interactions, we can forget that each of us has different emotions, ideas, desires, and perceptions and that each of us has the ability to make choices. Being patient means loving a person even when he makes choices with which we disagree.

Not everyone operates according to our priorities. We must accept that human element as a reality of relationships and include that reality in our expectations of others. Otherwise, we will continue to be impatient and express our impatience in condemnation that will not foster good human relationships.

The father of an eighteen-year-old boy told me, "I wish my son would go to college, but he is choosing to take a year off to travel. I don't know how he can afford to travel, and I don't understand how this could be helpful to him. But I choose to respect his choice." I appreciated the way this dad chose the attitude of patience even when he disagreed with his son's decision. Similarly, a young wife told me that for the first two years of her marriage she "nagged" her husband about sleeping in on the weekend when there was so much work to do around the house. "Now I realize," she said, "that he needs the freedom to use that time as he chooses. It seems to me he's wasting the best part of the day, but that's what he feels he needs to do. I get started with the work in the yard and wait for him to join me whenever he comes."

Each of us is in the process of change, sometimes for the better and sometimes for the worse. If we are conscious of this reality, then we will be more patient toward family members, coworkers, and friends who at the moment may not be making the choices we wish they would make. If we respect the process, we are more likely to have a positive influence on the outcome. We do not control other people, but we do influence one another. Patience creates an atmosphere that makes a positive influence possible.

REALIZE THE POWER OF PATIENCE

This leads me to a second reality that helps create a patient attitude. Just like every other characteristic of love, patience changes people. I'm reminded of one of Aesop's fables, "The North Wind and the Sun." Here is how it goes:

> The Wind and the Sun were disputing which was the stronger. Suddenly they saw a traveler coming down the road, and the Sun said: "I see a way to decide our dispute. Whichever of us can cause that

traveler to take off his cloak shall be regarded as the stronger. You begin." So the Sun retired behind a cloud, and the Wind began to blow as hard as it could upon the traveler. But the harder he blew, the more closely did the traveler wrap his cloak round him, till at last the Wind had to give up in despair. Then the Sun came out and shone in all his glory upon the traveler, who soon found it too hot to walk with his cloak on.[2]

This ancient fable shows a relevant truth for every one of our relationships. Harsh, stormy words only damage our connections with others and often cause people to increase their inappropriate or unloving behavior. It is patient, steady love that will change our friendships, marriages, and work relationships.

When I become impatient, lose my temper, and spout condemning words to my wife, Karolyn, I have become an enemy, not a friend. Karolyn's response is to fight the enemy or flee from the enemy. So we have a royal argument that no one wins, and both of us walk away wounded, or we have an estranged relationship in which we try to avoid each other. In either scenario we have lost the potential of positive influence. On the other hand, when I exhibit patience by controlling my temper and expressing my concern in a loving manner, I keep the relationship intact and strengthen the potential of positive influence.

Consider another example of the power of patience: On the hospital floor where Carol worked as an RN, none of the nurses wanted to be assigned to Mrs. Bradley. Recovering from a broken hip, Mrs. Bradley kept her nurse running all day: She was too hot or too cold; she needed fresh water; the nursing assistant didn't take her blood pressure correctly; she wanted her bed changed. . . . Her call button lit up every two or three minutes at the nurses' station. At times you could hear her yelling into the hall that she would be telling her family about the poor care she was receiving at this hospital.

"*You* try to make her happy," the night nurse said as she handed off her duties to Carol. Instead of trying to avoid Mrs. Bradley, Carol considered the relationship a challenge. That day, despite a full patient load, she determined to show Mrs. Bradley nothing but patience. Her goal was to meet this patient's needs before Mrs. Bradley could voice them.

"Do you have fresh water, Mrs. Bradley?" Carol asked, putting her head into the room. Five minutes later: "Are you comfortable, Mrs. Bradley?" Still later: "It looks as if you might like some sunshine. May I open these blinds for you?" Finally: "Did your lunch arrive on time today?"

At first Mrs. Bradley continued to press her call button every few minutes, but by midday Carol's patience had started to soften her. She rarely had to ask for help before Carol arrived to see what she might need.

"All this time we'd assumed she was a mean old lady, but I think she just didn't want to be alone," Carol says. "What I figured out was that she was afraid. When she knew I was aware of her, she was able to rest." Carol's patience created an environment in which Carol learned to value Mrs. Bradley for who she was and Mrs. Bradley gradually came to relax.

At the end of the day Carol was exhausted but satisfied. When Mrs. Bradley's son arrived around dinnertime, she actually seemed to be in a good mood. "This is Carol," she said. "She's the best nurse I've ever had."

It's much easier to be patient with people who are patient with us. But when we withdraw from the impatient person, we lose the chance to see the power that patience can have. Perhaps in these difficult situations more than at any other time, we will be amazed to see how patience can change people if we are committed to loving authentically.

HABITS TO ACQUIRE
When someone is particularly impatient toward you, consider it an opportunity to be particularly patient toward her.

Patience in Action

Patience does not mean we do nothing. I have known individuals who could sit stone-faced and listen to others rant and rave, then walk out of the room having given no response. That is not patience; it is isolation. It is self-centeredness. The stone-faced individual is unwilling to enter into the hurt of the other person.

Patience means caring enough to listen empathetically with a desire to understand what is going on inside the other person. Such listening requires time and is itself an expression of love. Patience might mean remaining calm when what the other person is saying is hurtful to you. Patience says, "I care enough about you that no matter what you say or how you say it, I will stay and listen instead of walking out on you."

CHOOSING TO LISTEN

Caryn says she learned this principle years ago after an argument with her husband when their children were very young. The argument began brewing when her husband, Steve, said he would be home from his new job by five-thirty, and nearly every day he walked in the door around six instead.

Caryn told herself that Steve's tardiness was no big deal, but any parent will tell you that a half hour at the end of the day with two children under the age of five is a *long* half hour. One evening, when Steve came home late again, Caryn lost it. "I feel like you're *lying* to me!" she said, sobbing.

Instead of getting defensive or contradicting Caryn, Steve sat down with her on the sofa and listened. "I don't think I'm lying to you," he said, "but I can see why you feel that way. I know it really hurts to be lied to, and I'm sorry."

Steve spoke words that affirmed Caryn's feelings and her needs. Then he explained how he often got a phone call at the end of the day and didn't want to lose the opportunity to talk to the person, especially if the call was three time zones away on the West Coast.

Because Steve's patience dispelled Caryn's frustration, she was able to hear from him that he wasn't trying to be deceptive; he just hadn't realized how important a half hour was to her. She chose to be more patient with him when he was running behind. More than thirty years later Steve still calls at the end of the day to let her know if he'll be home later than he said he would be. Mutual patience allowed this couple to make positive changes in their relationship that affirmed the feelings and value of each of them.

Patience is being willing to temporarily put up with unloving or emotional behavior in order to get at the issue that stimulates the anger. Patience means continuing to listen when you feel you are being wronged by the other person. It means acknowledging the person's feelings and making her feel heard.

GETTING THE FACTS

You cannot make a loving response until you have been patient long enough to get the facts. That means being willing to ask questions in order to understand another person's thoughts and feelings.

Michael, a single dad, struggled with his teenage son's constant demands for a car. Finally Michael asked, "Are you saying that you think I don't love you because I will not buy you a car?"

His son, Jason, responded, "I don't understand why you can have a car but I can't have a car."

"What do you think is unfair about that?"

"All my friends have cars!"

"Do you think their parents love them more than I love you?" Michael asked.

"No," Jason said, "but I don't understand why I can't have a car."

"Why do you think I'm not buying you a car?"

"You said it's because we can't afford it."

"Do you think I'm lying to you?"

"I don't think so. But why can't we afford it?"

"Would you like to sit down with me and look at our finances?" Michael asked. "I'd be happy to show you why we can't afford it."

"No," Jason said. "I believe you."

Then Michael asked, "If you had a car, what would you be able to do that you can't do now?"

"I could ask Ellen out on a date."

"Do you like Ellen?"

"Well, I'd like to get to know her. But if I can't take her out, I don't know how that can happen."

"Maybe I can help you make that happen," Michael replied.

They then discussed the possibilities of double-dating with an older teen who had a car, using Michael's car, or inviting Ellen over for dinner. By the end of the conversation Jason was excited about the possibility of getting to know Ellen.

Instead of becoming a barrier between Michael and Jason, the frustration of not having a second car strengthened their communication. Michael exhibited patience by listening long enough to find out what was really on his son's mind and to have a beneficial, loving response.

HABITS TO ACQUIRE
When someone is angry, use listening as a tool
to address his frustration.

Patience in Words

It was Saturday night at O'Hare International Airport in Chicago. I sat with a planeload of people near a closed gate, all of us restless to get to our final destination for the evening. The agent announced a delay in our departure because of weather. Outside, the rain cascaded from the heavens and the wind blew fiercely.

After we had waited thirty minutes, the agent announced an additional delay. The rain and wind were unabated.

Fifteen minutes later the rain slackened and the wind calmed. I assumed we would soon be able to board the plane. Instead, at 11:00 P.M. the agent announced that the flight had been canceled.

When the word *canceled* was announced, the man beside me sprang to his feet, dashed to the counter, and shouted loudly, "What do you mean, 'canceled'? It's stopped raining. It's not windy. How can it be canceled?"

The agent replied calmly, "Sir, it was not my decision. I am not in charge of such things—"

The man interrupted. "Well, someone needs to give us an explanation of why we are not flying. It's obvious the weather is not a problem."

The agent replied, "Sir, I'm sorry. I don't know why the flight was canceled."

Realizing he was fighting a losing battle, the man asked, "When does the next flight leave?"

"Tomorrow morning at six-twenty."

"*Tomorrow morning*? What do you mean, 'tomorrow morning'? I can't wait till tomorrow morning. I've got to get home tonight. What other airline is flying out tonight?" he yelled.

"There are no other flights, sir," the agent answered.

"Then what am I supposed to do? Spend the night in the airport?"

"No, sir. We'll put you up in a hotel."

"A hotel?" the man screamed. "I don't want to spend the night in a hotel. I want to go home."

"Then you can stay in the airport, sir. Or if you prefer, I'll call the police."

At the mention of police, the man calmed down and said, "I'll take the hotel room."

While the agent completed the paperwork for the hotel voucher, the man continued. "I can't believe this. What kind of airline would cancel a flight when it's not even raining? I'll never fly this airline again."

The agent handed him the hotel voucher and said, "Exit through baggage claim. Go across the street, and catch the shuttle to the hotel." The man walked off, still muttering to himself.

With his departure, the tension diminished, and we remaining passengers received our hotel vouchers and walked toward baggage claim. I doubt that any of us were happy to be spending the night in Chicago, but our fellow passenger's display of impatience reminded us that harsh words do not change reality. In fact after the episode the remaining passengers began to talk with one another about our past experiences in airline travel. The general consensus was that such cancellations were inevitable and we might as well enjoy our "vacation night" in Chicago. Of course, any of us had the right to ask, "Why was the flight canceled?" But none of us did. I think we all thought that the agent had been through enough for one evening.

FACING ANGER

We've all been in situations in which we or someone else has created extreme tension by getting impatient and failing to control his tongue. Anger in itself is not wrong. We get angry from time to time for one simple reason: People are not perfect! Thus we experience feelings of hurt, anger, disappointment, and frustration. Nothing is wrong with these emotions. The important thing is how we respond to them. If we lash out with harsh, bitter, condemning words, we make the situation worse. If we are patient with others, we give ourselves time to apply reason to our feelings.

Patience is not "agreeing" with the other person in order to avoid an argument. Patience is entering a dialogue to understand the other person's thoughts, feelings, and behavior. We may not like his behavior, but if we understand what has gone on in his mind and heart, we are able to give a more constructive response. And when we listen before we speak, we are more likely to speak healing words.

A POSITIVE VOICE

You are upset because your friend, who was to meet you at six that evening, has failed to arrive. When she shows up thirty minutes late, you have an option. You can launch into words expressing your anger and hurt. Or you can ask questions and listen.

Once you get the facts, you may realize that indeed her lateness can be attributed to her own irresponsible handling of her schedule. You may feel that your anger is legitimate. But even then you have an option on how to respond. Your words can express your impatience by condemning her behavior. Such words will probably get you into an argument and turn your evening into a fiasco. On the other hand, you can express your anger but choose to exhibit patience by saying, "I must confess I feel angry, hurt, and disappointed that you were late. But I don't think either one of us wants that to spoil our time together. So let's put that behind us and enjoy the evening." With such a patient response, you have salvaged an otherwise wasted evening. You were honest about your feelings, but you chose to be patient with the imperfections of the other person, and you expressed yourself in positive words.

Harsh and condemning words always create tension. Patience calls us to speak truthfully in love.

I recently had a chance to practice this wisdom. My wife and I had finished dinner when she said to me, "Honey, you remember when you made the trip to Germany about a month ago?"

"Yes," I said, wondering where this was going.

"Do you remember that we agreed that I would pay the bills while you were gone?"

"Yes," I said.

"Well, I paid some of them, but this morning I found this stack of bills in my closet and realized they had not been paid. And some of them are now overdue."

I looked at her, smiled, and said, "Karolyn, thank you for all the bills that you paid. I'll take care of the other ones, late fees and all."

Karolyn smiled. She and I both knew there had been a time when I would have gotten upset about the bills and spent a lot of energy being angry. What earlier in our marriage would have been a catastrophic evening of my condemning her turned out to be a moment of pleasure. The difference was my choice to be patient and express it in positive words.

Every time we are frustrated, we have a choice. We can lash out with hurtful words or we can ask questions, listen, seek to understand, and then choose to speak words that bring healing. We must never be satisfied with anything less.

The Efficiency of Patience

In the previous chapter we looked at the value our culture places on time. In many ways we hoard time even more than we do money. The idea of being patient can seem almost impossible as we move through a long to-do list for the day. What if patience turns into laziness or leads to missed deadlines? We barely have time to get things done as it is, how can we add another element to our interactions with people?

Authentic love calls us to love everyone with whom we relate, including coworkers, clients, and employers. But patience does not have to mean inefficiency. So how do we balance patience and our need to get things done?

QUALITY OF WORK

Emotions, conflicts, and human needs are rarely well organized, and we can't expect them to be. But learning to process them in a positive way is crucial. When we are patient, we acknowledge that relationships are more important than schedules. The surprise is that when we put relationships first and exercise patience at home and in the workplace, our productivity and quality of work actually increase.

One office manager told me her story of developing patience even when she feared it would hurt the bottom line: "I was distraught with the lack of productivity of one of my administrative assistants. I talked to my husband about it every night. One night he turned to me and said, 'There's probably something going on in her life that you don't know about that may explain her lack of productivity. Why don't you take time to talk with her?'

"Frankly, I didn't want to spend time with her, because I didn't particularly like her. It would have been easier to fire her. But over the next several weeks I had brief conversations with her, not so much about her work as about her life. At the end of the month I went to lunch with her and another administrative assistant. I talked about my son and some of the struggles we were having with him. When I did, the administrative assistant opened up and shared her struggles with her teenage son, who was on drugs. Now that I knew the problem, I could have a meaningful response. Over the next few weeks I helped her get her son into a treatment program.

"All that happened over a year ago, and she is now one of the best administrative assistants on our team. I realized through that experience that when people feel loved, they are much more productive in their work. I have thanked my husband many times for his encouragement to talk with my assistant rather than fire her."

Relationships don't have shortcuts. That doesn't mean we drop every project we're working on because someone needs to talk. It means that we are intentional about placing people before accomplishments in our actions and speech. We find success in relationships, not just in achievements. Every time we choose to be patient with someone rather than respond to confusing or inappropriate behavior in haste, we gain a deeper understanding of that person's value.

> Choosing to be patient can be one of the most efficient choices we make.

Letting Go of Hurry

In the book *Be Quick—But Don't Hurry!*, Andrew Hill, the former president of CBS Productions, writes about what he learned from the basketball coach John Wooden. Considered one of the best coaches ever, Wooden led UCLA to ten NCAA championships in twelve years. His former players, Andrew Hill among them, remember that one of his favorite phrases was *Be quick—but don't hurry*.

Coach Wooden recognized the importance of acting quickly, but he also knew that work done in haste would be wasted. Every young man on his team had been a star in high school. Each one felt himself capable of making any play necessary to win. "It was just not in their nature to ever think of slowing down; they all wanted to go faster and faster, which was why the job of slowing them down was such a priority for Coach," Hill writes. "He devoted more teaching to this one point than to any other."

Hill applies this principle to life outside the basketball court, writing that "impatience and unrealistic goals will sabotage a talented group of individuals in any workplace."[3] In a world of instant messaging and rush-hour traffic, we can get so caught up in getting things done that we forget how we are doing them—or the people we might be hurting in our quest for speed.

A hurried attitude, even when you're alone, affects your relationships. Have you ever tried walking quickly along the flat escalators, called people movers, at the airport and then getting off without missing a step? Your body is so used to moving that the unmoving ground feels unfamiliar. If you have a spirit of impatience about you all day, you will have trouble slowing down when you interact with the person at the grocery store that evening or greet your family at the door. When we love intentionally, we become conscious of the ways we are hurrying unnecessarily and we slow down—with all our relationships in mind.

THE MARSHMALLOW TEST

More than forty years ago Dr. Walter Mischel conducted an extensive long-term study at Stanford University that came to be known as the Marshmallow Test. In the study a researcher put a marshmallow in front of a four-year-old child and said, "You can have one marshmallow right now, or you can wait fifteen minutes while I do something else and then have two marshmallows when I come back."

Some of the kids ate their one marshmallow immediately. Others waited a few minutes before they ate their marshmallows. About one-third of the children waited until the researcher returned and then enjoyed the reward of two marshmallows. (Many of these kids sang songs, talked to themselves, looked the other way, covered their eyes, or even fell asleep as they waited.)

Fourteen years later Dr. Mischel interviewed the same kids again. He discovered that children who immediately ate the marshmallows were stubborn, impatient, and easily frustrated. Even as young adults these participants were willing to settle for less in the short term rather than patiently wait for something better.

On the other hand, the children who had waited for their marshmallows had better self-esteem and higher SAT scores and were considered more socially adept and trustworthy. As they looked to their future as adults, they displayed an ability to delay gratification with bigger goals in mind.

This famous Marshmallow Test reminds us not to get distracted with things that are tempting but not important. We could enjoy the power trip of getting angry at an employee when he does something wrong, but the feeling of superiority will likely wear off before he leaves the room. When we show patience with that employee, we look for progress even as we understand that he is not perfect. Our investment in that relationship can lead to long-term success for him as well as for us.

Cultivating the trait of patience increases our chances of success and contentment. When we commit ourselves to loving authentically, our attitude reflects our ability to focus on what is most important at the moment and patiently wait when necessary.

Becoming Patient with Ourselves

As we learn to be patient with others, we also need to be patient with ourselves. We too are in process, even when it comes to growing in patience. I like the illustration given by Erich Fromm, the world-famous psychoanalyst: "To have an idea of what patience is, one need only watch a child learning to walk. It falls, falls again, and falls again and yet it goes on trying, improving, until one day it walks without falling. What could the grown-up person achieve if he had the child's patience and its concentration in the pursuits which are important to him?"[4]

Most of us live under a fair amount of stress. This stress may come from too many responsibilities, too little money or time, poor health, or fractured relationships. Whatever the source of the stress, we are more likely to be impatient when we feel life pressing in on us. We become perfectionists. We want to do things right and timely. When we fail, we are irritated with ourselves and condemn ourselves with words: *I can't believe I did that. How could I be so foolish? Why didn't I take more time? I was so stupid.* Such self-talk does not engender growth. Instead, it drives us into further discouragement.

If we want to love others well, we need to be patient with ourselves.

If we are impatient with ourselves, we will likely be impatient with others. We hold others to the same high standard to which we hold ourselves. Often that standard is unrealistic for anyone.

The answer lies not necessarily in lowering the standard for ourselves but in cooperating with the process of growth. If you did a job with which you were not pleased, acknowledge the positive things you did and ask, *What can I learn from the experience?* When we are patient, we acknowledge to ourselves and others that every failure can be a stepping-stone toward success.

The Process of Developing Patience

As self-centered creatures we tend to do and say what we think is best for us. Our first instinct when we are hurt is to react to the person who hurt us. But every time we are impatient with others, we lose an opportunity to express love. Patience is not a little matter; it is a huge character trait that may well be the difference between leaving a positive legacy and leaving a negative one. So, what do we do when impatience is not only ingrained in the false self of our human nature but also has been entrenched in our habits for years?

Patience could mean the difference between leaving a positive legacy or a negative one.

BREAKING OLD PATTERNS

Often the road to patience begins by admitting past failures. I've found that when I am willing to apologize to others for impatient behavior, they are willing to forgive me. Apologizing is a way of admitting that I failed while also communicating that I am not happy or content with my failures. I realize that my failure has hurt others, and I become motivated to build bridges to the person I have offended so that I might express true love and open the potential for a future relationship.

Once we have cleared out the debris of past failures, we are ready to break old patterns of impatience and replace them with patterns of patience. The only way to break old patterns is to identify them. Ask yourself this: *What is my most common response when I am angry or disappointed with someone?* Answer that question, and you will have identified the negative patterns in your life that need to be replaced.

A friend of mine recently told me about a time when her husband came home from work without a can of formula for the baby. She'd had a long day with their infant and had called her husband as he was leaving the office to ask him to stop by the store and pick up the formula. "When he told me he had forgotten it, I said, 'How could you forget it? That's like forgetting that you have a baby. I've been here all day taking care of this baby, and you don't even appreciate me. I can't depend on you for anything.' Without a word my husband turned, got into the car, went to the grocery store, and got the formula. While he was gone, my words played over and over in my mind. I told myself, *That's the way you typically respond when you are frustrated with people's behavior.* I knew that my response was not loving. I knew that it did not exhibit patience. I knew that it was detrimental to my relationship with my husband, and I knew that it was demeaning to him as a person. When my husband came home, I apologized to him and told him how sorry I was that I had put him down. I said that I knew I also forgot things at times and I was sorry that I had taken my frustration out on him.

— "The following Sunday I was sitting in church and the guest speaker that day stood up and said, 'This morning I want to share some thoughts with you on how to control anger and frustration.' I could not believe my ears. I knew that this was for me. I got my pen and paper ready.

"The speaker shared two proverbs that changed my life forever. The first one said, 'If you have played the fool, . . . clap your hand over your mouth. For as churning the milk produces butter and as twisting the nose produces blood, so stirring up anger produces strife.'[5] The speaker emphasized 'clapping your hand over your mouth' when you realize that you are saying something that is judgmental. I took that literally, and for the next month I put my hand over my mouth several times. For me, it broke the habit of talking before thinking.

"Then the speaker talked about the proverb 'A soft answer turns away wrath, but a harsh word stirs up anger.'[6] The idea was that when we speak softly when we are angry, we are less likely to stir up anger in the heart of the other person. So when I removed my hand from my mouth, I started speaking softly. Those two things changed the way I responded when I experienced frustration. I feel so much better about myself, and I'm sure my family and friends appreciate the change that has taken place in my life."

This wife and mother demonstrated two important principles in developing patience.

1. *Find a method to break the negative patterns that have developed over time.* For some people this means covering the mouth. For others it means counting to one hundred before saying anything, or taking a walk around the block before responding to a situation, or simply leaving the room for a few minutes. Another woman told me that when she is upset or angry, she waters her flowers. "The first summer I tried this," she said, "I almost drowned my petunias." Better to have waterlogged petunias than to continue in a negative lifestyle. These are ways of consciously stopping old patterns and setting the stage for positive change.

2. *Replace negative behavior with positive behavior.* For this wife, the positive behavior was learning to speak with a soft voice. I know a mom who whispers to her young children when she has important instructions to give. The children lean forward, wide-eyed, to hear what she has to say. If she yelled her instructions or even spoke them in a normal voice, her children would be more likely to ignore her or react in fear. Speaking softly causes others to listen.

Others have learned to write what they will say before they say it or write out questions they would like to ask so they can understand the situation more clearly before they give a response.

One man shared with me that what helped him establish new patterns was to begin the conversation with the following words: I want to say this as positively as I can because I believe in you and I value our relationship.

"That statement," he said, "reminded me of how I wanted to express myself and also assured the other person that I was looking for a solution and not trying to hurt him."

ACCEPTING REALITY

Another step in the process of developing patience is to realize, often through experience, that impatience does not change the situation. After all his harsh words, the man in the Chicago airport who got irate with the airline agent still spent the night in a Chicago hotel. We can express impatience with negative words and behavior, but when all is said and done, the situation remains unchanged. On the other hand, our negative reaction has probably hurt others and embarrassed us. Most important, it has not demonstrated authentic love. Such impatient behavior is not only futile but also detrimental to the cause of a love-filled life.

SOLVING THE PROBLEM

The final step in developing patience is to focus on the solution rather than the problem. My friend whose husband forgot to bring home the baby's formula reacted to his actions, but the main issue was not his forgetfulness but how to feed the baby that evening. When she focused on what she considered his irresponsible behavior, she came across as condemning. Had she chosen to focus on the solution, she might have said, "Honey, we're still out of food for the baby tonight. Do you want to keep an eye on her while I go to the store, or would it be easier for you to go to the store?" However her husband responded to the choice she offered, he would most likely have had a much more positive attitude and their relationship would not have been fractured by condemning words.

Patience focuses on the problem, not the person.

When negative feelings arise from the behavior or words of another person, the problem will not evaporate with the passing of time. The problem needs a solution. Since patience allows someone else to be imperfect, when imperfection causes problems, patience focuses on solving the problem rather than condemning the person.

The Competitor to Patience: Pride

The obvious competitor to patience is impatience. But what causes impatience? Often it is our pride that causes us to react harshly to others. Pride says, "I am right, and you are wrong. I want you to know how angry I am so you know how right I am. I can't be patient with you because that would be giving in, and you don't deserve that."

The Pulitzer Prize–winning writer Will Durant once said, "To speak ill of others is a dishonest way of praising ourselves." We often put others down through impatient remarks and angry rages in an unconscious effort to look better. We want to be recognized for how we have been inconvenienced, hurt, or mistreated.

If we want our feelings to be recognized because we want stronger, more honest relationships, we are acting out of love. In that case, we speak the truth softly, with respect for the other person. But when we wallow in self-righteous anger because we want others to notice that we are "better" than someone else, we are acting out of pride. Pride keeps us from seeing that the person we are angry with has just as much value as we do and that we are just as likely to make a mistake as anyone else. When we stubbornly focus on the error or weakness of someone else, we ignore what it will take to solve the problem at hand.

Patience gives us the freedom to let go of our need to be right all the time. It allows us the peace of putting relationships before the selfish desires that rob us of joy.

A New Agenda

Keri's four-year-old son, Andrew, fought asthma episodes on a regular basis. Despite steroids and medical help, sometimes the only thing he could do during an acute attack was wait it out. After any kind of respiratory illness, that waiting required extreme patience for the whole family as Andrew whimpered with pain and fear.

Keri was married to a doctoral student at a major university. During her husband's final stretch of dissertation research, knowing their family was already greatly stressed, Keri did everything she could to keep Andrew healthy. Even so, Andrew caught a cold, and then a bronchial infection settled in his lungs. As he struggled to breathe, the only thing that soothed him was resting in Keri's arms. Every few moments he grabbed her shirt as he struggled to get his next breath. If he fell asleep briefly, Keri eased him out of her arms so she could use the bathroom or get something to eat. But soon he was awake again, scared and screaming for Mommy.

After a full day of this Keri was ready to scream herself. Her house was a mess; her older son would be coming home from school soon; her husband would be walking in the door tired at the end of a long day at the library. She was in the exact place she had been that morning. She had done nothing that day except hold Andrew. She hadn't even had a chance to take a shower.

Then Keri looked down at her sleeping son. *How many more months or years will I have to hold him like this?* she wondered. *It must be so scary not to be able to breathe. This is one day. This is just one day.* With conscious effort, she chose to be patient—that evening and through the next "one day," and the next, until the wonderful moment when Andrew lifted his head and asked for animal crackers.

Rather than think Andrew was trying to ruin her plans, Keri recognized that he was simply responding to his fear in his four-year-old way. Instead of feeling frazzled or focusing on all she wasn't getting done, she was patient with who Andrew was in that moment. Her relationship with him was more important than her plans for that week.

Anger and frustration would not help Andrew breathe more easily. But self-control allowed Keri to feel peaceful in a difficult situation. It allowed her to demonstrate the patience we offer to others and ourselves when we live out of authentic love.

If you are facing a situation with a child, friend, colleague, or spouse that seems to be taking over your life, consider what it would be like to exchange your agenda in the relationship for an attitude of patience and understanding. That may seem an impossible idea at first, but deciding to be patient even for just one moment can make a difference. Like every trait of a loving person, patience begins with one choice followed by another until it becomes a beautiful habit.

What Would Your Relationships Be Like If You . . .
- Treated everyone, including yourself, as a person in process rather than as a machine that performs?
- Showed in your words and actions that you valued relationships more than time?
- Listened long enough to understand what another person was thinking and feeling?
- Gave up harsh and condemning words and learned to speak softly?
- Focused on finding solutions to problems rather than finding someone to blame?

Making It Personal

QUESTIONS FOR DISCUSSION AND REFLECTION

1. What is the most common sign of impatience in our culture?
2. Do you believe our society is more or less patient than it was one hundred years ago? Why do you think this is the case?
3. When have you seen the patient attitude of a person change someone else for the better?

4. Think of the most recent time you were impatient with someone. How did you react? What is most likely to make you impatient? Why?

5. Do you consider yourself patient with yourself? Why or why not? When was the last time you were impatient with yourself?

6. Think of two or three examples of someone being patient with you. How did another person's patience affect your attitude?

OPTIONS FOR APPLICATION

1. In what ways could you express patience this week with yourself, your spouse, your kids, or another loved one? Whom do you most need to listen to this week?

2. Over the past week do you remember a time when you were verbally out of control? What did you say? How did it affect your relationship with the other person? If your words were damaging to your relationship, are you willing to confess your failure to the other person? If so, do it as quickly as possible.

3. Write the following statements on an index card, and read them once a day for the rest of the week:

- People are not machines. They have ideas, emotions, desires, and perceptions that are different from mine.
- People don't work according to my priorities. Their agendas may be different from my own. I choose to respect the choices of others.
- People are always in process. I choose to give them time for growth.
- My patience creates a more productive atmosphere for helping others.

CHAPTER FOUR

Forgiveness

FINDING FREEDOM FROM THE GRIP OF ANGER

Forgiveness is not an occasional act; it is a permanent attitude.
—MARTIN LUTHER KING, JR.

On October 2, 2006, Charles Carl Roberts walked into a one-room Amish schoolhouse in Nickel Mines, Pennsylvania, and killed five schoolgirls before shooting himself. His actions shocked the country. Yet the story that shook the public even more was that hours after the shooting Amish neighbors reached out to Roberts's wife and three children with compassion. They made it clear that they held no malice toward Roberts and that they desired reconciliation with his family. Days later members of the Amish community attended Roberts's funeral and set up a fund to help support his wife and children.

Forgiveness is so much a part of this community's attitude that it doesn't question whether to extend justice or mercy to a killer. Love is truly a way of life for them.

FORGIVENESS: using honesty, compassion, and self-awareness to reconcile with someone who has hurt you.

Violence, though horrific, is expected in today's culture. Forgiveness catches us off guard. It goes against our assumptions. The world would have understood if the families of those five schoolgirls had reacted in hate and vengeance. But the Pennsylvania Amish community knew they would find healing only through forgiveness.

You and I may or may not need to forgive someone in such dramatic circumstances. But no matter what our circumstances, forgiveness is one of the seven essential characteristics of love; if we want to be loving people, then we must learn to forgive. We must forgive the deepest hurts of life as well as the daily offenses of a family member or a clerk's overcharging us at the hardware store. Whether the offense is large or small, forgiveness requires us to seek reconciliation if our relationships are to have a positive influence on our lives.

How Well Do I Forgive?

1. When someone wrongs me, I am most likely to . . .
a. Stop speaking to the person until he or she apologizes.
b. Ignore what happened and move on.
c. Confront the person with my feelings.

2. If someone I love refuses to apologize to me, I . . .
a. Get angry and leave the room.
b. Pretend it doesn't matter to me.
c. Tell him or her that I am ready to forgive at any time.

3. When the memory of a wrong done to me comes to mind, I . . .
a. Remind the person of the pain he or she caused.
b. Tell myself I shouldn't remember that kind of thing.
c. Try to release my anger and spend my energy thinking about something else.

4. When I make a mistake, I am most likely to . . .
a. Explain why it wasn't my fault.
b. Dwell on my mistake privately and feel bad about it.
c. Go to the person I wronged and ask for forgiveness.

5. When someone confronts me with something I did wrong, I . . .
a. Get defensive and blame someone else.
b. Change the subject.
c. Confess what I did wrong and ask for forgiveness.

As you look at this brief test, how often did you answer *a?* If that was a common answer, you are likely to react in anger when someone hurts you; you might need to become more aware of how your anger affects you. If your most frequent answer was *b*, you probably try to avoid conflict in a relationship—even if it means allowing a barrier to remain between you and someone else. The goal in this chapter is to understand why confrontation, forgiveness, and release—those *c* answers—are so important to loving with an authentic love.

A Passion for Justice, a Capacity to Love

I remember the husband who told me, "I was so angry with my wife and her lover. I wanted both of them to pay for the pain they had caused me and our children." Such feelings are perfectly normal given the sense we each have of what is right and wrong. We are incurably moral creatures. When we are wronged, something inside us says: *That's not right. Whoever did this must pay for it.*

The transforming power of authentic love does not remove this plea for justice. It explains why we want justice in the first place. We are created to love and be loved. Certain natural laws govern our decisions, and a desire for justice is deeply rooted in our being.

True forgiveness can come only when justice and love work together.

At the same time, we each have the capacity to extend forgiveness through love in every relationship. Most children love their parents because something deep within them says, *Parents should love their children, and children should love their parents.* Most people exhibit some level of love toward their neighbors, coworkers, and even strangers.

The balance between justice and love creates a tension that is played out in courtrooms and relationships every day. Listen to people's comments when a judicial verdict has been reached:

- "The cause of justice was thwarted in this case."
- "She got what she deserved."

- "I think probation was a good decision because it was his first offense and he seemed genuinely repentant."

The challenge of living a life of true love is that in this tension we must offer forgiveness to those who have done us wrong even as we acknowledge the hurt they have caused. The husband whose wife left with another man later told me, "She returned after three months and told me that she had made a terrible mistake and wanted to work on our marriage. I didn't think I could ever forgive her. It didn't happen overnight, but as I realized that she was sincere, I found the ability to forgive. Today we have a great marriage. I'm so glad I did not let my pride keep me from loving her."

THE CHOICE TO FORGIVE

Victoria Ruvolo had every right to be angry. As the district attorney in her case said, a crime had been committed against her for which no punishment seemed harsh enough.

Ruvolo was fortunate to be alive after an eighteen-year-old prankster threw a twenty-pound frozen turkey from a speeding car into her windshield, breaking nearly every bone in her face. He and his friends had purchased the turkey with a stolen credit card and gone on a "senseless shopping spree, just for kicks."[1] Ruvolo endured ten hours of surgery, a medically induced coma, and a month in the hospital before she was able to return home, where she faced months of rehabilitative therapy.

Yet Ruvolo maintained contact with her assailant throughout her ordeal and expressed forgiveness for his actions. One particular courtroom scene amazed onlookers when the young man "carefully and tentatively made his way to where Ruvolo sat in the courtroom and tearfully whispered an apology. 'I'm so sorry for what I did to you.' Ruvolo then stood, and the victim and her assailant embraced, weeping. She stroked his head and patted his back as he sobbed, and witnesses . . . heard her say, 'It's OK. I just want you to make your life the best it can be.' According to accounts, hardened prosecutors and reporters were choking back tears."[2]

When her assailant was sentenced, Ruvolo asked the judge to be lenient. In her statement to the defendant, she said, "Despite all the fear and the pain, I have learned from this horrific experience, and I have much to be thankful for. . . . There is no room for vengeance in my life, and I do not believe a long, hard prison term would do you, me, or society any good."

And so the teenage prankster, who could have spent twenty-five years in jail, instead served six months. Ruvolo went on to say in her statement: "I truly hope that by demonstrating compassion and leniency I have encouraged you to seek an honorable life. If my generosity will help you mature into a responsible, honest man, whose graciousness is a source of pride to your loved ones and your community, then I will be truly gratified, and my suffering will not have been in vain."

Ruvolo did not ignore the fact that a longer prison sentence would have been justifiable. But as she later told the media, "What would vengeance do? God gave me a second chance, and I'm just passing it on."[3] She saw forgiveness as a greater good than justice.

Ruvolo's actions remind us of the power of forgiveness to change lives. As her brother-in-law commented after the emotional courtroom scene, "She held him like a mother would. She told him, 'I want you to be somebody,' and he said, 'I will, I will, I promise.' "[4]

WHY WE NEED FORGIVENESS

Forgiveness is a radical concept in today's courtrooms as well as in our homes. Yet it is an essential element in human relationships. This is true for two reasons:

1. *Human beings are truly free—free to love, free to hate.* Because of this freedom, people sometimes make wrong decisions and walk in the wrong direction. When they do, they hurt themselves and those around them.
2. *Forgiveness is necessary in human relationships because our freedom almost always takes a self-centered path.* Our default mode is *What is best for me?* Left to our false selves, we often make decisions for our own good even at the expense of others. We see this reality throughout history. We see it paraded across TV screens and printed in newspapers every day. We see it in international tragedies and in local stories of embezzlement, rape, murder, and

stealing. And these are only the most visible selfish acts. If the walls of homes across the country could talk, how many would reveal harsh words, demeaning conversations, and physical or sexual abuse that will never be reported in the media?

To live is to have the potential of hurting others and being hurt. Without forgiveness, we are left *only* with justice when wrong is done. If justice were meted out today to everyone, most of the populace would end up in prison. When it comes down to it, do you truly want justice for all *your* actions? The question becomes this: *Since we are free to act on our selfish natures, how can anyone live a life of love?*

We all have the opportunity to overcome our self-centered natures and learn to live for the benefit of others. That means forgiving those who offend us. It does not mean ignoring wrongs done to us. Our sense of justice will not allow us to overlook unloving actions. If it did, evil would prevail in the world. But in the tension between justice and love, love can be the more powerful reality. Forgiveness is the choice to love rather than demand justice. When we are living out of our true selves, even greater than our desire to get even is our desire for reconciliation.

Learning to Forgive

Let's look at the progression of events when we forgive out of authentic love. First, a wrong is committed; a brother, sister, friend, or spouse treats us unjustly. We are hurt and angry because our sense of right has been violated. Our first response is clear: We are to rebuke the person who wronged us. The word *rebuke* means to "place a weight upon," "to bring a matter to the attention of another." In short, we confront the other person with her wrongdoing. It is usually best to take time to cool down emotionally before making this rebuke. Authentic love requires us to show respect for the other person in spite of what she has done. When we love, we confront the other person with gentleness, truth, and an offer of forgiveness. We confront because we do not want anything to mar the relationship.

The next step, ideally, is that the other person owns up to the wrong and expresses a desire to not repeat it in the future. This is our deepest desire when we confront the person who has offended us because then there can be genuine forgiveness. We lift the penalty of our anger and receive the individual back into a restored relationship with us. We begin the process of rebuilding trust. We refuse to allow the person's misdeed to thwart future growth in the relationship, and we do not allow our feelings of hurt and disappointment to control our behavior. This kind of forgiveness requires another person's participation as well as our own.

We cannot truly forgive without the participation of the person who hurt us.

The Limits of Forgiveness

As forgiveness becomes a natural part of all our relationships, we need to be aware of what it does *not* do.

- *Forgiveness does not come easily.* A woman whose husband had taken their money to go gambling—again—wept as she asked, "How can I forgive him when he has hurt me so deeply? How could he lie to me like that when I just want to help him? I feel so violated." It took time, but when her husband broke off his connections to the gambling world, admitted that his behavior was wrong, and committed to a rehabilitation program, she began to work toward forgiveness. Five years later she told me, "It was the hardest and best choice I ever made. I am so glad I didn't give up on him."

- *Forgiveness does not remove all the consequences of wrongdoing.* Let's say that as a young father I spend little time with my children. When we are together, I speak harsh, critical, demeaning words and show little love. Years later I go to my children, who by this time are in their late teenage years. I confess my failures as a father and ask their forgiveness. Let's assume they choose to forgive me. Their forgiveness does not heal all the emotional scars of the past. It does not bring back to me the lost opportunities of spending positive, loving time with my young children. What forgiveness does is open the possibility for a better relationship in the future. With time, additional conversations, and perhaps counseling, my children may come to find healing from the wrongs I've perpetrated upon them. Forgiveness provides the platform on which this healing can take place.

- *Forgiveness does not immediately restore trust.* The young woman who has been hurt by her friend's dishonesty may indeed forgive her upon her confession and a change in her behavior. But betrayal destroyed her trust. That trust can be rebuilt only by her being trustworthy in the future. Forgiveness opens the door for the possibility of renewed trust in time.

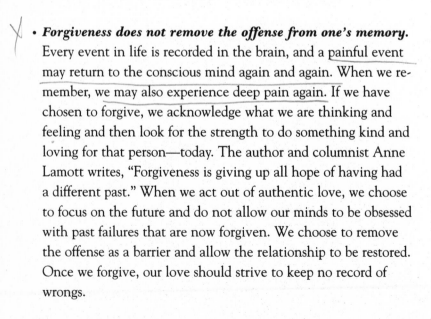

Forgiveness alone does not restore trust, but without forgiveness, trust cannot be restored.

- *Forgiveness does not remove the offense from one's memory.* Every event in life is recorded in the brain, and a painful event may return to the conscious mind again and again. When we remember, we may also experience deep pain again. If we have chosen to forgive, we acknowledge what we are thinking and feeling and then look for the strength to do something kind and loving for that person—today. The author and columnist Anne Lamott writes, "Forgiveness is giving up all hope of having had a different past." When we act out of authentic love, we choose to focus on the future and do not allow our minds to be obsessed with past failures that are now forgiven. We choose to remove the offense as a barrier and allow the relationship to be restored. Once we forgive, our love should strive to keep no record of wrongs.

Negotiating Differences

"Our thirty-five years of marriage have not been perfect," Gail says, "but Don and I still love each other, still enjoy being together, and still have to negotiate with each other—every day! Sometimes I think the hardest things to understand are those everyday habits. Don hardly ever puts his arm around me unless I ask him to, and he loses track of time so easily he almost always makes us late. He hates clutter so much that he picks up after me in the kitchen when I'm not even done using the things I've gotten out! I know there are a lot of things he'd like to change about me too. If you want to know the truth, we're still learning how to live together well."

Gail and Don have made many mutual concessions over the years. When they were first married, their arguments were almost always over keeping the house clean. Gail didn't mind shoes in the entryway, books and papers covering the kitchen counter, and clothes on the floor of the closet. Not only did Don mind these things, but Gail's messiness shocked him; he'd always pictured himself being married to a tidy woman. Gail, on the other hand, was hungry for Don to express his love to her with touch and words, but he seldom did. More than once he joked, "I love you. If that changes, I'll let you know."

After more than three decades of marriage Gail and Don are still learning to love each other despite their weaknesses. Don has much greater tolerance for clutter around the house. Gail tries to pick up the common areas of their home more often because she realizes that is a way to love Don. She reminds herself that Don is expressing love to her every time he fixes her car or makes her dinner. He in turn tries to affirm his wife, not just on anniversaries and birthdays but on ordinary days.

Simple irritation with someone's behavior does not call for forgiveness and apology. Irritation instead calls for negotiation that may lead to the person changing his behavior or may lead to an acceptance of his behavior. Likewise, personality conflicts do not call for forgiveness. One person is by nature organized, while another is spontaneous. If these two people work or live together, they may create tension. Tension calls for conversation, understanding, and acceptance of differences. It does not call for forgiveness.

Of course, learning to negotiate differences is not always easy. Sometimes our response to irritations is to lash out with harsh and condemning words. When this happens we need to apologize and seek forgiveness. Anyone in a strong marriage or friendship knows that love means saying you're sorry many times, simply because you know that your behavior has hurt the other person. As Don and Gail have discovered, being willing to forgive small offenses is a step toward experiencing love as a way of life.

HABITS TO ACQUIRE
Practice forgiveness in small ways and offer apologies even for small offenses.

When You Need Forgiveness

The Pennsylvania Amish shooting might not have occurred if the killer had sought and received forgiveness for an incident in his young adulthood. In a suicide note, Roberts claimed he was haunted by memories of molesting two young family members twenty years earlier.

We'll probably never know the full truth behind Roberts's words or how his past wrongdoing affected his actions that October day. We do know that forgiveness—both given and received—can bring healing and change lives. To love authentically, we must confess and turn from our own failures even as we extend forgiveness to others.

If you are the one who has committed the offense and hurt someone else, take the initiative to seek reconciliation with the one you have offended. If you do not immediately seek forgiveness from the person you have offended, and if he chooses to confront you with your wrong behavior, you would be wise to confess wrongdoing and seek reconciliation with him.

If you are caught up in trying to shift responsibility for your own actions, or if you have been unwilling to confess and repent of your wrongdoing, I urge you to reconsider the path you have chosen. Failure to apologize and seek forgiveness allows the offense to remain a barrier between you and the other person. Every barrier you erect leads you deeper into isolation. Forgiveness is critical to your own healing as well as that of others.

When we offend others, the challenge of a love-filled life is to accept responsibility for our failures, to turn from our wrongdoing, and to seek forgiveness of the one whom we have offended. When we do this, relationships can be restored. No long-term positive relationship exists without confession, a change in behavior, and forgiveness. We need not be perfect in order to have good relationships, but we must be willing to deal with our failures realistically.

> **No long-term positive relationships exist without forgiveness.**

Loving the Person Who Refuses to Apologize

If you lovingly confront someone who hurt you, in many cases the person will admit the wrong and ask forgiveness. On the other hand, the person may deny any wrongdoing and be insulted by the accusation. If you know that your information is correct and you present the "evidence" to the offender, he may be forced to admit that he has wronged you. But he may be unwilling to change his behavior. Your commitment to authentic love calls on you to act and think in a different way.

> **HABITS TO ACQUIRE**
> If the person who hurt you will not or cannot apologize, remember that it is still possible to release your anger toward her.

1. RELEASE

Jamie managed a fitness center for two years before it came to light that the owner of the center was embezzling money and lying compulsively about everything from his childhood to his family to his financial status. All of Jamie's excitement about the future of the center, and all the plans she'd daydreamed about with the owner, suddenly fell flat. The employer she trusted had betrayed her. She couldn't even carry on a rational conversation with him because he continued to lie. In the midst of this, Jamie faced treatments for cancer and an unexpectedly increased workload.

"I was so angry at first," she says. "Then during one of my treatments I thought, *I don't want anger to take up space in my brain right now.* I decided that the treatment attacking my cancer that day would attack my anger as well. I could almost feel the bitterness leave my body."

Though Jamie is still negotiating the repercussions of her employer's actions, she speaks with no bitterness about the situation. She is letting love be more powerful than the wrong done to her.

When someone has wronged you and refuses to apologize, the challenge is not to forgive the unapologizing offender but to *release* him, along with hurt and anger. If the offender confesses his error and makes a positive change in his life, you can then forgive. If not, the consequences of his actions will find him in time without any help from you. Releasing a person is very different from forgiving. It does not lead to reconciliation, but it does free you emotionally and spiritually to become the person you were meant to be.

As a minister in the Christian tradition, I encourage people to release the person to God, whom I believe to be both just and loving. I view God as one who stands ready to forgive all who confess their wrongdoing and who desire his forgiveness. I am not compelled to seek revenge, because I have made the choice to release both my anger and the person who wronged me to God's justice and love. I am now ready for step two.

2. CONFESS

The second step in being freed from the pain and anger of being mistreated is to confess your own failures in the situation. If you have been wronged, your anger is legitimate; you should feel angry. But anger was designed to be a visitor, not a resident. Anger motivates you to confront the person who wronged you and seek reconciliation. When you hold anger inside and brood over it, it becomes bitterness and later hatred. These emotions and attitudes are destructive to anyone who harbors them. They might even cause you to strike out in violence against those who hurt you.

Anger should be a visitor, not a resident.

We all have read of angry employees who return to shoot their supervisors or coworkers. More commonly, we all have probably unleashed verbal tirades against a person who wronged us. When we become obsessed with our own hurt and anger, we are guilty of misguided passion. If ever there is a time when we need help and guidance in handling our emotions, it is when we have been wronged by a friend or family member. Confessing our own failure to handle hurt and anger in a positive way liberates us from further resentment.

3. RETURN GOOD FOR BAD

The third step is a giant step. You return good for bad.

By nature we are kind to those who are kind to us; we show love to those who love us. But when love is a way of life, the standard is much higher: We express love even to those who mistreat us.

One woman, Elise, shared with me that as a young girl she often wanted to lean her head against her mother's fur coat when they sat next to each other in church. She loved the softness of the fur against her cheek and the comfort of being close to someone. Her mother, though, was critical and distant and always pushed Elise away so the child wouldn't get dirt on the coat.

As an adult Elise worked for years to sort through the feelings of rejection and pain she'd felt as a child. When she tried to talk about her feelings with her elderly mother, her mother changed the subject.

When Elise's father died, Elise watched her mother carry her grief alone. When she saw her mother sitting silently in the front pew at the funeral, Elise sat down and put her arm around her. Without a word, her weary mother leaned her head against Elise's shoulder and closed her eyes. For Elise, it was a significant moment of healing as she let her mother rest like a child against her in a way Elise had not known herself. She demonstrated true love by responding with compassion to the person who hurt her.

4. USE YOUR PAIN WELL

If you are dealing with a person who refuses to apologize, your own inner reflection is vital in learning how to implement these three steps and alleviate your own inner turmoil. When you release the person who has wronged you, recognize your own failures in the situation, and seek to love the offender, you will be liberated to go on with your life and use your time and energy in a constructive way.

I doubt that Victoria Ruvolo would be able to offer her assailant a better life if she had not released her anger toward him. Like so many stories in our own lives, her story of pain and forgiveness shows the human capacity to hurt others as well as the ability we each have to release our anger and use our time and energy to help others.

∼ Competitor to Forgiveness: Fear

At the point of deciding whether to seek reconciliation or not, it helps to name the fears that stand in our way:

- The person will refuse to apologize.
- We will have to admit that we have been hurt.
- We will have to confess our part in the wrongdoing.
- The other person will see forgiveness as permission to do wrong.

When we acknowledge these fears, we can respond to them with the truth about forgiveness:

- Even if the other person's refusal to apologize means we can't reconcile, we still have the choice to release our anger.
- Vulnerability is an important part of relationships. If we admit we have been hurt, other people are more likely to admit the hurts they caused.
- Confession teaches us about the power of forgiveness and must be part of our lives if we are to love authentically.

- We can't control how the other person will react to our forgiveness. If we have the opportunity to forgive in a relationship, authentic love calls us to forgive.

Fear is a competitor to forgiveness, but it is not as strong as love. When we love others who wrong us, we will find a freedom from our fears that allows us to enjoy our relationships like never before.

Becoming a Forgiving Person

For two years, Courtney had made a meal for her son's teacher at the end of the school year. Relating to Hunter's second-grade teacher, Mrs. Cooper, however, was a continual struggle. Hunter had dreaded going to school all year because of Mrs. Cooper's sharp words and quick anger. Courtney thought that Mrs. Cooper's teaching style was harmful to Hunter and the other children. Despite meeting with Courtney and the principal numerous times, Mrs. Cooper never wavered from her style of teaching and continually said Courtney was being too easy on Hunter.

Courtney struggled to release her anger toward this woman who had made her son's school year miserable and never admitted any fault. But she also knew that Mrs. Cooper had constant back pain, a difficult home life, and a lot of grading and paperwork to do in that last week of school. So Courtney made not just a small meal but a large, deep-dish pan of baked chicken and mashed potatoes. When she took it to Mrs. Cooper on the last day of class, Courtney thanked her with genuine appreciation for her commitment to Hunter's education. She recognized with words and actions that Mrs. Cooper was being the best teacher she knew how to be under trying circumstances and that she too had had a difficult year.

With her predisposition to forgive rather than to judge, to show mercy rather than to require justice, Courtney showed the traits of a forgiving person. A forgiving person stands ready to forgive when an apology is offered. When no apology is forthcoming, a forgiving person will take the initiative to lovingly confront the person in the wrong and offer forgiveness. A forgiving person will not wallow in hurt or lash out in anger but will spend energy seeking reconciliation.

How, then, do you become a forgiving person?

STEP ONE: FORGIVE YOURSELF

Over the years I have known people who continually put themselves down because of their failures. To flagellate yourself with condemning words is self-destructive. Saying, "I can't believe I did that. I was so stupid. How could I have been so insensitive? I have hurt the person I love the most. I don't know that I can ever forgive myself for what I did," may be appropriate as part of your confession, but once you have received forgiveness, those words are no longer needed. When the memory of past failures comes back to your mind and the emotional pain returns, you must forgive yourself just as others have forgiven you.

STEP TWO: APOLOGIZE FOR YOUR OWN FAILURES IN RELATIONSHIPS

Being honest about our offenses leads us to understand how important forgiveness is if we want our relationships to thrive. One young man told me, "I've always felt that people should not be so sensitive. For years I told jokes that were racially focused. I thought nothing of it until one day an African-American friend at work whom I really like talked to me about how hurt he was by my jokes. It was a wake-up call to me. I apologized to him and later to our whole department. I've become much more aware of how my words and behavior affect others." He added, "I'm doing a lot more apologizing these days."

You are still in process. It should be no surprise that sometimes you will say and do things that are painful to others, words and actions that are not kind and not loving. Choosing to apologize is a major step in the process of becoming a forgiving person.

Apologizing . . .

- Shows that you are willing to accept responsibility for your wrongful behavior: "I was wrong."
- Expresses regret: "I'm sorry that my actions hurt you so deeply. I feel bad for what I have done."
- Seeks to make restitution: "What can I do to make this up to you?"

- Expresses a genuine desire to change behavior: "I don't ever want to do that again."
- Asks for forgiveness: "Will you please forgive me?"[5]

When you ask for and receive the forgiveness of others, you experience the joy of reconciliation. When others refuse to forgive you, you experience the pain of rejection. Both these experiences motivate you to become a forgiving person when others apologize to you.

STEP THREE: HAVE AN ATTITUDE OF AUTHENTIC LOVE TOWARD OTHERS

In your efforts to forgive, you may become exasperated when one person continues to offend. Yet when you love authentically, you strive to become a conduit for forgiveness at all times. This kind of love is learned in daily, ordinary ways. Your attitude shows the other person that you are always ready to restore the relationship. Authentic love calls you to be open to forgive, no matter how long it takes.

"Getting Angry Won't Correct the Past"

When Michael Watson faced Chris Eubank at White Hart Lane in London on September 21, 1991, the boxing world waited to see who would take the world middleweight title. Watson's dream was to become a world champion boxer, and he was on his way, enjoying the rise of a celebrity career complete with "fast cars, expensive clothes, and girls." Then, at the end of round eleven, Eubank delivered a blow to Watson that nearly ended Watson's life. Just after the referee stepped in to stop round twelve, Watson collapsed. He spent the next forty days in a coma, and a blood clot left him partially paralyzed.

Watson writes that he emerged from the coma confused, frustrated, and struggling to face reality. Then he thought of how much Eubank must be suffering and how the incident could have happened the other way around. "Getting angry won't correct the past," he realized as he began to focus on the future. "If I had animosity about what Chris had done to me, I'd be breaking myself down mentally as well as physically. How could I then move on?" As Watson began to heal emotionally and physically, he found a new peace and strength. "Now I feel brand new. I love the way I am because I've got a lot of love in my heart."

Forgiving someone is a way of recognizing that we are imperfect people living in an imperfect world. Some of the events we need to forgive come from malicious intent, but many of them come simply from human weakness, whether we need to forgive a spouse who left the kitchen a mess or a doctor who made a medical error while caring for us.

When someone is hurt, it's tempting to try to figure out who is to blame, but in reality it's impossible to assign percentages of blame to everyone or every circumstance involved. Sometimes we simply need to acknowledge that a relationship needs healing, and the chances are good that some weakness on our part played a part in the damage. Admitting this may encourage the other person to do the same. It can be difficult to apologize for something we feel was out of our control, but authentic love calls us to reconcile with those we hurt and those who hurt us. When we spend our energy on restoring the relationship, we are far better equipped to love others in the future.

In 2003, Michael Watson completed the London Marathon . . . six days after beginning the race. Chris Eubank accompanied him on the final leg.[6]

A Heart Set Free

The abuse started when she was five. Katie experiences physical pain and gagging just talking about it; she can't eat for hours after counseling. Her father sexually abused her and made death threats throughout her childhood. After her parents divorced, Katie's stepdad continued the abuse until Katie was fifteen. Both men invited others to participate in unspeakable acts against this young girl.

For years Katie knew she had been abused but did not remember the details of her father's involvement. As her counseling continued, she began to wonder how much her dad had been a part of her pain in childhood. At times her anger was overwhelming. Yet she persisted in sorting through her feelings because she longed for freedom.

Katie lived in the same town as her father, who acknowledged nothing of the past. Again and again Katie released her anger toward her abusers until her hate subsided and she experienced a new freedom in her thoughts and emotions.

When her father was diagnosed with terminal cancer, Katie didn't want him to face death alone. Over the next two years she stood by him through doctors' appointments and hospital stays as the slow-growing cancer took over his body. After he had had surgery for tumors on his spine, she knew he didn't have long to live. She stayed at the hospital around the clock for a week, caring for him and loving him though he was often unaware of her presence.

Then one Friday he started speaking his memories: being under the hood fixing the car, hanging out with friends in high school . . . and abusing Katie. In his delirium, all the violence of those years came pouring out of his mouth in vulgar language and horrid detail. For a day Katie endured listening to this confirmation of her fears. When she could bear it no more, she went home.

"I didn't know if I could go back into that hospital room," Katie says. "But I had a chance to offer him pure love. I had a chance to bring redemption to this experience."

When she returned to the hospital thirty-six hours later, Katie carried deep pain. It was because of this man in the hospital bed that she looked for an exit in every room she entered. It was because of this man that she had nightmares of being trapped. This man had adversely influenced her marriage, her relationships with her kids, and her thoughts of God. But she had resolved years before to release her father and her anger.

"He's my dad, and I love him. I don't understand all that has happened in the past. All I know is I love him now."

That day, Katie's father revealed nothing of his recent tirades. "I really want some chocolate," he told his daughter. "I would give anything for some chocolate." In great pain and paralyzed from the tumors on his back, he hadn't had solid food for four days.

"Dad, I'm going to go get you chocolate," Katie said without hesitation. She went to a specialty candy store and bought a pound of fudge.

Back at the hospital, she sat on the bed and fed her father pieces of the chocolate he craved. His head sank back against the pillow, and he smiled. Katie delighted that in the midst of his misery she could bring joy to him.

Katie was the only person with her father when he died the next week. In his final days in hospice she spent hours singing lullabies to calm him.

When he died, he had made no apologies to Katie. He could not take away the pain of the past, and Katie never denies that pain. But she chose to give to him when he'd taken so much from her. She chose to extend mercy though it didn't make sense. She chose to offer love when he deserved justice—love, piece by piece, from a heart free to forgive.

What would your relationships be like if you . . .
- Believed that anger and love are not incompatible?
- Took the initiative to seek reconciliation rather than let resentment grow?
- Learned how to forgive or release the offender and knew when to do each?
- Confessed wrongdoing readily to give someone else the opportunity to practice forgiveness?
- Had the attitude of true love toward those who offend you and lived out forgiveness in relationships as a way of life?

Making It Personal

QUESTIONS FOR DISCUSSION AND REFLECTION

1. Victoria Ruvolo forgave the person who nearly killed her and asked that he receive a light sentence for his crime. Do you think her response was appropriate to the situation? Why or why not?
2. Are the choices you make in your daily life more likely to show justice or love, or both? Why?
3. When have you seen someone return good for bad in a relationship? What effect did it have on the people involved?
4. Think of one situation in the past week when someone hurt or inconvenienced you. How did you respond? In what way did your response reflect an attitude of true love? If you had it to do over, what might you do differently?
5. When someone confronts you with something you did wrong, how do you usually respond?
6. Think of an instance in your life when you apologized to someone else. What did that experience teach you about forgiveness?

7. We looked at four steps to loving the person who refuses to apologize:

a. Release.

b. Confess your own failures.

c. Return good for bad.

d. Use your pain well.

Which one of these steps is most difficult for you? Why do you think that's the case?

OPTIONS FOR APPLICATION

1. Think of an offense that someone has committed against you and that stands as a barrier in your relationship. Are you ready to forgive that person? What is one step you could take to lovingly confront that person and seek reconciliation?

2. Have you offended someone, and does the offense stand as a barrier between you two? What step will you take to confess your failure and request forgiveness of the person you have offended?

3. Think of someone who is unable or refuses to confess a wrongdoing to you. What would it look like to release the person and let go of your anger?

 Courtesy

TREATING OTHERS AS FRIENDS

Be kind, for everyone you meet is fighting a great battle.
—PHILO OF ALEXANDRIA

Early in his career, Andrew Horner dreamed of owning his own company, but in 1950s Dallas he was having trouble finding a job at all. The youngest of thirteen children born in Belfast, Northern Ireland, Horner had recently emigrated to the United States from Canada with his wife, Joan. After several unsuccessful interviews, he overheard someone mention a job opening at S. C. Johnson & Son, also known as Johnson's Wax. The only problem was that it required a college degree, and Horner had dropped out of high school at age sixteen.

Undeterred, Horner drove to Johnson's Wax and interviewed with Mr. Lansford, the regional manager. Mr. Lansford said he was considering a candidate with a degree from Notre Dame, but he would be in touch. "I knew I could handle the job," Horner writes. "As I left the building, I introduced myself to all the ladies in the office. Every day I went to check if Mr. Lansford had hired anyone yet, and when I did, I stopped to talk to the women, asking about their families and getting to know them. After about a week of this, Mr. Lansford decided that he would let the women in the office decide who they wanted to be their boss. They unanimously said, 'That nice young man from Canada,' and I was hired."[1] Horner says that he likes to tell this story because "it demonstrates the power of building relationships."[2] He did not have the experience or education the company required, but he noticed people, showed interest in their lives, and was courteous to them.

Horner's commitment to building relationships became part of every job he had. In 1985 he and his wife founded Premier Designs, Inc., in Irving, Texas. The company's philosophy is based on the same principle that Horner acted on back in 1951: Every person has value. Today this national jewelry sales company has more than 250 employees and brings in more than $200 million in sales annually. And it might not exist at all if not for an attitude of courtesy.

COURTESY: the act of treating everyone as a personal friend.

The Value of Relationship

The popular conception of courtesy is to be well mannered. The word *courtesy*, however, is much richer; it means to be "friendly-minded." In the world of relationships, not everyone will choose to be our friend, but courtesy motivates us to *treat* all as friends in our speech and behavior.

Courtesy seems to be a small thing compared with acts of patience or forgiveness. But courtesy is rooted in a belief crucial to every relationship: Everyone we meet is worthy of our friendship; beneath every exterior is a person worth knowing. When we truly believe this, courtesy is not only possible but inevitable.

When we are courteous to someone, we acknowledge our desire to form a relationship with him, even if just for the moment it takes to pull into his lane of traffic. When we are discourteous, we are acting as if we were the most important person in the world at that moment. Courtesy in fact is often the first step toward friendship. When you treat someone as if she were a friend, you open the door to an expanding relationship.

If we believe every person we meet is valuable, courtesy will be inevitable.

In the mornings, my friend Angie frequently goes to a sandwich shop to write. She noticed that the same young woman usually cleared her table and had a considerate spirit about her. One morning in December Angie took this woman a holiday candle and thanked her for her service over the past year. Three years later the young worker still smiles at Angie every time she comes in. Sometimes they chat about events in their lives. The mutual courtesy of these women gave them the opportunity to form a relationship. They may not become best friends, but their enjoyment of each other brings pleasure to an ordinary day.

Courtesy is an essential part of making love a way of life because it places value on relationships. Without courtesy to strangers, friends, and our family members, we cannot build positive relationships that recognize the worth of others.

❧ Am I Courteous?

Answer the following questions on a scale from one to five, one being "rarely," and five being "usually."

1. I send birthday cards and thank-you notes.   /

2. I enjoy looking for ways to be polite to others.   5

3. When someone gives me something I don't need, I respond with genuine gratitude.   5

4. I go out of my way to be courteous to the people I am closest to.   3

5. I look for ways to be courteous to people who seem to be having a hard day.   3

Count up your answers. If your score is from twenty to twenty-five, you are well on your way to loving people through courtesy. If it's lower, you might appreciate the reminders in this chapter about how courtesy is a way of recognizing the value of others.

Treating Others with Courtesy

Some time ago I was traveling with a group of teenagers on a trip to help needy people in Haiti. In one of our domestic airports we had to ride a bus from one terminal to another. I noticed that three or four of the teenagers immediately gave up their seats when older people walked onto the bus, while other teenagers remained seated as older adults stood all around them. I assumed that those who stood had been taught this courtesy by their parents and that those who remained seated had not. I made a mental note and later encouraged our leader to make courtesy a topic for discussion at one of our group meetings.

If courtesy is one of the qualities of love, and if we want to be excellent lovers, then shouldn't courtesy be a frequently discussed topic? For the person who loves authentically, courtesy is a way of life. It is also a source of joy. The more we are courteous, the more we delight in seeing others respond to our kindness.

Opportunities to treat someone as a friend are not hard to find. If we have not developed an *attitude* of courtesy, we fail to recognize the opportunities. Let's look at some of the ways we can develop this attitude of love.

SEIZING THE MOMENT

The British writer Evelyn Waugh once warned Lady Mosley that he would respond to her every time she wrote to him. He explained that his father, the editor and publisher Arthur Waugh, had "spent the last twenty years of his life answering letters. If someone thanked him for a wedding present, he thanked them for thanking him, and there was no end to the exchange but death."[3]

Courtesy means acknowledging the presence or efforts of someone else—perhaps not to the extent of Arthur Waugh but certainly more than we typically do today. I recently gave each person in a group of about thirty people a copy of one of my books. Within the next two weeks I received three thank-you notes. My wife concluded: "Only ten percent were taught by their mothers to send thank-you notes." She was probably right, but I couldn't help wondering if the 90 percent were courteous in other areas of life. I wanted to believe that more than 10 percent of us have developed some level of courtesy toward others. I also knew that some people enjoy expressing and receiving love in words, while that never occurs to others. Even so, I appreciated the fact that a few people took the time to express gratitude for a simple gesture; they treated me like a friend rather than a hired speaker.

Courtesy is often as simple as remembering birthdays and anniversaries or sending a get-well card when someone is sick. What has been most meaningful to you in times of celebration or grief? Be aware of how you can love others in the same way you want to be loved.

ON THE ROAD

When two cars approach a vacant parking spot, are you the driver who defers to the other, or are you the driver who dashes to get the spot as if you'd scored a touchdown? It seems that when some people get behind the wheel of a car, everyone else becomes their enemy. They are out to win a race, and all tactics are fair play. Tailgating, horn blowing, obscene gestures, and refusing to change lanes for incoming traffic all seem to be legitimate maneuvers.

Perhaps on the road more than any other place, we notice when people are courteous in their actions. I am always filled with gratitude when a driver pauses long enough to let me enter a crowded street from a restaurant parking lot. I have an idea that the courteous driver also feels good about himself. What would happen in this country's streets and parking lots if each of us treated other drivers as though they were our personal friends?

LIKE A GOOD NEIGHBOR

Courtesy is a synonym for being a good neighbor. That means treating our actual neighbors as friends. Perhaps that will involve mowing their grass when they are hospitalized, volunteering to collect their mail when they are traveling, or making our tools available when they are working on a project. Being a good neighbor means being aware of our neighbors' needs and having a positive influence in their lives.

Such simple acts can have major effects on a neighborhood. In his book *The Tipping Point*, Malcolm Gladwell shows how when community activists in New York City focused on "small" things like rowdiness and neighborhood cleanliness and began showing a desire to make positive change, crimes such as rape and murder declined. "The small number of people in the small number of situations in which the police or the new social forces had some impact started behaving very differently," and their behavior caught on.[4] Who knows what effect your act of courtesy may have in your community?

CAN YOU HEAR ME NOW?

The proliferation of cell phones has introduced a whole new arena for courteous or discourteous behavior. I will never forget the first time I felt the brunt of this reality. I was in the middle of a counseling session with a client when his cell phone rang. He said, "Excuse me," then answered his cell phone and proceeded to have a five-minute conversation with the person on the other end. After the phone conversation he repeated, "Excuse me," and we continued our conversation as though nothing had happened. Later I had a hard time believing this had actually occurred. Since then, though, I have had similar experiences on many occasions, not necessarily in the counseling office but in private conversations and in public places.

Cell phones have become such a source of discourtesy that July has been declared National Cell Phone Courtesy Month. It apparently is not helping the situation. In a recent survey, 91 percent of the respondents said they had been victims of "technology-related public displays of insensitivity." It's interesting to note that in the same survey, 83 percent of respondents said they never or rarely were guilty of committing such acts.[5] As with so many acts of discourtesy, we notice the actions of other people but remain unaware of our own.

How often have we seen two people sitting across from each other at a restaurant, one talking away on her cell phone while the other stares out the window? I don't know where we got the idea that the person who is calling is more important than the person in front of us. I understand there are exceptions for emergencies or certain on-call jobs. In the normal flow of life, however, the rule of courtesy is: *Don't answer your cell phone when you are talking with someone.*

MAKING THE SATISFYING CHOICE

Courtesy transforms moments of annoyance into opportunities for grace. The remarkable thing is that it takes less time and energy to be kind than it does to get angry.

I spend a great deal of my time on airplanes. I am regularly given the opportunity to accommodate a husband and wife or a mother and daughter who wish to sit together. I must be honest and say that I genuinely prefer the aisle seat. But the question is, *How would I treat a friend?* Middle seats are not so bad when you have the satisfaction of knowing you have enhanced the trip for others.

Then there is the matter of relating to telemarketers, especially those who interrupt dinner to sell vinyl siding for a brick house. Rather than treat them rudely, how about saying, "Don't need the vinyl siding but glad to see that you are working hard. I wish you well. Have a great day"? It takes less work to treat the person courteously than it does to vent irritation, and when we are courteous, we feel much better after the encounter has ended.

RECEIVING WITH GRATITUDE

Courtesy also means receiving from others with gratitude. Some of us find it easier to give than to receive, but graciously receiving acts of kindness is a way to treat others courteously.

I remember one particular instance of speaking in another country on marriage and family topics. At the end of my stay there one of my hosts gave me a gift. I knew it was costly; I knew my host could not afford the gift. It was a gift of sacrifice and love. Everything inside me wanted to say, "You need the money more than I need the gift." But I knew that would be extremely rude. I accepted the gift with gratitude.

When others want to do something for you or give you something as an expression of love, it is discourteous to refuse them the opportunity.

Receiving from others is a way of showing love.

GIVING BAD NEWS

We are also called upon to be courteous when we have difficult decisions to make. Many of us occupy supervisory roles, and sometimes, because of finances or other reasons, we have to dismiss employees. Even this should be done with courtesy. James M. Braude, a California manufac-turer, tells this story: "One of the most courteous men I ever knew was the man who fired me from my first job. He called me in and said, 'Son, I don't know how we are ever going to get along without you, but start-ing Monday we are going to try.' "[6] There is a way to treat people cour-teously even when we are informing them of something unpleasant.

SAYING I'M SORRY

I recently read this suggestion for etiquette in a rare circumstance:

> *What would be the proper thing to say if, in carving a duck, it should skid off the platter and into your neighbor's lap?*
> *Be very courteous. Say, "May I trouble you for that duck?"*[7]

Courtesy plays an important role when we make a mistake or have an accident that inconveniences someone else. A friend recently told me of his experience at a restaurant: The waiter dropped a plate of food on his shoulder that proceeded to dribble down his shirt and slacks. The waiter said, "Oh, I'm so sorry." He returned with paper towels that he used to brush the food from my friend's clothing. The waiter again said, "I'm so sorry." But he made no offer to give him a free meal or to pay for cleaning or replace his clothing.

The friend said to me, "That's the last time I'll ever go to that restaurant." It was an accident, to be sure. But "I'm so sorry" was not enough courtesy to bring him back to the restaurant. Had the waiter informed the manager, and had the manager offered a free meal and compensation for the cleanup, chances are that the man would have returned to the restaurant.

We all make mistakes. Courtesy calls us to put ourselves in the place of the other person so we can apologize in the most loving way.

PAYING ATTENTION

The story is told of a time when Czar Nicholas I of Russia asked Liszt, the great pianist, to play at court. In the middle of the opening num-ber, the great musician looked at the czar and saw him talking to an aide. Liszt continued playing but felt irritated. When the czar did not stop, Liszt finally quit playing.

The czar sent a messenger to ask why he was not playing. Liszt said, "When the czar speaks, everyone should be silent." After that there was no interruption in the concert.[8]

Paying attention is a way of being courteous. That may mean attending the piano recital of someone's child and giving the music your full attention even though you would rather be home. It may mean letting someone tell you what you already know. When you interrupt and say, "Yes, I've already heard that," you take from the person an opportunity to share something that is important to him. Your courtesy enriches the life of the speaker, and that is what love is all about.

⁓ Looking for Change

It seems most of us would like to experience more courtesy in everyday life. The policy think tank Public Agenda recently conducted a nationwide survey about what Americans think of rude behavior, whether on the road, in restaurants, or in the workplace. Here are the findings:

- 79 percent: Think lack of respect and courtesy is a serious national problem.
- 73 percent: Believe Americans treated one another with greater respect in the past.
- 62 percent: Are bothered a lot by witnessing rude and disrespectful behavior.
- 49 percent: Have been subjected to loud and annoying cell phone conversations.
- 44 percent: Hear foul language (and 56 percent said it bothered them a lot).
- 41 percent: Confess to having acted rudely or disrespectfully themselves.[9]

Speaking with Courtesy

Courtesy is perhaps best shown in the way we listen and the way we speak. Words give us the opportunity every day to affirm the importance of relationship.

THE ARGUMENT CULTURE

People in Western society have been greatly influenced by what social scientist Deborah Tannen has called the argument culture. She writes: "[We have come to] approach public dialogue, and just about anything we need to accomplish, as if it were a fight. . . . Our spirits are corroded by living in an atmosphere of unrelenting contention. . . . When you are having an argument with someone, your goal is not to listen and understand. Instead, you use every tactic you can think of—including distorting what your opponent just said—in order to win the argument."[10]

Watch any television talk show and you will quickly see what Dr. Tannen is talking about. Speakers interrupt one another in the middle of sentences, raise their voices as if loudness were more convincing than softness, attack the other people rather than those people's ideas, try to push their opponents in a corner by asking yes and no questions, then slam them to the mat. If all else fails, they give their opponents demeaning labels. Few individuals seek to listen to other people's viewpoints. The objective is to win the argument, not to enlighten the audience.

Is this the way to build relationships? Straight talk certainly has its place, but when we speak to others discourteously, we may end up winning the argument and losing the relationship.

If we have a courteous attitude, we initiate every conversation as though the person were a friend. Our first goal should always be to preserve the relationship, not to win an argument. When the other person walks away, we want her to know that we respect her as a person even if we disagree with her ideas.

HABITS TO ACQUIRE
Initiate every conversation as though the person you are talking to is a friend.

Most of us will speak courteously to others if they are speaking courteously to us. The sign of mature love is to speak courteously to those who are not reciprocating.

Rob was having a performance interview at work. His supervisor pointed out two areas where he thought Rob was not performing satisfactorily.

Rob said to me later, "I knew my supervisor had drawn his conclusion by talking with someone else because he himself had not been in a position to observe me. My first thought was to say to him, 'I think it's unfair that you are judging me on the words of someone else.' But I heard your words ringing in my mind: 'Speak to him as though he were your friend.' So I said, 'I can appreciate what you are saying. To be honest with you, that is not the way I see it, but I know you have legitimate reasons for reaching your conclusion. And I respect that. So, what suggestions do you have on how I could do the job more effectively, because that's my desire?'

"From that point on," Rob told me, "the conversation was as friendly as it could be. When I left, I said, 'I've enjoyed our conversation, and I appreciate your perspective. I will certainly try to learn from the suggestions you have made. Please know I am open to other ideas you have in the future. Thanks for your time.'

"Since that conversation, all our interactions have been positive. That experience taught me that when I speak to someone as though he were my friend, he is more likely to become my friend."

When we find ourselves in a conversation that is far from friendly-minded, it takes discipline to respond with words of courtesy. But our choice to be disciplined may soften the words of the other person, creating space for a true friendship to develop.

So, what does it mean to speak with courtesy? Let me suggest some practical ideas.

- *Initiate conversation.* This is easy for some people because they are talkers by nature. For a more introverted person, this will be more difficult. When you consider everyone you encounter a potential friend, however, you are motivated to get to know him or her. Initiating a conversation communicates: I think you are worth knowing; I value you as a person.

Of course there are people who will not reciprocate when you open the door to a friendly conversation. To be courteous is to respect their choice. Courtesy does not impose itself on others.

Often conversations can be initiated by asking the other person to do something for you. If you have a coworker or someone in your community who has expertise in a particular area and you have a need, asking a favor is treating the other person as though he were your friend and leaving room for further conversation to develop. A friendly relationship is often begun by making a request.

- *Give your undivided attention.* If you are talking with someone in the hallway and others pass by, maintain eye contact with the person in front of you. If you are sharing a meal together in a crowded dining room, focus your attention upon the person with whom you are eating. Focused attention communicates: You are the most important person in my world at this moment; I value what you have to say. When you maintain eye contact, your mind is less likely to wander to other subjects, and the other person knows you are focused on the conversation.

- *Listen to understand, not to judge.* You naturally evaluate the words of other people as they talk. You may agree or disagree with their ideas, but it is courteous to make sure you understand their ideas before you express your own. When you disagree too early in the conversation, you stop the flow of communication. Take time to discover what the other person is trying to communicate before you respond. Otherwise, you may respond inappropriately.

When you disagree, express your disagreement as you would to a friend, not an enemy. "I understand what you are saying, and it makes a lot of sense. Let me share my perspective, which is somewhat different." Then share your ideas. Expressing respect for another's ideas before sharing your own keeps the conversation friendly and less likely to become adversarial.

Recognize that differences of opinion are part of life. If we refuse to have friendly conversations with those who disagree with
us, our circle of friends becomes smaller and smaller. If, on the
other hand, we learn to speak with courtesy, our circle of friends
broadens. Never force another person to agree with your opinion.
Remember, you are not trying to win an argument; you are seeking to build a relationship.

Hope for Peace

I was once guiding a discussion among college students. The group was
composed primarily of American students, but it included one young man
from Israel, who was Jewish, and another from Egypt, who was Muslim.

Since the discussion was open-ended, the young man from Egypt
raised a question about what Americans think of the tensions in the
Middle East. My first response was: "I cannot speak for all Americans, I
can speak only for myself, but it is an excellent question." I opened the
floor for opinions. Several students shared their perspective. Some
were more pro-Israel; some were more pro-Arab.

I summarized by saying, "It appears to me that we are saying that the
religious and cultural differences between Jews and Muslims are very
real and that the perspectives on the history of these two groups are
also quite different. I think we agree that there has been mistreatment
and misunderstanding on both sides. What we would hope for is that a
new generation might come to listen to each other, trying to find a
meeting place that shows respect and dignity for both groups. After all,
isn't that what we are trying to do in this discussion?"

After the meeting was over, both the Jewish and the Arab students
approached me individually to express appreciation for showing some
understanding of their positions. The Arab student said, "In most of the
discussions I have been in, people are either pro-Jewish or pro-Arab and
show little respect for the other's position. I think respect is the big issue, and listening to each other is our only hope for solving the problem." I agreed with him. I'm not suggesting that a friendly talk will solve
all of the world's cultural and religious tensions. I am suggesting that if
we want to be a part of the solution, rather than a part of the problem,
we must learn to speak with courtesy.

- ***Don't raise your voice.*** Never resort to name-calling or loud, harsh, condemning monologues. Raising your voice and lashing out with condemning words create more heat than light. The other person and those who may be listening to the conversation will likely not hear what you say but will be distracted by how you said it. So not only do such antics tend to create enemies rather than friends, but your rudeness detracts from any truth that might have been in your statement.

- ***When you must reject an idea, do it with grace.*** Always speak out of a desire to preserve the relationship. For example, you might say, "I appreciate your sharing your idea. I personally can't accept it as being true, but I respect you as a person, and I hope that our disagreement on this issue will not hurt our relationship because I think you have a lot to offer me and perhaps I have something to offer you." Reject ideas, but never reject people.

- ***Apologize when needed.*** The reality is that sometimes we speak rudely. This does not have to end a relationship. If we are willing to apologize, often the other person is willing to forgive us, and the relationship can continue. A sincere apology will deepen the relationship rather than destroy it.

If we learn how to speak with courtesy, even when we disagree with others, we can keep the doors of communication open and perhaps retain a friendly atmosphere rather than create enemies.

How Do I Become Courteous?

Let's be honest, some people irritate us. Yet with discipline we can be courteous even when we're irritated. So, how do we practice courtesy, whether we struggle to be polite to the person chewing too loudly next to us at breakfast or to the driver who just cut us off? If we keep three realities in the forefront of our minds, we'll find that courtesy becomes a natural way of interacting with others.

EVERY PERSON YOU MEET IS VALUABLE

A little before 8:00 A.M. on Friday, January 12, 2007, a young man in jeans, a T-shirt, and a Washington Nationals baseball cap stepped inside Washington, D.C.'s L'Enfant Plaza, just outside the Metro, and took a violin out of its case. Leaving the open case at his feet, he tossed in a few dollars, turned to face the businessmen and -women rushing through the Metro doors, and began to play.

Sixty-three people passed by the violinist before one man briefly turned his head as he walked by. A few seconds later a woman put in the first donation of the performance, a dollar. Six minutes into the performance, someone stood against a wall nearby and listened.

In the forty-three minutes that the violinist played, seven people stopped to listen to the performance for at least a minute. Twenty-seven people tossed money into the case. One thousand seventy people rushed by, just a few feet away, without seeming to see or hear the musician.

What these hurried commuters didn't know was that they could have enjoyed a free concert that morning by the internationally acclaimed violinist Joshua Bell as he played some of the most stunning music ever written—on a 1713 Stradivarius violin. The *Washington Post* had arranged the performance as an experiment. Would people stop to notice beauty amid the bustle of rush hour? Far more people stood in line for a lottery ticket at the kiosk at the top of the escalators nearby.

"It's a strange feeling, that people were actually . . . *ignoring* me," Bell says, laughing. In the three-quarters of an hour that he played that day, he earned $32.17. In more typical settings his talents can bring in up to $1,000 a minute.[11]

Busy people on their way to work overlooked Joshua Bell's value as a violinist. How often does our busyness keep us from seeing the value of every person around us? Of course, not everyone can play an instrument as well as Joshua Bell can. But everyone we meet has an unquantifiable value that we will see if we only take the time to watch and listen. When we are rude to an employee, a store clerk, or the person in front of us on the sidewalk blocking our way, we may as well be walking by a world-class violinist while wearing earplugs.

Courtesy gives us the *opportunity* to notice the beauty and gifted-ness of the people we encounter every day. It reminds us of the joy we find when we put aside our agendas for a moment and simply stop to listen.

EVERY PERSON YOU MEET IS STRUGGLING

The film director Stanley Kramer tells the story of directing Vivien Leigh, best known for playing Scarlett O'Hara in *Gone with the Wind,* in her final role in the 1965 film *Ship of Fools:* "On the set one morning she was making up for a scene when she fooled around at the makeup table for a long time and made life pretty miserable for all the makeup people for a period of about two and a half hours." When Kramer walked into the room, Leigh looked at him and said, "I, . . . Stanley, I can't do it today." Weak from depression and tuberculosis (which took her life two years later), Leigh was asking for grace. At an appreciation for Leigh held at the University of Southern California after her death, Kramer said, "I knew she was ill and that she couldn't do it. I'll never forget that look. That was the look of one of the greatest actresses of our time. From that moment on I became . . . the most on-purpose, understanding, and patient person that I could possibly be. She was ill and had the courage to go ahead. . . . What is there then that one can say?"[12]

Behind every face is a struggling human spirit. Sometimes the struggle is rooted in physical pain or disease. Sometimes it grows out of wounded relationships or difficult finances. But every person we meet today will be struggling in some way. Henry Wadsworth Longfellow once said, "Every man has his secret sorrows, which the world knows not; and often times we call a man cold when he is only sad."

The other night I overheard a library clerk snap at a patron that she had come in too close to closing time to be checking out so many books. Instead of responding with defensiveness or anger, the patron said, "It sounds as if you've had a long day."

The librarian immediately softened her tone and smiled as she started to scan the stack of books. "It *has* been a long day. See that line over there of people waiting to check out books? When people come in so late, we don't get out of here until nine-thirty."

"I can see why you want to get home! I'll try to get here earlier next time." And the patron left with her bag of books as the librarian called the next patron in a considerably gentler voice.

When I observe what appears to be arrogant, hostile, or distant behavior, my instinct is to respond with anger. But if I reflect on the struggle behind the behavior, I am far more likely to have a courteous response to the individual. I may still feel irritated, but if I look beyond the outward appearance, I am motivated to respond with courtesy.

HABITS TO ACQUIRE

When someone is particularly rude or distant, take a minute to consider what might be the underlying cause.

EVERY EXPRESSION OF COURTESY ENRICHES SOMEONE'S LIFE

When I was in graduate school, Karolyn and I had very little time or money. Both of us worked, and I carried a full academic load. We lived in student housing and became good friends with John and Jane, who lived in the apartment above us. About a year later Jane's mom and dad came to visit for a week. We met them briefly the day they arrived, and Jane introduced us as her "best friends." Later that week I came home to find that Jane's dad had washed and waxed my car. I could hardly believe my eyes. When I went to thank him, he said, "A friend of Jane's is a friend of mine." To this day I remember him with fondness. He demonstrated love by treating me as a friend, even though I was only an acquaintance.

No one outgrows the desire to be treated with courtesy. When we express courtesy to someone, we can know without a doubt that we have made his day brighter. We have lightened his load and encouraged him to be courteous to others as well. We feel good about being friendly-minded, and the other person feels good that someone has treated him with respect.

Courtesy Begins at Home

Recently I visited the city of Baton Rouge. I was met at the airport by a twenty-three-year-old man. As he drove me to the hotel, I noticed that he responded with "Yes, sir" or "No, sir" to every one of my questions. My first thought was that he had recently served in the military, but I was wrong.

The next day, I noted that when a woman spoke to him, his response was either "Yes, ma'am" or "No, ma'am." It was obvious to me that he had been reared in a Southern home where he had learned this common courtesy: Address a man as "sir" and a woman as "ma'am." Courtesy was a natural part of this young man's speech.

Each culture and subculture has its own list of common courtesies, courtesies that are expected of everyone. Usually these are taught and learned in the home. Here are a few of the common courtesies I learned growing up in a middle-class working family in the Southeast.

- When someone gives you a compliment or a gift, always say, "Thank you."
- Don't talk with food in your mouth.
- Ask permission before playing with your sister's toys.
- Don't take the biggest piece of chicken.
- When it comes to food, taste it before you reject it. Then say, "I don't care for that. Thank you."
- Never enter someone's room without knocking. Then say, "May I come in, please?"
- Do your chores before you play ball.
- When you see your mother or father doing something, always ask, "May I help you?"
- Wait your turn to ride the scooter.
- When Aunt Zelda arrives, meet her at the door with a hug.
- If you want Johnny to come out to play, knock on the front door and ask his mother, "May Johnny come out and play with me?" If she says, "Not now," say, "Thank you," and leave.
- Say "Yes, ma'am" or "No, ma'am" to your mother and "Yes, sir" or "No, sir" to your father.
- Don't scream at your parents or your sister.
- When someone else is talking, don't interrupt.
- When you enter a room, take off your cap.
- Look a person in the eye when you speak to him or her.
- When you want salt at the dinner table, say, "Please pass the salt."
- When you leave the dinner table, say, "May I please be excused?"

All these "common courtesies" are designed to show respect for family members and neighbors. They are not universal norms, but they are common enough that you probably identified some of them as behavior your own parents considered courteous.

TEACHING COURTESY TO OUR CHILDREN

As adults we affirm or reject the common courtesies we were taught as children. For example, I was told as a child, "We don't sing at the table." Years later I discovered that my wife had been taught the same thing. When we were drawing up our guidelines for the children, we included "We don't sing at the table."

On numerous occasions our preschool children would burst out singing at the table. We would immediately stop them with "We don't sing at the table." Soon my wife said to me, "I think our rule about not singing is stifling the kids. It doesn't seem consistent with the idea of expressing joy."

We discussed it and agreed that "no singing at the table" was a common courtesy we had learned as children that we would consciously choose to reject. After that, our children could freely sing at the table as long they didn't have food in their mouths.

Whatever courtesies you were taught as a child probably still strongly influence your behavior as an adult. Those of us who were raised in homes where common courtesies were taught have a head start on developing this characteristic of love. With that in mind, if you are a parent, I want to encourage you to identify the common courtesies you are teaching your children. You may want to add to or subtract from your list as you reflect upon the question, *What are the common acts of courtesy that I would like my children to learn?*

Children need to be taught that there are certain things we do or don't do because we respect one another. If the child learns to respect parents and siblings, the child is more likely to respect teachers and other adults outside the home. The teenage son who screams at his parents is likely to scream at his wife someday.

If you grew up in a home where little emphasis was placed upon common courtesies, you might want to talk with other families about what courtesies they are teaching their children. Then formulate your own list and help your children take a step toward loving others.

As difficult as it can be to extend courtesy to a stranger, it can be a real test of love to extend courtesy to those who are closest to us. Even relationships with good friends, a spouse, or family members should include some common courtesies.

Here are some courtesies that my wife and I have adopted through the years. We've framed these in the context of marriage, but they apply to any close relationship.

- *Never speak for each other.* If someone asks me a question about what my wife thinks, wants, or desires, my response is: "You will have to ask her about that; I can't speak for her" or "I'll be happy to ask her and get back to you." When you speak for someone, you are circumventing her individuality.

- *Listen to each other empathetically.* When I am listening empathetically, I am trying to understand not only what my wife is saying but also how she is feeling. In order to accomplish this goal, I do not interrupt her but rather ask clarifying questions to make sure I understand what she is saying and feeling. "What I hear you saying is that you feel angry because you had to ask me three times to take out the garbage. Is that what you are saying?" This kind of reflective question focuses on understanding rather than judging. When Karolyn feels fully understood, then I can share my perspective on the topic and she will listen empathetically to me. Once we understand each other, we can then solve the problem. In the earlier years of our marriage, before we learned how to listen to each other empathetically, Karolyn and I spent much of our time arguing with each other. Arguing is not courteous.

- *Ask for what you want.* Some time ago a wife said to me, "I wish my husband would do something special for my birthday."

  "Have you told him that is what you wish?" I asked.

  "No," she said. "If I have to tell him, then it doesn't mean as much."

  "I hope you live a long time," I said, "because the chances of your husband reading your mind are slim indeed. God didn't give most husbands the gift of mind reading."

Learn to ask for what you want. If the other person chooses to do it, it is still an act of love. She didn't have to do what you requested. So accept it as a gift.

- **When you have a conflict, focus on finding a solution rather than on winning.** When I win, my spouse loses. It's not much fun to live with a loser. Resolving conflict calls for respecting each other's ideas and then looking for a solution that will affirm our love for each other. The best solution is one in which both Karolyn and I feel positive about the outcome.

- **Make requests, not demands.** Demanding something of my wife makes me a slave driver and her a slave. Nobody wants to be controlled by someone else, but most of us are open to a sincere request.

- **Before you make a request for change, give your spouse two or three compliments.** Verbal appreciation communicates "I like you. I appreciate you. I respect you." When I tell my wife things that I appreciate about her, she feels respected and appreciated and is far more open to receiving an honest request.

- **Once a failure has been confessed and forgiven, never bring it up again.** I cannot erase failures, but I can forgive them. Once they are forgiven, there is no value in raising the issue again. My choice to condemn Karolyn for a past failure is evidence that I have not yet forgiven her. I need to learn what I can from the experience, but once the process is ended, I need to let it be history.

These common courtesies that my wife and I extend to each other have enriched our marriage greatly. Perhaps you have discovered some of these for yourself in your close relationships. I suggest that you and your family members make lists of the common courtesies you have learned to extend to one another. Then make lists of things you all would like to add to your common courtesy repertoire.

If we learn to treat one another with courtesy within the family unit, we are far more likely to express courtesy to those outside the family. Indeed, courtesy begins at home.

∽ *Competitor to Courtesy: Busyness*

When was the last time you had an opportunity to be courteous to someone and didn't take it? Why did you let that opportunity slide by? I would venture a guess that most of us would say we lose the chance to be courteous when we are particularly busy.

Just like the businessmen and -women who walked by Joshua Bell that January morning, we are distracted people. Courtesy, like each of the other six characteristics of a loving person, is countercultural. In a driven world, getting things done is more important than affirming the value of other people.

As the author Evelyn Underhill wrote more than seventy years ago, "Fuss and feverishness, anxiety, intensity, intolerance, instability, pessimism and wobble, and every kind of hurry and worry—these . . . are signs of the self-made and self-acting soul. . . ."[3] Because busyness makes us self-focused, we often see impoliteness as someone else's problem, not our own. We see our acts of discourtesy as one-time events because we are on our way somewhere, we have so much on our minds, or we have too much to do.

I trust it's clear by this point in the book that no one is expected to love authentically 100 percent of the time. Our human weakness makes that impossible. Loving others in "small" ways as well as grand acts, however, can always be our goal. Every "one-time event" of rudeness deprives us of the possibility of strengthening a relationship with someone.

When we live a life of courtesy, we are always on the lookout for what people do well. We are not so consumed with tasks and deadlines that we are unaware of the value of the person next to us. Like so many worthwhile things in life, being polite can seem overwhelming but in fact takes very little time. When our attitude changes, acting courteously becomes a natural part of making love a way of life.

A Friend in Disguise

Booker T. Washington, the renowned black educator, relied on friend-ships and hard work to strengthen the relationship between races in the post–Civil War era. His efforts helped establish more than five thousand schools in the turn-of-the-century southern United States, and his autobiography, *Up from Slavery*, is considered one of the most influential books in U.S. history. Well respected and well known, Washington interacted with some of the richest and most famous lead-ers and politicians of his time.

The story is told that shortly after he took over the presidency of Tuskegee Institute in Alabama, Professor Washington was walking in an exclusive section of town when a wealthy white woman stopped him. Not knowing the famous Mr. Washington by sight, she asked if he would like to earn a few dollars by chopping wood for her. Because he had no pressing business at the moment, Professor Washington smiled, rolled up his sleeves, and proceeded to do the humble chore she had requested. When he was finished, he carried the logs into the house and stacked them by the fireplace. A little girl recognized him and later revealed his identity to the woman.

The next morning the embarrassed woman went to see Mr. Wash-ington in his office at the institute and apologized profusely. "It's per-fectly all right, madam," he replied. "Occasionally I enjoy a little manual labor. Besides, it's always a delight to do something for a friend." She shook his hand warmly and assured him that his courteous and gra-cious attitude had endeared him and his work to her heart. Not long afterward she showed her admiration by persuading some wealthy acquaintances to join her in donating thousands of dollars to the Tuskegee Institute.

Washington was free to show courtesy to this woman because he considered her a friend, not an imposition. When we live with a simi-lar freedom, we see just how big an impact small courtesies can have.

What Would Your Relationships Be Like If You . . .
- Treated every individual as a potential friend?
- Made choices as you drove, talked on the phone, traveled, and interacted with your neighbors that showed you value every person's worth?

- Received others' acts of kindness and generosity with graciousness?
- Spoke courteously with everyone, even those with whom you disagree?
- Learned to express common courtesies to the people you love the most?

Making It Personal

QUESTIONS FOR DISCUSSION OR REFLECTION

1. During the past week, has anyone spoken rudely to you or acted discourteously toward you? If so, what was your response?
2. When has someone else's courtesy changed your mood?
3. Think of a time in the last week when you treated someone courteously and felt good about it. What motivated you to be courteous?
4. Think of a time in the last week when you treated someone discourteously. What could you have done to be more courteous in that situation? Is it still possible to apologize?
5. When are you most likely to be discourteous: in the car, on the phone, at work, at the end of the day, with your family? Why do you think that is?
6. What is your most common response when someone disagrees with your opinion?
7. What are the common courtesies you were taught as a child?

OPTIONS FOR APPLICATION

1. Do you agree with the following five statements?
   a. All people are valuable.
   b. All people have the potential to be a part of positive relationships.
   c. All people are struggling.
   d. All people need love.
   e. All people will be enriched by courtesy.
   Consider writing these five realities on an index card. Then think of one person you interact with regularly who is often difficult to love. Put that person's name in place of "all people" (and make the verb singular), and keep these five realities in mind when you relate to that person.

2. Initiate a conversation this week with someone you don't know very well. This might be a coworker, someone in your neighborhood, or someone you meet in a public setting. Learning to initiate conversations is a major step in speaking with courtesy.

3. If you live with parents, children, a spouse, or a roommate, make a list of common courtesies you want to practice in your home.

 Humility

STEPPING DOWN SO SOMEONE ELSE CAN STEP UP

*Humility is a most strange thing. The moment you think
you have acquired it is just the moment you have lost it.*
—BERNARD MELTZER

When the author Jim Collins and his team of researchers studied the
secrets behind the most successful companies in the country, they
came across some unexpected findings. Collins's book *Good to Great*
details what turns a good company into a great one in terms of long-
term profitability. It includes a study of the leadership styles of the
good-to-great companies' CEOs.

"We were surprised, shocked really," writes Collins, "to discover
the type of leadership required for turning a good company into a great
one. Compared to high-profile leaders with big personalities who make
headlines and become celebrities, the good-to-great leaders seem to
have come from Mars. Self-effacing, quiet, reserved, even shy—these
leaders are a paradoxical blend of personal humility and professional
will."[1]

The humility of these business leaders came out especially in how
they talked about themselves—or, rather, *didn't* talk about themselves.
Collins reports: "During interviews with the good-to-great leaders,
they'd talk about the company and the contributions of other execu-
tives as long as we'd like but would deflect discussion about their own
contributions. When pressed to talk about themselves, they'd say
things like, 'I hope I'm not sounding like a big shot.' Or, 'If the board
hadn't picked such great successors, you probably wouldn't be talking
with me today.' Or, 'Did I have a lot to do with it? Oh, that sounds so
self-serving. I don't think I can take much credit. We were blessed with
marvelous people.' "[2]

Despite their noticeable humility, all these CEOs were very high achievers. They led their companies to stock returns that were nearly seven times higher than those of the general market over a period of fifteen years.

My guess is these CEOs didn't spend a lot of time thinking about being humble. They concentrated instead on following sound business practices and building good rapport with employees and customers. Their attitude causes us to look at humility in a new way.

Many of us think of humility as a weak character trait, something we are supposed to show but only if we want to risk professional success and put up with people walking over us in our own homes. Ask most people to define "humility," and you probably won't hear words like *success, satisfaction, respect*, or, most important, *relationship*. Yet these are the words most important to the humble CEOs of good-to-great companies.

In fact humility is not an option on our way to making love a way of life. Like the other characteristics of a loving person, humility affirms the worth of someone else. And just like every other act of love, stepping down so someone else can step up gives us the opportunity for great joy.

∼ *Am I Humble?*

Humility in the abstract matters little; it's how humbly we act in normal, everyday circumstances that determines whether we build up or tear down those we love. It's worth considering how we would handle some true-to-life situations where we have a choice to act with pride or humility.

1. If someone else tells a story about something he achieved or acquired, I usually . . .
a. Interrupt to top his story with an even more impressive story about myself.
b. Say nothing but let my body language convey that I don't think much of the story.
c. Show interest and ask questions.

2. At work, when higher-ups are around, I usually . . .

a. Try to make myself look good, even if it means taking credit for others' accomplishments.

b. Mention my own work for the company, when given an opening.

c. Point out the contributions of others, while letting my own actions speak for themselves.

3. When a family member or close friend has achieved something in an area where I like to excel myself, I usually . . .

a. Find fault with her accomplishment and then try to turn the attention to myself.

b. Ignore her achievement.

c. Congratulate her and make sure others learn of what she has done.

4. If someone I dislike fails at something, I usually . . .

a. Consider how his failing might benefit me.

b. Casually mention the incident to someone else.

c. Look for an opportunity to affirm him.

5. When I become aware of a weakness or failing in myself, I usually . . .

a. Think about who might have contributed to the weakness.

b. Try not to think about it at all.

c. Take steps to correct that weakness in the future.

Give yourself zero points for each *a* answer, one point for each *b* answer, and two points for each *c* answer. The higher your score, the farther along you may be on the road to genuine humility.

Peaceful Living

Have you ever stood back and watched people waiting to check out at the grocery store? Once most of us finish our shopping and get to the cash register, we show our unrest in our faces and fidgety mannerisms: *Why is this taking so long? Get me out of here.* We shimmy our carts into the shortest line, accepting our right to that position regardless of the person coming down the aisle ten seconds behind us. Meanwhile, we keep an eye out to see if another register will open so that we can be first in line there. Rarely do we say, "You go ahead. I'm in no hurry." Our desire to be first overtakes any thought of putting others before ourselves.

This desire to be first is so ingrained in us that some may question whether humility can really be learned. The reality is that if we ever become humble in spirit, it *must* be learned. Have you ever seen a humble toddler? Our instinct from the time we are born is to get what we want.

If we view humility as a way to experience the joy of loving others, it will become part of our attitude. The official definition of humility is "to bow, or to lower oneself." We could also say that humility replaces the anger, ambition, and selfishness of the false self with the peacefulness of the true self. Humble people are secure in who they are. They recognize their own value as well as the value of others and are therefore pleased to see others succeed. Humility is not a popular theme in Western culture, but it is an essential and satisfying characteristic of love. That's not to say that humility comes easily.

HUMILITY: a peacefulness of heart that allows you to stand aside in order to affirm the value of someone else.

Anonymous

One of the key principles of Alcoholics Anonymous, as even its name suggests, is anonymity. In AA there are no big shots; all are equal as people who have become enslaved by alcohol and are working together to live free of addiction. You might think, then, that Bill Wilson, who founded Alcoholics Anonymous in the 1930s, would have been a master of humility. And he was—eventually. But it took him a long time to get there.

In *My Name Is Bill*, the biographer Susan Cheever gives a vivid example of Wilson's struggle with a desire for distinction. Years after Wilson had established AA and its twelve-step program, officials from Yale University expressed their wish to give him an honorary degree because of his achievement. Wilson wanted that degree and the honor that went with it. Yet by that point in his life he "was sufficiently sophisticated in his own principles to know that accepting it was somehow a bad idea."[3]

This was the man who once wrote that the principle of anonymity "reminds us that we are to place principles before personalities; that we are actually to practice a genuine humility." He also said, "Moved by the spirit of anonymity, we try to give up our natural desired-for personal distinction."[4] Even so, Cheever writes, Wilson "struggled with desire as he reached for humility."[5]

Wavering about his response to Yale, Wilson sought the advice of AA's board of trustees. "His spirits were buoyed to find that all but one of the trustees thought he should accept the degree," Cheever says. The dissenter among the trustees was Archibald Roosevelt, the son of former president Theodore Roosevelt. The younger Roosevelt explained to Wilson that his father had been concerned about his own attraction to power and had decided never to accept a personal honor, making an exception only for the Nobel Prize.

Cheever writes, "Bill knew that he was hearing the right message" from Roosevelt.[6] Wilson refused the degree for himself (even when Yale offered to give it to him as W. W. rather than use his full name) but asked that it be given to Alcoholics Anonymous as an organization. Yale rejected the suggestion.

Cheever's book describes Wilson's eventual progress in humility. "Later he declined to be on the cover of *Time* magazine, even, as the editors suggested, with his back to the camera. He also turned down at least six other honorary degrees and a number of overtures from the Nobel Prize Committee."

Here was a man with the same natural tendency toward pride that we all have. Yet having seen the benefits of anonymity within his organization, he chose the humble route over the one that would have brought him more public renown. In so doing, he preserved his credibility and influence among the fellow alcoholics he had dedicated his life to serving.

I tell this story not to say that it's wrong to receive the recognition of others. Often awards and accolades are inspiring to those involved and help promote good works. But Bill Wilson's struggle with wanting to be recognized yet wanting to be humble reflects the tension many of us feel. Wilson was obviously fearful of the distraction recognition could bring. Humility and recognition are not always opposed to each other, but constantly seeking affirmation can keep us from loving well.

What we don't realize when we let ambition take over our thoughts is that the energy we use in trying to look good could instead be used to build relationships. Whether those relationships will lead to the success we want, we don't know. The important thing is that we're acting in love, and the more we act humbly, the more our priorities change.

When seeing through the eyes of authentic love, we realize that humility . . .

- Reflects an awareness of one's own place in the world.
- Takes the opportunity to put others first, even if that means making a sacrifice.
- Shows strength, not weakness.
- Recognizes that the needs of others are just as important as our own needs.
- Affirms the worth of others.
- Doesn't waste energy in pride, resentment, or anger.

With these things in mind, let's look at what it means to love others with an attitude of humility.

Becoming Aware of Your Place

Jim is a prominent leader of a nonprofit organization in India, a man with a deep laugh, strong opinions, and a great desire to help others. Jim says his grandmother, who raised him, used to tell him, "Just remember, no one is better than you. And just remember, no one is worse than you." It takes humility to live as no better *and* no worse than you are. That means recognizing that you are just as valuable, and just as weak, as the people you are called to love.

HEAD OF THE LINE

Many people say the first step in acquiring humility is to realize that we are proud. When we acknowledge the desire to be bigger and better than others, we are liberated to understand the people we were meant to be.

G. K. Chesterton was a prolific writer at the turn of the twentieth century whose words inspired Mohandas Gandhi to lead a movement to end British colonial rule in India and prompted Michael Collins to fight for Irish independence. Chesterton was once asked to contribute to a series in *The Times* (London) on the question, What is the problem with the universe? He answered, "I am. Sincerely, G. K. Chesterton."

When we are tempted to think of ourselves more highly than we should, it helps to remember that we have just as much potential to hurt others or make mistakes as anyone else. When we see the pride in ourselves, we don't fall captive to it.

Desire for affirmation is not pride. Pride is desire for acclaim outside a love-filled life. When humility is part of making love a way of life, our desire is to be all we were created to be—nothing more and nothing less.

Recognizing our own worth is a step toward loving others more authentically.

PRIDE IN REVERSE

Pride is not the only enemy to humility. Failing to recognize our own worth also keeps us from loving others.

Bill Wilson of Alcoholics Anonymous once wrote, "We are apt to be swamped with guilt and self-loathing. We wallow in this messy bog, often getting a misshapen and painful pleasure out of it. . . . This is pride in reverse."[7] If we are truly humble, we will not put ourselves down. Just as love calls us to recognize the value of others, it also calls us to affirm our own value.

I often see how poor self-esteem keeps us from giving and receiving authentic love. Colin, a thirty-something man living in Seattle, struggled with depression and loneliness. He was engaged to a successful young woman who seemed to adore him. Yet he had trouble expressing his love to her and even broke the engagement once before committing to the relationship again. He was the overseer of a dozen employees and worked in a middle management position, but he had no true friends in the workplace. Relationships seemed to hold more pain than joy for him.

As we talked in my counseling office, our conversation turned to Colin's childhood. Like many of the people I meet with, Colin had grown up in a home that was critical and unaffirming. Words of condemnation rang in his ears as an adult: "You are irresponsible, ignorant, ugly, fat, worthless." The more we talked, the more I saw that Colin couldn't truly care for someone else until he realized that he himself was valuable. In other words, he couldn't show love through humility or in any other way until he knew he deserved love.

For individuals like Colin, the first step to love is recognizing their own self-worth. That means giving thanks for who they are and for the gifts and talents they have. They cannot step down until they first step up and acknowledge that the messages of childhood are false. As they begin to recognize their own value, they become capable of true humility.

HABITS TO ACQUIRE

If you are preoccupied with getting the attention you think you deserve, change your attitude by asking someone a question about herself and paying attention to the answer.

Being Willing to Sacrifice

Over the years I've observed in my personal counseling that without humility we get angry at whatever or whoever we think is holding us back from being first. When we are not making progress toward our goals, we get discouraged, even depressed, and look for someone to blame.

This is particularly true in the workplace. Almost every person I've met who is struggling in his vocation speaks of someone who made a derogatory statement about him that influenced the supervisor to overlook him for a promotion. Now he's on a level that he believes is too low for him. If allowed to fester, his anger will stay in his mind for years because someone interrupted his rise to the top.

Contrast that self-centered attitude with the perspective of Josh, a recent college graduate employed by a large and progressive company. His supervisor called him into her office one morning and said, "I've got an opening that I think you might be interested in. It's between you and Tim. I think you have more potential, but Tim has more experience. I'm talking to each of you to hear why you think you deserve the promotion."

"How old is Tim?" Josh asked.

"Around forty-five," the supervisor answered.

"I think you should give it to him," Josh said. "I'll have other opportunities, but this may be his last chance. I think you should honor his experience with the company."

Tim received the job because of Josh's choice to step aside. As a result, Josh was in a position to learn from Tim in a mentoring relationship. Over the next few years they developed a significant friendship that benefited both of them personally and professionally.

True humility is more concerned with sacrificing so that someone else can get ahead than with pushing to get ahead ourselves. When an attitude of humility comes naturally to us, we are always alert to what sacrifices we might need to make to help someone else.

HUMILITY IN MARRIAGE

This attitude of sacrifice can make all the difference in a marriage. Put two people with different personalities, priorities, and gifts in the same household, and someone is going to have to sacrifice for the other at some point.

When Bruce Kuhn, a former Broadway actor, met Hetty, he knew he'd found the woman of his dreams. The only problem was that Bruce's work took him all over the United States. Hetty, an artist, lived in the Netherlands. *Her* client base was across the ocean. So Bruce, at midlife, and without knowing a word of Dutch, moved to the Netherlands, where Hetty could continue her work. After pulling back on his demanding schedule, he now makes a transatlantic commute when he can and helps raise their two children.

He says, "My artistic ambitions were the whole center of my universe. [But] I came to the point of saying, *I will purposely put you in front of myself,* and she did the same. . . . She honors and respects my work enough to put her work on the line, and she's as committed to her artistic life as I am."

Bruce acknowledges that adjusting his career and moving a world away have not been easy, but the joy he discovered in the sacrifice is obvious.

Humility in marriage might mean sacrificing a job, your first choice of how to spend the weekend, or simply the need to win an argument. It can be tempting to push a spouse to agree with you about something as minor as what year you went to the Grand Canyon. Humility sometimes calls you to sacrifice your own need to be right for the sake of a relationship.

ROOM FOR RELATIONSHIP

Loving someone through humility does not always require sacrifice, but it does require a willingness to sacrifice if doing so would enhance the lives of others. Being humble might mean sacrificing the best seat in a restaurant, an hour of time to help your spouse prepare for a big interview, or the opportunity to impress your supervisor. When we recognize that all these things were *gifts* to us in the first place, we are free to give them to others rather than spend energy clinging to them. Neither Josh's choice nor Bruce Kuhn's choice led to immediate worldly success, but their decisions left room for relationships to grow.

If you want to show true love to someone, sacrifice something of value for the sake of the relationship.

Discovering the Strength of Humility

Historians tell us that before the American Revolutionary Army disbanded in 1783, some of the officers who were encamped at Newburgh, New York, grew angry about the back pay still due them. They threatened to confront Congress to give them what was owed. A military takeover of the national government was a real possibility.

General Washington sympathized with the men but knew that this uprising could damage the democracy of the new country. He called a meeting on March 15 at which he faced his angry and disrespectful officers.

After giving a short speech about the finances of the nation, Washington reached into his pocket for a letter from a member of the Second Continental Congress stating that it was working to come up with the salaries that had not been paid. Rather than read the letter immediately, however, he fumbled with the paper without speaking. Then he took a pair of reading glasses from his pocket.

"Gentlemen," he said, "you will permit me to put on my spectacles, for I have not only grown gray but almost blind in the service of my country."

Washington was fifty-one years old at the time, having taken command of the American forces at the age of forty-three. His moment of vulnerability in front of the men who had followed him for eight and a half years dispelled the tension of the moment. The officers were reminded that Washington had sacrificed for their country as much as or more than they had.

After Washington left the room, the army reaffirmed its loyalty to the cause. Washington's humility about his weakness, rather than bravado about his power, had softened the soldiers. As one witness wrote, "There was something so natural, so unaffected, in this appeal, as rendered it superior to the most studied oratory; it forced its way to the heart."[8]

That's what humility will do: force its way to the heart. In showing our weaknesses, we are actually showing strength of character. That might mean admitting we need help even when we want to prove ourselves.

This is particularly difficult in a work or family situation in which others are watching to see if we'll succeed. The author Joy Jordan-Lake writes in *Working Families* about the struggle and privilege of raising children while pursuing a career. "My family insists they will etch 'I Can Do It Myself' on my tombstone," she says. At the same time, she acknowledges that being successful in both working and family relationships often means enlisting the help of others.[9]

Consider Amy, who wanted to impress her mother-in-law, Becky, with elaborate home-cooked meals and desserts on Becky's first visit. It was also the first visit since Amy and Mark's son had been born three weeks earlier. Exhausted and emotional, Amy did everything she could to be the consummate hostess, in between feeding the baby and trying to get a few hours of sleep. She refused all of Becky's offers to help in the kitchen, insisting that she had it under control.

On the third day of the visit Amy noticed that Becky seemed hurt by her refusals of help. Amy also knew that she couldn't keep up her activity level much longer.

"You know, I do need help," she told Becky toward the end of the day. "I guess if you wouldn't mind putting dinner together, that would be great. All the ingredients are out on the counter already." Becky readily agreed, and the women chatted in the kitchen while Becky cooked and Amy sat doing nothing for the first time in days. Not only did dinner get made that evening, but Amy and Becky grew closer in their enjoyment of each other.

Accepting the help of others is one of the best and most difficult ways of fostering loving relationships.

While we naturally want to hide our failings and showcase our better qualities, a humility that lets others know exactly who we are has the potential to revolutionize our relationships. Humility, like every other loving character trait, is countercultural. It goes against the go-for-it mentality of our culture and acknowledges that relationships are the most important part of living well.

Recognizing the Needs of Others

It's often easier to show humility around strangers than around those closest to us. I've seen this for years in marital relationships. The husband gets angry with the wife, or she with him, because each thinks, *I am not getting the support I deserve. My spouse is hurting me instead of helping me. Why should I do something for her?*

With this attitude, couples lash out in anger and become adversaries instead of lovers. Self-advancement becomes more important than caring. True humility means putting aside your own concerns and imagining what it would be like to be in the other person's place.

Deb and Kevin are a young career couple who have been married several years. Recently, Deb was busily making plans to meet her parents for the weekend at a nearby ski resort. She casually mentioned the idea to Kevin and assumed he would be eager to go. Kevin, however, was exhausted from sales meetings at work and wanted to spend a quiet weekend at home. In fact the last thing he wanted to do was spend hundreds of dollars to drink cocoa with his in-laws in a bustling ski lodge.

When Deb excitedly told her husband that she'd found the perfect condo for the four of them, Kevin finally lost it. "Why do you always want to *go* somewhere? What's wrong with our house? Don't you care that my job is exhausting, or are you as oblivious as my boss?"

Deb was taken aback. "I don't *always* want to go somewhere, but once in a while it would be nice! Why are you trying to keep me from having a relaxing weekend with my family?" She stormed out of the house and got in the car, not knowing where she would go but needing to get away for a few hours.

As Deb and Kevin stewed over their argument in separate corners, each began to consider the other's situation.

He works so hard, and I never really asked him about going away. I guess we haven't had much time just the two of us lately. . . .

She planned this weekend thinking I would like it. She works hard too, and this is her way of relaxing. . . .

By the time Deb came home later that evening, she had the idea of waiting until later that spring to go skiing. At the moment it was more important for the couple to have quality time with each other.

Meanwhile, Kevin had found a secluded rental home near the ski lifts that would be peaceful for him but still allow Deb to have time with her parents. As they compared notes, they realized their new dilemma was deciding which plan to choose!

Deb and Kevin were both humbly aware of how the other received love: Deb craved activity and time with her family, while Kevin longed for quiet and time alone with his wife. They showed humility by putting themselves in each other's place.

HABITS TO ACQUIRE

When you believe you've received unfair criticism, don't strike back. Take the time to consider the truth behind the criticism, and be willing to learn from the situation.

Using Your Energy Well

On the eve of the April 2007 annual film festival for overlooked movies, the film critic Roger Ebert wrote a newspaper article for his fans.[10] "I have received a lot of advice that I should not attend the Festival," he said. "What will I look like? To paraphrase a line from *Raging Bull*, I ain't a pretty boy no more." It was to be Ebert's first major public appearance since having had a cancerous growth removed from his right lower jaw. Doctors had taken a portion of the jaw during surgery and also opened his windpipe so Ebert could breathe better. As a result, he temporarily could not speak.

Ebert wrote that when he arrived at the festival, "I will be wearing a gauze bandage around my neck, and my mouth will be seen to droop. So it goes. I was told photos of me in this condition would attract the gossip papers. So what? I have been very sick, am getting better and this is how it looks." Ebert continued. "We spend too much time hiding illness." The evening of the film festival he spoke through written notes and hand signals as he enjoyed the festival with friends and fellow critics.

Many of us are embarrassed to be seen not looking our best. But this Pulitzer Prize–winning journalist would not let pride keep him from what he loved. Ebert's humility inspired thousands of cancer survivors and their families who are tired of "hiding illness." He reminded us that we aren't always able to show our "good side" to the world and that sometimes showing our weakness can be a gift to others.

The loving person doesn't waste energy with pride. He has a great sense of what is most important in life and lives out his desire to love others.

> **Our weaknesses can become strengths when we see them through humble eyes.**

True Versus False Humility

The person who is tempted to write a book titled *Humility and How I Attained It* is not writing a book on humility but rather a book on *How to Camouflage Pride*. Humility is determined by attitude, not behavior, and comes first from our desire to love.

LOOK AT ME!

Observe any group of kindergarteners and you will see a familiar glance when one child shares a crayon or puts away a toy without being asked. Nonverbally he or she is asking, *Did you see me do that? What do I get?* Children know that when they do good things, they are likely to be rewarded.

As we mature in humility, we do good simply because another person is worthy of our love, not because we expect something in return. Waiting for someone to affirm our "humble" act distracts us from loving others. You may have heard it said that when you're twenty, you worry about what everyone thinks of you. When you're thirty, you don't care what anyone thinks of you. When you're forty, you realize no one was thinking of you anyway. With maturity, we allow our actions to fade into the background and don't worry if no one applauds them.

As we've seen throughout this book, authentic love does not love out of selfish ambition but simply for the sake of love. One question to ask yourself when you perform a humble act is this: *Am I doing this for something in return?* We might receive honor for our humility, but that shouldn't be our motivation. Performing what is perceived as an act of humility to gain the attention of others is just another form of pride.

A NEW FOCUS

If someone goes around saying, "Oh, I'm nobody," and, "What I think doesn't matter; forget me," she may appear to be humble at first, but she is actually showing pride. Instead of always talking about herself, a truly humble person shows a genuine interest in others, wanting to know what their stories are, what they think about things, where they excel. She is the kind of person others want to be around. She is not thinking about how humble she is, much less telling others about it. She probably isn't thinking about herself at all.

THE BEST MOTIVATION

True humility is sensitive to what actions would be most helpful to others. It is willing to give up food if in so doing, others can be fed, to forgo sleep so others can sleep more peacefully. The goal is not to gain merit for oneself by sacrificing but to foster the well-being of others.

When Henri Nouwen, the internationally renowned author and Catholic priest, left his prestigious teaching position at Harvard University and moved to the L'Arche Community of Daybreak near Toronto, Canada, a home for those with developmental disabilities, he did not do it in order to demonstrate his great humility. He did it because he was truly humble. He said, "After twenty-five years of priesthood, I found myself praying poorly, living somewhat isolated from other people, and very much preoccupied with burning issues. . . . I woke up one day with the realization that I was living in a very dark place and that the term 'burnout' was a convenient psychological translation for a spiritual death."[11]

For Nouwen, Daybreak was his homecoming. He lived in one of the homes and was asked to help Adam Arnett, a man with a severe disability, get dressed, bathed, and shaved in the morning. Nouwen's book *Adam, God's Beloved* describes how Adam became his friend, his teacher, and his guide. In his humility Nouwen learned from the one he helped. It is in our humility that we often accomplish our greatest good and often receive great good in return.

Humility has nothing to do with our status in the world. Someone can be lowly in status and prideful in heart, or the other way around. In the same way, when one is truly humble, it makes no difference whether one is teaching at a prestigious university or helping a disabled man; both are expressions of true love.

Humility as a Way of Life

Reflecting on these three realities is the key to living out true humility:

1. I have nothing that I have not received.
2. My knowledge of the universe is limited.
3. I am utterly dependent on something outside myself for life.

When we integrate these three realities into our attitude, humility is inevitable.

1. *I have nothing that I have not received.* If you have taken step one toward humility by admitting your propensity toward pride, you are ready for the second step. You proceed to walk down the road of humility by reflecting on the truth that you have nothing that you did not receive. Life itself was not your choice. Once you were born, someone met your physical needs for several years. Your brain and physical abilities were gifts for you to develop. The blood that keeps your body functioning does not flow by your efforts. Whatever you have accomplished has been with the help of others.

Alex Haley, the late author of *Roots*, had a special picture in his office. Framed on his wall was a shot of a turtle sitting on top of a fence post. Haley prized the picture because it was a reminder of the lesson he had learned long ago. "If you see a turtle on a fence post, you know he had some help. Any time I start thinking 'Wow, isn't this marvelous what I have done?' I look at that picture and remember how this turtle, me, got up on that post."[12] So, if you are sitting on a fence post enjoying the view, remember that you had help.

2. *My knowledge is limited.* The wisest among us holds only a thimbleful of knowledge. Sir Isaac Newton, acclaimed as one of the greatest minds in the history of human thought, once said, "I seem to have been only like a boy playing on the seashore and diverting myself in now and then finding the smoother pebble or a prettier shell than ordinary whilst the great ocean of truth lay all undiscovered before me."[13]

   Newton spoke for all of us. The person who holds a PhD in aerodynamics may know little about human relationships. The person lettered in psychology may know almost nothing about physics. While we may develop a great deal of knowledge about one small facet of the universe, we remain ignorant beside the immense ocean of knowledge. In the light of our great ignorance, where is the rationale for pride?

3. *I am utterly dependent on something outside myself for life.* Everything we have is a gift, including our next breath. I personally believe that God created us and that his provision sustains us. I find in God my source of strength, wisdom, direction, and life itself. I look to him for purpose and meaning.

   Even if you don't share an allegiance to God, you will likely agree that none of us is self-made. It is impossible to take full credit for success in life or even for our survival on the planet. We all depend on something outside of ourselves in some way.

   Albert Schweitzer, the physician who invested his life in helping lepers in French Equatorial Africa, did not go to Africa to make a name for himself, although in 1952 he was awarded the Nobel Peace Prize.

   Once he was asked, "If you could live your life over again, what would you do?"

   He answered, "If I should live again, I would take the same path, for this is my destiny. My life has not been an easy one. I have had many difficulties. Yet, I belong to the privileged few who have been able to follow the ideal of their youth, and I am deeply thankful."[14]

   For a lifetime Schweitzer quietly gave each patient his attention. Before procedures he explained, "You'll go to sleep, and in a while you will wake up and the pain will be gone. Don't be afraid." And the patient was calmed.

Hours later, in the dark dormitory, Schweitzer watched while his patient wakened. When the patient thanked the doctor for taking away the pain, Schweitzer replied that it was not his doing. It was love that had brought him to Africa, love that had compelled others to give medicines and bandages, and love that had kept Schweitzer and his wife there.[15] For Schweitzer, humility was a way of life.

Pride is reliance on our own abilities; humility means recognizing how dependent we are on power outside ourselves.

Competitor to Humility: Pain

Anita had no inkling of it, but when she got together with her sisters, all of them now in their forties, she reenacted patterns engraved in childhood. The middle child in her family, Anita had always thought that her older sister received attention as the "leader," while her younger sister was adored as the "clown." Anita was all too often overlooked within the family, or so she believed. Without realizing it, she compensated by pushing herself forward.

When the three women got together at family reunions, Anita tried to get attention by speaking about recognitions she had received at work, reviews of her roles in community theater, and the good grades her children were earning at school. In other words, her pain from feeling ignored drove her to focus on herself. She attributed the distance between herself and her sisters as further proof that she was the outcast of the family, rather than recognize that she herself was creating the distance. She was so preoccupied with proving herself that she was driving her sisters away instead of building a relationship with them. If she had shown an interest in them instead of speaking about herself, she would have found opportunities to cultivate those relationships.

Hurts from the past can easily hinder our attempts at humility. It's not just hurts from past family dynamics, as in Anita's case. The pain may come from being passed over for a promotion at work, having a friendship go cool, or losing a spouse who has become attracted to someone else. Whatever the situation, our desire not to be hurt again can make us defend ourselves by trying to impress others. In short, it can make us appear prideful, forgetting the art of humility.

Only when we seek healing from our hurts, relying on the other six characteristics of love, are we free to take our mind off ourselves and pay more attention to those we love.

True Friendship

Today we think of Meriwether Lewis and William Clark as equals in their extraordinary endeavor that mapped much of the western United States in the early nineteenth century. That's how the members of their expedition looked upon them as well. But if it hadn't been for an act of sacrifice on the part of Captain Lewis, the trip might have gone down in history as the Lewis Expedition instead of the Lewis and Clark Expedition.

In 1803 President Thomas Jefferson commissioned his valued assistant Lewis to lead the expedition across the uncharted western region of the nation, and Lewis in turn immediately wrote to his good friend Clark to describe the expedition in the making. As one historian writes, "Lewis went on to make a most extraordinary offer. If Clark could come, Lewis promised him a captain's commission and co-command of the expedition. Lewis had talked to the president and obtained Jefferson's permission to add another officer. But Jefferson thought he had in mind a lieutenant as second-in-command, and certainly had not authorized Lewis to offer a captain's commission."[16]

Clark accepted the offer Lewis wasn't authorized to make. Several weeks later Lewis learned that the War Department had commissioned Clark as a lieutenant. The easiest course at this point would have been for Lewis to apologize to his friend for the mix-up and ask Clark to accept second place in their command of the expedition. Despite his strong desire to be a captain, Clark probably would have agreed to being his friend's second-in-command. But that wasn't Lewis's plan.

He wrote to Clark and said, "I think it will be best to let none of our party or any other persons know any thing about the grade."[17]

Clark gratefully accepted this offer. And so, while officially Clark headed west as a lieutenant, both men referred to him as Captain, as did the unsuspecting members of their mapping party. Lewis could have pulled rank on Clark during the dangerous four-thousand-mile wilderness journey, but he never did.

In this way Meriwether Lewis gave up his chance for sole command and greater glory in the annals of history. Their names have come down to us, linked forever, as Captain Lewis and Captain Clark, cocommanders of the greatest exploratory trek in American history and an example of one of the truest recorded friendships in history.

This is the joy of true humility: loving others so much that our desire for their affirmation is greater than any selfish ambition.

What Would Your Relationships Be Like If You . . .
- Were willing to forgo your own "rights" when doing so would benefit others?
- Would seek a place of service rather than a seat of authority?
- Used your possessions, abilities, and status in life to help others succeed?
- Saw any talent, time, or position you possessed as a gift?
- Did not harbor anger when others put themselves first?

Making It Personal

QUESTIONS FOR DISCUSSION OR REFLECTION

1. As you reflect on the past month, what behavior have you observed in others that reflected an attitude of humility?
2. When have you gained something because of someone else's loss?
3. Humility means recognizing our own worth as well as the worth of others. Do you find it more difficult to accept your unique gifts or someone else's? Why do you think that is?
4. What makes you valuable?
5. What is the most difficult thing for you to sacrifice?

1. Who is the hardest person in your life to put ahead of you? What is one thing you could do this week to step down so that person could step up?

2. This week, look for an ordinary place—the grocery store, the kitchen, the break room—to ask, "Would it be helpful to you if I did . . . ?" If the answer is yes, then do it.

3. Think of someone you relate to on a regular basis. Practice humility by putting yourself in that person's situation right now. What would be the best way to express love to him or her today? Will that act of love involve sacrifice on your part?

CHAPTER SEVEN

Generosity

GIVING YOURSELF TO OTHERS

Love in a word is the gift of self.
—POPE JOHN PAUL II

Dr. Jack McConnell grew up in "the last house in the hollow" in the coal mining community of Crumpler, West Virginia. His father never earned more than $150 a month and never owned a car, yet during the Depression, McConnell's parents often served lunch to forty or fifty people a day. Drifters riding the rails saw a mark on the McConnells' front gate and knew that they could find food there. "We didn't have much," McConnell says, "but we had a big garden and they could pick corn and tomatoes and we would find a chicken somewhere and make a meal for everyone."[1] McConnell remembers that one of his father's favorite questions to his seven children at the dinner table was: "And what have you done for someone today?"[2]

That spirit of giving made a lasting impression. Today the retired Dr. McConnell is known for starting a clinic on Hilton Head Island, South Carolina, that provides free medical care to those who can't afford it. He donates his time to helping thousands of "friends and neighbors who don't feel well" and inspiring other local retired doctors and nurses to give their time too.[3] The success of the Volunteers in Medicine has led to the formation of more than fifty similar clinics nationwide.[4] When asked how he likes working for nothing, McConnell responded, "I make a million dollars every day. What I get from this clinic you can't buy with money."[5]

We often think of generosity as the decision to donate money to a worthy cause or buy a meal for someone on the street. Those are indeed generous acts, but generosity in the context of authentic love is much more than financial giving. When we love authentically, we have an attitude of generosity in all we do. We are alert to how others need the money, time, energy, attention, and ability that we have to give. That might mean staying up late to talk with the teenage son who opens up about his feelings just when we're ready to go to bed. It might mean noticing that a friend could use a ride to the doctor even though he won't ask for it or that the single mom next door could use some extra help with the yard work on weekends.

The word *gift* is the translation of the Greek work *charis*, which means "unmerited favor." Every time we give our money, talents, or time, we are acknowledging that these things were gifts to us in the first place. Our gifts to someone else are not based upon the person's performance or what the individual has done for us but rather flow from our love for him or her. When we live with a generous spirit, it's amazing to watch the opportunities to love that come our way.

How Generous Am I?

Rank the following statements on a scale from one to five, one being "rarely" and five being "usually."

1. One of my favorite things to do with my family is spend time with them.

2. I am intentional about using my abilities to help others.

3. When I talk with someone, I focus my full attention on her.

4. I enjoy giving away money because I believe it helps others know they are valuable.

5. When one of my possessions is lost, broken, or stolen, it doesn't take me long to let go of it emotionally.

Count up your answers. If your score is from twenty to twenty-five, you are probably alert to ways you can love others through different kinds of generosity. If it's lower, consider whether you struggle most to give away time, ability, or money.

The Gift of Yourself

Generosity may end with actions, but it begins with an attitude of the heart. When we generously give our whole selves, we show others how much we value them.

A couple who have been married over thirty years shared this story with me: Early in their marriage Peter often traveled for his work, leaving Sharon and their two young children home alone. Most of Peter's trips were brief, but any young parent knows how stressful it can be to take care of preschoolers alone. During those years Sharon also struggled with depression and anxiety. When Peter was away, the burdens of the day and the fears about his safety sometimes overwhelmed her.

On one particular trip, Peter left before Sharon and the children had gotten up. He was headed to New York for five days and had an early plane to catch. He called Sharon from the airport as she was getting the girls their breakfast. Sharon knew he was just calling to check in and say good morning, and she tried to sound cheerful. Even so, she couldn't hide the discouragement she felt over facing another week on her own.

"I'm fine, really, I'm fine," she told him when he expressed concern. It was her familiar mantra. When she hung up, she sat down at the kitchen table that was covered with milk and soggy Cheerios and cried.

Thirty minutes later she was helping the girls get dressed when she heard the garage door go up. Soon Peter walked into the room.

"What are you doing? Your meetings! You'll lose your job!" Sharon looked with dismay at the suitcase on the floor.

"You need me more now than New York does," Peter said. "I called my boss and told him I had to take a few days off. They'll be fine." He knelt to help his daughters get dressed while Sharon looked on.

Sharon realized what her husband had done—given up something important to him to show her how much he valued their relationship. As Peter and Sharon took the girls to the park and later sat down to talk as a couple, Peter focused only on his wife and daughters. He gave his whole self to them that day to show them that he was always ready to love them abundantly.

Generosity involves more than material possessions. Above all, generosity involves empathy, compassion, transparency, and the ability to listen. In a marriage relationship in particular, it can be easy to take the other person for granted. When we are generous with those we love, we give them our full attention when they speak. We strive to meet their needs as we can, not halfheartedly but extravagantly. That doesn't mean we have to cancel every business trip we're on when a loved one needs us. It means we have a generous spirit so we are alert to the times when we can give more of ourselves to show love.

Decades later Sharon remembers the details of that day as if they had just happened. Peter's "wasteful" act of generosity told her she was valuable in a way she will never forget.

> GENEROSITY: giving your attention, time, abilities, money, and compassion freely to others.

The Giving of Time

During my sophomore year in college I was surprised one day when my professor Dr. Harold Garner invited me to lunch on my birthday. Three days later, on a cold January day, we walked three blocks from campus to a nice restaurant. I don't remember what I ate, nor do I remember anything about our conversation, except that he asked me about my extended family. But what I do remember is that I felt his genuine concern for me as a person. From that day I was far more attentive in his classes.

In all my undergraduate and graduate education, I never had another professor invite me to lunch. To this day I have a special place in my heart for Harold Garner because he gave me the gift of time.

In today's culture, time is one of the most important things we can offer someone. To give someone your time is to give him a portion of your life. An hour invested in listening to a child talk about her first day of school is an hour you might have spent playing golf, cleaning the house, or answering your e-mails. The child might never know your sacrifice, but the time you give is a powerful expression of love.

To love people is to be willing to give your time to get to know them. The writer James Vollbracht tells the story of a grandmother, Ruth, who lived in a gang-infested neighborhood. She went out for a walk alone every day, despite the protests of her friends who worried about her getting mugged. "But Ruth had a unique strategy. Rather than avoid the kids, she'd engage them. She'd approach them, ask their names, tell them stories about the neighborhood and about their parents, grandparents, and aunts and uncles."

Ruth didn't fear for her safety because the gangs on the street knew she cared for them. "All these kids really want is to be recognized and respected," she said. "A gang provides them with what they haven't got from their family or community. I try to give them some of these essentials whenever I can."[6]

Taking time to inquire about another person's family relationships, vocation, social interests, and physical health communicates to others that you care about them. As you spend time with people, you discover their needs and their desires. Only then are you able to express love in other ways. Until you take time to know someone, you are not likely to help him. We cannot give the gift of time to everyone we pass on the street or encounter on the subway, but we can give the gift of time to someone every day.

Asking questions of someone is one of the most loving ways of relating—and one of the most rewarding. In his book *The Healing Art of Storytelling*, Richard Stone writes about the importance of asking older people to tell us the stories of historical events, such as Pearl Harbor, the Korean War, or the Cuban missile crisis. We can learn so much from others by hearing where they were when history happened or simply what it was like when they first fell in love, first saw the ocean, or got their first jobs.

Before the printing press, storytelling was common in communities; stories were told over and over, and younger generations carried on the tradition. Now, in a world of e-mails and text messaging, we sort through many words every day, but rarely do we truly connect with someone's experience.

Taking the time to ask good questions—at a business lunch, when your spouse gets home at the end of the day, when a friend calls just to say hello—helps build relationships and shows that you value the other person.

HABITS TO ACQUIRE
When you don't know how to show love to someone,
ask her about herself.

TIME TO HEAL

When Kara's infant son died, she didn't know if she would ever move past her grief. Just a few months after his death, Sophie, the elderly mother of a friend of hers, lost her husband to cancer. Although Kara and Sophie didn't know each other well, Kara, knowing how painful holidays could be in the midst of loss, called Sophie on Thanksgiving morning that year. After talking for a half hour or so, the two women made plans to get together in December. Soon they were getting together regularly, poring over Sophie's wedding album and the baby album Kara had kept for her son. They asked each other questions, called each other on hard days, and went out for lunch on anniversaries of difficult memories. As they gave each other the gift of time, they found healing.

Almost everyone we encounter is struggling in some way. The trouble may be poor health, a damaged relationship, vocational stress, or feelings of low self-esteem or depression. Offering a listening ear could go a long way in bringing hope and help to these individuals. As Kara and Sophie discovered, the wonderful thing about giving time to those who are hurting is that we ourselves are helped as we help others.

FAMILY TIME

Over the years I have heard countless spouses in my office say in one way or another what a wife told me recently: "I feel like I am not important to my husband. He has time for everything else but no time for me. We seldom ever talk except about logistics." This marriage is dying because what the wife desires most is quality time with her husband, yet the husband is unaware of how she needs to be loved.

It's easy to think we don't need to be purposeful about spending time with those we live with because we see them every day. But being generous in offering time to our families is an important step in giving well.

Children long for this expression of love. One young man said to me recently, "My parents are too busy to have children. I don't know why they had us." I was reminded of the poignant Harry Chapin song "Cat's in the Cradle," about a son who wanted time with his father. As the father hurried to catch planes and pay bills, his adoring son asked when he would be home. His father said he wasn't sure.

> *But we'll get together then.*
> *You know we'll have a good time then.*

The "then" never came as the boy grew up and became busy with a family of his own. When his father called, the grown son replied that he didn't have the time to see him. The father realized his son had grown up to be just like him.

We often think we'll just get through the summer or the next deadline or the next set of visitors and *then* change how we use our time. But as Annie Dillard writes, "How we spend our days is, of course, how we spend our lives."[7] The choices we make today about investing in our closest relationships probably reflect the choices we will make over a lifetime if we don't change our attitude.

None of us will ever love our families perfectly. When we cultivate a generous spirit, we become more aware of investing time in the most important thing, which may not be the thing that appears to be most urgent.

The most important thing may not be the most urgent thing.

The Sacrifice of Time

You might be thinking: *This sounds great, but I cannot add anything more to my life right now. I would love to spend more time with people, but I also need to make a living and keep the house together.* If you think you can't do it all, you're right. You won't be able to find that elusive "balance" of friends, family, work, and rest because relationships and life don't happen that neatly.

True generosity requires sacrifice. It requires a change in perspective. One young mother I know says that when life gets to the point where the details of the day feel too overwhelming, she asks herself: *What's not working right now?* You might be able to change more about your day than you think you can. Maybe increasing your hours at work has provided for a nicer vacation this year but cuts into the time you can give to caring for your elderly parents. Maybe when you stop to think about it, your preschooler has been staying up later than he needs to; an extra half hour in the evening could give you a little more space. Maybe you and your spouse have slipped into the habit of watching television at night instead of talking.

When the financier J. P. Morgan was asked, "How much is enough money?" he reportedly quipped, "Just a little more."[8] I venture to say that many of us would say the same thing about time: We will never have all we want or feel we need. Every "extra" bit of time we have is eaten up in the tasks of the day unless we are determined to put relationships first.

Our incomes and abilities may differ, but we all have the same amount of time in a day. Subtract the hours we spend sleeping, and you discover the available hours for giving people the gift of time. Certainly our vocation or education requires a number of these hours. But even in those contexts we have opportunities to give others undivided attention and express interest in their well-being. If we have hearts set on giving, we'll be looking for opportunities where we can give the gift of time.

RADICAL CHANGE

You are the only one who can decide how you will invest your time. It is possible that reading this chapter and seriously trying to implement its message will mean making radical changes in the way you use your days.

I am reminded of Robertson McQuilkin, the president of Columbia International University, who gave up his presidency when his wife began to experience dementia. The only time she was at peace was when he was at home. For him it was not a hard decision. He said, "She has cared for me fully and sacrificially all these years; if I cared for her for the next forty years I would not be out of her debt. . . . But there is more: I love Muriel." For the next thirteen years he gave the gift of time by caring for his wife. Only after her death did he continue pursuing his own goals.[9]

For many of us, changing our attitudes toward time will not be so radical. It may be as simple as setting a goal to have a quality conversation with at least one person every day. That conversation may be brief or extended but deeper than talking about the weather and sports. The gift of time is a powerful expression of love, one for which there are many would-be recipients.

The Giving of Abilities

It was a cold Friday night in January. I was out of town leading a marriage seminar. When I called my wife to check in with her, she told me that the pilot light on the furnace had gone out and the house was getting cold. I suggested that she call our friend Larry and see if he could come over and light it. When I called back in thirty minutes, Karolyn said, "The house is getting warmer." Larry had responded immediately, lit the pilot, and brought warmth back to our house. He expressed his love by using an ability he had that Karolyn did not possess. Incidentally, Larry has many abilities, among them baking cookies and preparing meals. He uses these abilities regularly when he volunteers to be the cook at a youth camp each summer and when he shares his cookies with us and others.

I personally don't know how to cook meals or bake cookies. And to be perfectly honest, it would have taken me much longer than Larry to light the pilot on our gas furnace. In the area of culinary skills and technical abilities, I fall in the category of "challenged." You may be more like Larry or more like me, but the good news is that all of us have abilities to do something, and these abilities can be used as an expression of love.

FINDING SATISFACTION

Anne Wenger was a dear friend for many years. She was a speech pathologist who, at the age of fifty-four, experienced polio and from that point on walked with difficulty. For many years she sat in her home with an unlocked door, inviting parents to bring their children who needed the services of a speech pathologist. She invested hours in the lives of children without charge and used her abilities to express love to others. I have never met a happier, more fulfilled woman than Anne Wenger. She knew the joy of loving others by giving away her abilities.

A few years ago I traveled to Southeast Asia to encourage workers who had responded to the tsunami catastrophe of 2004. During that time I met Gary and Evelyn. He was eighty-five; she was eighty-one. Gary was trained as an agriculturalist, and he and Evelyn had invested twelve years of their lives on the island of Antigua in the Caribbean. Upon retirement at the age of sixty-five, they began to look for opportunities to help in other places around the world. They went to Southeast Asia and discovered a deep hunger on the part of nationals in different countries to learn English. They quickly trained themselves how to teach English as a second language. They were soon invited into Buddhist monasteries, government hospitals, and other places to teach English.

Over the past twenty years Gary and Evelyn have developed and published numerous books that are designed to teach English. They give them away to anyone who would like to use them and have given permission for others to copy them freely without royalties. When I asked how they finance this project, Gary said, "By Social Security and a small retirement check that we receive from our former employer."

"How long do you intend to continue this?" I inquired.

"As long as we have health and energy," Gary responded. Here is a couple who have discovered the joy of taking a simple ability—teaching English as a second language—and using it to express love to thousands of individuals.

We don't have to go overseas to love generously. Using our abilities to love others can be simpler and much more satisfying than we imagine.

A CALL TO LOVE

When Bill entered a nursing home and was less able to manage his own bank account and money decisions, he became almost panicked about what would happen to his finances. His daughter called Keisha, a woman at a local bank who worked with a number of people at Bill's nursing home. Keisha spent hours of time talking with Bill and his daughter about his financial future and gave him advice that saved the family thousands of dollars.

After Bill grew too ill to leave his room, he began ordering clothes, gardening equipment, and various tools from catalogs. Everything went to a post office box, and someone from the bank always had to pick up what he ordered. Rather than chastise Bill for using his money in this way or for taking up her time, Keisha picked up the packages and made sure they were delivered to Bill's door. When he ordered a new jacket from L. L. Bean, Keisha made a special trip to the nursing home to watch him open it because she knew he was excited about it.

At the time of Bill's death several years later, Keisha continued to use her abilities, even beyond the context of her job, to help the family sort through remaining financial questions. She did more than her job called for because she was aware of her vocation, her calling to love others.

THE POWER OF VOCATION

The word *vocation* means "calling." Our overarching calling is to enrich the lives of others by making love the fundamental purpose of our lives, which is what this book is all about.

All of life, including our callings, is sacred. Most of us are compensated financially for using our abilities to fulfill a specific calling. We take these funds to support our families and to help others. But the vocation itself is an expression of love because it is meeting the needs of others.

This is why there are some occupations that those living in love choose not to pursue. They fall into three categories: (1) occupations dealing with matters that are likely to hurt others (such as illegal drug trafficking); (2) occupations that do not provide any useful service to society; and (3) occupations that, though permissible in themselves, are harmful for the particular person (such as working as a janitor in a bar if you are an alcoholic). This is why some individuals have left one vocation and followed another as they mature on their path of love. How tragic to invest large portions of one's life in a vocation that does not enhance the lives of others! To do so is to waste the abilities given to us.

When a vocation helps others in some physical, emotional, or spiritual way, then the vocation itself is an expression of love. That doesn't mean you have to be in a traditional helping role, such as a minister, rabbi, nurse, or teacher.

Whatever your job is, you can look to serve the people with whom you work. If you dislike your current workplace—if it is more a job than a calling—you might move on to something else someday, but in the meantime, living with a generous spirit toward others around you can be a sacrificial expression of love.

Your calling right now might be to step down in your job, or away from it completely, to care for a family member or elderly parents. In this way, you are sacrificing some of your abilities to use other abilities for the sake of love. Perhaps you are called to follow a spouse across the country so she can pursue her calling. This too is generosity when it is done in a spirit of love for the sake of relationship.

Whatever your job is today, it can become an expression of love.

BEYOND NINE TO FIVE

All of us have opportunities to use our abilities to love others even beyond our vocational involvements. I know a man who teaches school as a vocation but who spends hours using his abilities to help underprivileged children by tutoring them without charge. I know a group of retired women who invest one morning a week in making quilts for the homeless. I know a wife who stays up late most evenings helping her husband type his dissertation.

A common way to use our abilities to help others is in our homes.

Cooking, cleaning, diapering, fixing the computer, mowing the lawn, and changing lightbulbs are all ways we use our abilities to love our spouses, children, roommates, and parents well.

One of the reasons it's important to see our own worth is that when we know our value, we are alert to the ways we can use our gifts for others. If you want to be generous with your abilities, you must believe that you play an important role in the world. No one else can take your place. Your abilities are needed. As you use your abilities to express love, not only are you becoming a loving person, but you are also helping make love a way of life for others.

The Giving of Money

When Microsoft's founder, Bill Gates, the world's richest man, formed a charitable foundation in 1994 and made an initial contribution of ninety-four million dollars, it made headlines. Since then Gates and his wife have donated more than sixteen billion dollars to such good works as providing drinking water in Africa and fighting AIDS. Then, in 2006, Warren Buffett announced that he would be donating to the Gates Foundation shares of stock totaling more than $30 billion. Again, this was, understandably, front-page news across the country.

Contrast this with the actions of Albert Lexie, a developmentally disabled shoeshine man in Pittsburgh, Pennsylvania. Lexie, charging three dollars per shine, makes only about ten thousand dollars a year from his work, yet he makes many lives better every day.

In the early 1980s Lexie heard about the Free Care Fund to raise money for children's medical care at the Children's Hospital of Pittsburgh. Though he had so little himself, twice a week Lexie started making the trip to Children's Hospital to shine shoes and donate his tips to the fund. Since that time he has donated more than one hundred thousand dollars to the children's fund.

When we see Lexie's contributions through the eyes of authentic love, we recognize that his generosity is just as significant as Gates's or Buffett's donations to important charities. In the course of human history the everyday gifts of people of goodwill have established hospitals, universities, homes for the homeless, and clothing and food distribution centers around the world.

If we have the physical and intellectual ability to work, love calls us to invest our energies in making money so that in turn we can provide for the needs not only of our families but also of others. The desire to give money is one of the most satisfying, practical aspects of valuing other people. Just like everything we own or enjoy, money is a gift to us in the first place. The joy we get from giving it away is just one of its many benefits.

HOW MUCH SHOULD I GIVE?

Some people reason that if their incomes were greater, they could afford to give more to good causes. How much money we have is not as important as our attitude toward money and our attitude toward relationships. As the author W. S. Plumer said, "He who is not liberal with what he has, does but deceive himself when he thinks he would be liberal if he had more." In other words, if we don't give from our "little," we do not give out of our "much."

In a sense, it doesn't matter how much we give, as long as we give with a generous spirit. However, it does help us to have a goal when we set out to be more generous people. With that in mind, I believe that giving 10 percent of one's income ought to be the minimal goal for every person, regardless of his or her means. If everyone consistently did this, there would never be a need for fund-raising events.

Well-known financial advisers back me up. David Bach, the author of *The Automatic Millionaire* series of books, encourages readers to give 10 percent of their incomes for the sake of others *and* for the sake of building up wealth. "The more you give, the wealthier you feel," he writes. "And it's not just a feeling. As strange as it may seem, the truth is that money often flows faster to those who give. Why? Because givers attract abundance into their lives rather than scarcity."[10] Other financial gurus point out that when we set aside certain portions of our monthly incomes to give away, we are more careful with the remaining 90 percent and therefore accumulate more money over the long term.

The more you give, the more true wealth you have.

C. S. Lewis, the author of *The Chronicles of Narnia* series, once wrote: "I do not believe one can settle how much we ought to give. I am afraid the only safe rule is to give more than we can spare. In other words, if our expenditure on comforts, luxuries, amusements, etc., is up to the standard common among those with the same income as our own, we are probably giving away too little. If our charities do not at all pinch or hamper us, I should say they are too small. There ought to be things that we should like to do and cannot do because our charitable expenditure excludes them."[11]

If you live on a fixed income, you may not be able to give what others can give, but you can give something. Some of the most generous people I've known have started with the smallest amounts of money. John D. Rockefeller, one of the wealthiest men of the last century and a model for modern philanthropy, reportedly gave away 10 percent of the first paycheck he ever received and simply increased his giving from there. Imagine what good we could do if we all began to give 10 percent of what we had to affirm the value of other people!

If our hearts are focused on others, we shall want to invest everything we have in relationships; if our hearts are centered on self, then we seek to accumulate all we can for ourselves. That doesn't mean we throw out our 401(k)s. It means we enjoy the present and plan for the future with a spirit of generosity, not hoarding unnecessarily but planning and giving out of love for those close to us and others who are in need.

HABITS TO ACQUIRE
Whatever your habit of financial giving is this year, increase it by 1 percent next year and every year following.

WHY DO WE GIVE?

When Steve heard that the receptionist at his company was facing unexpected surgery just weeks after her husband had lost his job, he bought her a fifty-dollar gift card to a discount store. Fifty dollars won't go far toward hospital bills, but it can buy essential groceries. More important, it communicated to the receptionist that someone noticed her and cared for her. This is the best use of money possible: to strengthen relationships.

If our giving is done not for the sake of relationships but to receive the accolades of people, we are not truly generous, and we miss out on the joy of giving for the sake of love. The Christian Bible puts it this way: "If I give all that I possess to the poor and surrender my body to the flames, but have not love, I gain nothing."[12] When genuine love for others motivates our giving, generosity is not a burden but a joy. We give because we recognize the priceless worth of others.

THE DANGER AND POTENTIAL OF MONEY

As John D. Rockefeller's wealth from the oil industry accumulated, one adviser told him, "Mr. Rockefeller, your fortune is rolling up, rolling up like an avalanche! You must keep up with it! You must distribute it faster than it grows! If you do not, it will crush you and your children and your children's children."[13] Any amount of money has the potential to do more harm in our lives than good if it comes between us and other people instead of helping relationships grow. When we give it away, we remember the importance of other people in our lives. When we keep it to ourselves, we may have an easier material existence, but we will suffer from a narrowness of spirit.

Perhaps the most infamous miser in American history was a woman who lived at about the same time as Rockefeller, Hetty Green (1834–1916). Green inherited money, married into money, and made plenty of money of her own through shrewd investments, yet her stinginess made her a legend. To save money, she never turned on the heat or used hot water in her home. She wore one old dress that she changed only after it had worn out. When her son Ned broke his leg, she wouldn't get him the treatment he needed at a hospital, causing him to lose his leg to gangrene. After her husband died and her children left home, she moved repeatedly among small apartments in different states to avoid establishing a residence that would gain the attention of tax officials. In old age she suffered from a hernia that she refused to have fixed because the operation would have cost her $150. When she died, her net worth may have been as large as $200 million, making her perhaps the richest woman in the world at the time, yet her soul was afflicted with penury.

Imagine what Hetty Green could have done for the people close to her and to the needy of her time with all that money! Still, she kept it all to herself, sacrificing peace and relationships for the sake of something that didn't make her happy on earth and that she couldn't take with her when she died. The vice of miserliness, hoarding money for ourselves well beyond what we need, will, by its nature, turn our focus upon ourselves and cut us off from healthy relationships with others. Whether we have as much as John D. Rockefeller and Hetty Green or as little as a shoeshine man, a grasping attitude will impoverish our relationships while a giving attitude will strengthen them.

HOLDING IT LOOSELY

Dennis has bought a new car, straight from the dealer, only once in his life. He researched what he wanted and added a lot of extras. The first weekend he owned it, he went to visit his mother. While he was there, his sister and her kids came over in a truck with the kids' bikes. Soon after they arrived, Dennis heard a scream: "Look out for Uncle Dennis's car!" Then his nephew came in "with his lower lip hanging down to the floor," as Dennis tells it, and told Dennis he'd scratched the new car with his bike.

"It's okay. I'm glad you told me," Dennis said. Then he saw the scratch. It was all the way down the side of the car. The only thing to do was to get it fixed.

Just a few weeks later Dennis was parked in the driveway of a friend's house when his friend's wife arrived home and drove her car into the passenger side of Dennis's car, badly damaging the exterior.

"Both times I didn't really feel upset," Dennis says now. "I loved that car, but it was just a car." Because he held his possessions loosely, he was able to show the traits of love generously. He valued relationships more than what he owned, and he experienced the freedom of living out that priority.

The author Sheldon Vanauken once wrote about purchasing his first car with his wife, Davy. The couple were thrilled to own a new vehicle, but the first thing they did when they got it home was hit it with a hammer "to make it comfortably dented." Vanauken writes that they didn't want anything "that might divide lover from lover." They concluded that "overvalued possessions . . . were a burden, possessing their owners." Generosity requires us to keep earthly possessions from becoming more important than they should be.[14]

PROJECT GIVING

Many people are challenged by what I call project giving. I remember the man who said to me, "I was captivated when I heard Joni Earickson Tada, who is a paraplegic, tell of her Project Wheelchair. She collects used wheelchairs, has them refurbished, and ships them to third world countries. This touched me, and I wanted to be a part of it. I couldn't travel to other countries, but I could give money to the project." This man was receiving the joy of participating in the work of love someone else initiated.[15]

Where Should I Give?

A good place to begin giving financially or otherwise is to local organizations that you trust, such as homeless shelters, schools, hospitals, food programs, and religious associations. I once read the story of a mother who volunteered at the preschool that her special needs son had attended before he died. "It was where he was the happiest. . . . I can help because I know what it feels like to be a parent with a special needs child." This woman later trained as an occupational therapist so she could help other families in need of care.[16]

If you want to give money to a charitable cause but you aren't sure where to start, go to www.justgive.org. Before donating money to an organization, find out more about it through the Better Business Bureau (www.bbb.org) and the IRS (www.irs.org).

MORE THAN WE THOUGHT WE HAD

Winston Churchill once said, "We make a living by what we earn, we make a life by what we give." Only when we give away a portion of our money and possessions will we be aware of how much we have left. This is one of the many paradoxes of living a life of authentic love.

When giving flows from a grateful heart, we are humbled rather than prideful in our gifts. We give not out of a sense of duty but out of a heart of love.

The grave of Christopher Chapman in Westminster Abbey bears the date of 1680 and the following statement:

> What I gave, I have
> What I spent, I had,
> What I left, I lost,
> By not giving it

As we learn the art of giving, we find we have more than we ever realized.

The Simple Joy of Giving

When Amber Coffman's mother wanted to volunteer at Sarah's House, a homeless shelter near her home in Maryland, she decided she would volunteer only if eight-year-old Amber came with her. As mother and daughter spent time with homeless children and their parents every week, Amber learned the joy and the pain of getting to know others' stories. The desire to live generously grew from the relationships she built with the homeless community, and three years later, in 1993, eleven-year-old Amber started the Happy Helpers for the Homeless program to aid Baltimore's poorest population. She started by recruiting other kids her age to make cheese and bologna sandwiches in her home every Saturday morning and distribute them to homeless people. Today Coffman continues to direct the organization she founded, which has helped more than thirty thousand people and spawned forty-nine similar programs in the United States and abroad. And every week six hundred bag lunches are distributed to the homeless in Baltimore, Maryland.

EVERY PERSON IS A RELATIONSHIP

We are not generous because we want to start a program that will become known internationally and help thousands of people. We are generous because we care about relationships. Amber's mother cared about passing on the spirit of generosity to her daughter, and her daughter cared for the people she met.

Mother Teresa, whose generosity of spirit has brought healing and peace to tens of thousands, once wrote: "I never look at the masses as my responsibility. I look at the individual."[17] These are good words to remember when we're feeling overwhelmed with all the people, many of them in our own families or workplaces, who need help. We are called to be generous not to a statistic but to the person in front of us. A spirit of generosity can bring healing to more people than we can imagine, one relationship at a time.

No matter what or how you give, remember that it is an individual you are serving.

SIMPLE CREATIVITY

When citizens of Roswell, New Mexico, got together to brainstorm ways to help the kids in their community, they concentrated on Boys & Girls Clubs, the YMCA, theater, and youth sports. Then a middle-aged woman raised her hand and said, "I have an acre of gardens in my backyard. I have always had a dream that the children and the adults in our community could come garden together. When you garden, something magical happens. . . . You build something together that lasts a lifetime."[18] The room fell silent when she finished speaking. The idea was so simple and so authentic. It just might work.

Look for creative ways to give your time, money, and abilities away. Start by asking, *What do I have that other people don't have?* Maybe you are not called to adopt a child, but you have the funds to help another couple adopt. Maybe you don't have the funds to help another couple, but you have the ability to mobilize an effort on the Internet to raise money for that couple. If you have any kinds of special resources, consider them things that are given to you so you can share them with others. That change of mind-set will open up many possibilities for generosity.

GENEROSITY LEADS TO GENEROSITY

Story after story shows us how one act of generosity can lead to the participation of countless other people.

On August 1, 2007, twenty-six-year-old Marcelo Cruz was driving on the Interstate 35 bridge in Minneapolis when it began to collapse. He kept himself from plunging into the Mississippi River by deliberately crashing his van into the wall. Cruz, a paraplegic, could not get out of his specially equipped van because it was on a slant. After two people pulled him free, others got him to the emergency room to get help for his injured back.

Lawrence Pleskow, the head of a California-based charity called When U Dream a Dream, saw Cruz's story on the news and called Cruz to tell him he would come to Minnesota that week to present him with a new van Cruz could keep until he got a replacement for the one he crashed. Pleskow's charity also wanted to fly Cruz and his mother to California so they could tour Disneyland, meet celebrities, and enjoy vacation time together.

Cruz is in a wheelchair because seven years ago he was shot by an unknown assailant in a street fight. He says now he is overwhelmed with the generosity of others who have heard about his situation. It started with one person's doing what he could to help and led to a chain of kindness that could change a life.[19]

In the same way, one simple act of generosity in your home or workplace can lead others around you to respond generously. One person decorating someone's cubicle on her birthday can lead to someone else's bringing in flowers for the front desk. Even something as small as picking up a friend's favorite coffee drink, with just the amount of whipped cream that she likes, contributes to a spirit of generosity in the friendship.

GETTING TOGETHER

Thinking creatively might lead you to discover new ways of spending time with friends and coworkers. Families, such as Amber Coffman and her mother, can strengthen their own relationships as they build relationships with others by volunteering together. Similarly, business offices are often brought together through helping others. When Justin's wife was killed in a car accident, his entire office brought in toys, games, books, and favorite foods for his three children, still recovering from the accident. As departments focused outside themselves, they found that they worked in better unity and discovered positive traits about one another they had not known before.

If you're in a family, marriage, or community group that's experiencing a lot of tension, consider donating a Saturday morning to raking yards or serving soup together. You might be surprised at the results.

"It Energizes Me"

Between his junior and senior years at LeTourneau College in Texas, David took an engineering job in Wausau, Wisconsin, for the summer. Just a few weeks into the summer he unexpectedly lost his housing. The elderly couple who owned the room he rented decided "it wasn't working out" and asked him to leave—now. So David, who was trying to earn money for the rest of his education, had a summer job in a strange town, a car full of his earthly possessions, and nowhere to live. He went to several apartment complexes but couldn't even get an apartment manager to show him a room since it was Sunday. He called friends, looking for options. Finally, a friend called him back. A young couple might have a room they could spare:

He drove to their house. The three of them sat in the small kitchen that afternoon and chatted, laughing as they became more comfortable with one another.

"So, how soon do you need a place to stay?" the wife asked.

"Well, all my stuff is in my car," David confessed.

The couple looked at each other and then smiled. "We would love to have you stay here," they both said at once. Their charge for room and board would not have covered meals somewhere else. Yet the couple seemed delighted to be able to help someone in this way. Their attitude of generosity not only initiated a friendship that endures twenty-five years later but also later inspired David and his wife to open their home to a coworker in need of a place to stay.

A young mother, Jana, speaks of a similar excitement in a friend who has discovered the joy of giving. Every time Jana and her family go on vacation, this friend checks on the house and brings in the mail.

The day before Jana and her family get back, she stocks their shelves with all the essentials and then some.

"Laundry soap, soup, milk, cereal—I keep discovering new things for about three days after we get home!" Jana says. "When I thanked her this last time, she told me, 'I just love doing it. It *energizes* me.' "

Generosity does not need to be a burden in any of our relationships. While it can require sacrifice, as all love does, the rewards of improved relationships bring an energy and enthusiasm that nothing can replace. To have an opportunity to build relationships through helping those in need is one of life's highest privileges.

Competitor to Generosity: Our Own Agenda

Life is filled with trying to meet the latest deadline; get the kids to bed on time; stop by the store for essentials; watch investments; go to ball games, board meetings, and parent-teacher conferences; get the oil changed in the car; stop off at the gym for a workout; mow the grass; and load the dishwasher—again.

With these things and much more filling up our schedules, it's easy to keep our focuses inward, to parcel out our time, money, and energy for the things we want to accomplish rather than remembering the people we want to accomplish them for. When we get wrapped up in our own plans for the day, we can overlook what those around us truly need, and we can miss the opportunity to serve them.

Magazine articles tell us we need to slow down for the sake of our health and well-being. That may be true, but we also need to slow down for the sake of loving relationships. How can we know what people need, much less help with those needs, if we are distracted by our own agendas all the time?

How many of us have rushed past a homeless person on the street without noticing the look on his face? In the same way, every day we hurry by people, sometimes in our own kitchens, whose needs we could meet if we would set aside our to-do list for a few minutes.

Of course we each have certain things we need to get done each day. But as Augustine of Hippo once said, "Nothing worth doing can be accomplished in one's lifetime." When our long-term perspectives carry more weight than our short-term checklists, we realize that generosity is often simpler than we realize. The good lover's question, *What can I do for you?*, doesn't take long to ask. Pausing to listen to the answer can make all the difference to someone in need of love.

Getting a Generous Life

Divorce, poverty, and neglect characterized author Barbara Curtis's childhood. As an adult she drank heavily, did drugs, and neglected her two daughters. After she had overcome her addictions with the help of Alcoholics Anonymous, she realized what a poor mother she had been. "When you're not raised with parents who are lavish in loving you," Curtis says, "generosity doesn't come naturally to you. It's a switch you have to discover and turn on yourself. When I first got sober, I had to confront the fact that I had to do things differently. I went to the park and watched moms with their kids to see what loving moms did, because that wasn't my experience."

Now, at age fifty-nine, Curtis says she is learning new truths about loving generously. After having had nine children by birth, including a son with Down syndrome, Curtis and her husband adopted three more boys with Down syndrome. She says it sounds more heroic than it is.

"Some days when the kids were little, I didn't want to get out of bed and face the day. I felt I couldn't give any more. But those days were expanding my capacity to love. Now I'd like to sit and write all day or go on a cruise with my husband instead of cleaning the house or fighting the school system for my teenagers. But I believe that my work cleaning bathrooms is just as important as writing for thousands of people or speaking in front of a group of five hundred. Giving away your time and energy in parenting or any other relationship can be thankless. The important thing is that you have a generous spirit. Whether or not it's acknowledged in any way, acting out of love stretches you to be a more loving person. If it's not costing you anything, then what difference does it make?"

Barbara Curtis clearly takes delight in helping others. "I love people by serving," she says. "I could spend the rest of my life helping people and never do enough to show my gratitude for the chance to turn my life around. As you get older, you see how much more work there is to do in your soul before you can love authentically—so much more to do in your heart to become a more generous person."[20]

Every part of our lives changes when our attitudes toward our time, money, possessions, and abilities change. As Anna Quindlen writes, "You cannot be really first-rate at your work if your work is all you are." The same could be said for your attitude toward your home, education, and even hobbies. When we concentrate too much on what we do, we forget the value of the people we encounter every day. Generosity moves our minds and hearts out of the ruts they fall into and brings us back to relationships. It gives us new eyes to see the beauty of people who could use our gifts. Quindlen writes, "Get a life in which you are generous. Look around at the azaleas making fuchsia star bursts in spring; look at a full moon hanging silver in a black sky on a cold night. And realize that life is glorious, and that you have no business taking it for granted. Care so deeply about its goodness that you want to spread it around. . . . All of us want to do well. But if we do not do good, too, then doing well will never be enough."[21] One of the most satisfying, joy-filled choices we can make is to "get a life" full of generosity, gratitude, and the beauty of giving ourselves away for the sake of relationships.

What would your relationships be like if you . . .
- Held your possessions in open hands, ready to release them when they were needed?
- Gave 10 percent of your income to others?
- Took time daily to show an acquaintance, a friend, a child, or a spouse that you were interested in his or her well-being?
- Used your abilities to benefit others in creative ways?
- Found joy in having a generous spirit toward others, no matter the circumstances?

Making It Personal

1. What was a time you experienced the joy of giving?
2. As you analyze your patterns of giving over the past few years, how would you describe your attitude toward giving? Selfish? Inconsistent? Moderate? Generous? How satisfied are you with this pattern?
3. What is most likely to keep you from giving money to someone? From giving time? From giving abilities?

1. Make a list of some of the big gifts you have received in your life. These might include education, loving·parents, intelligence, a job opportunity. . . . Giving begins by accepting this reality: *All that I am and possess is a gift.*
2. Are there people in your family or circle of friends with whom you desire to spend more time? If so, what can you do to begin to make this happen?
3. What is one thing you could do right now to become more sensitive to the opportunities you have daily to give people your undivided attention?
4. Are you presently giving one-tenth of your income to causes that help people in need? If not, do you see this as a goal you would like to attain? Why or why not?
5. Make a list of the gifts of money you have made over the past month. Are there other individuals, churches, community groups, or projects that you would like to add to your list next month?
6. Make a list of some of the abilities you think you possess. How have you used your abilities to help others in the past? What steps could you take to use your abilities to a greater degree? In what ways can you use your abilities to express love to others?

 Honesty

REVEALING WHO YOU REALLY ARE

Truth is such a rare thing, it is delightful to tell it.
—EMILY DICKINSON

Joy and Becca started working at the marketing department of a phone company within a few months of each other. Eager to start her career well, Joy worked long hours to make the best possible impression in the company. Becca also wanted to please their supervisor, but she saw her job primarily as a chance to make money before she got married and had a family.

The young women enjoyed chatting at lunch breaks and sometimes had dinner together after work. They grew closer while commiserating about their hard work, tiny cubicles, and low pay.

Then one afternoon Becca excitedly shared the news that she had been offered a promotion. Her new role would offer her a better salary, a real office, and more authority. She was on her way up.

Joy tried to sound excited, but she found it difficult to keep her voice light. *Why should she get the promotion when she doesn't even want to continue with the company?*

Over the next few months Joy made frequent excuses to avoid spending time with Becca. Eventually Becca stopped sending "I'm about to eat my fingers. Are you ready for lunch?" e-mails. Joy brought Becca a plant for her new office but didn't stay to talk. Soon the young women tried to avoid each other in the halls.

"Didn't you and Becca use to be friends?" a coworker asked Joy casually one afternoon. The words stuck with Joy the rest of the day and evening. She realized her pride was keeping her from admitting to Becca what was really bothering her, and she was losing a friendship because of it. She got in her car and headed to Becca's apartment.

"I was jealous," she said at the door. "I wanted that job, and you didn't even seem to notice. You don't even *care* about that place! But I'm sorry I reacted the way I did."

Becca invited Joy in, and together the women spoke honestly about their hurt. Both felt raw at the end of the conversation, but something had shifted in their relationship. In the weeks to come, they gradually renewed their friendship and determined not to let anger simmer but to speak truth to each other. Because she was finally honest about her own feelings, Joy was able to celebrate Becca's achievement with her, while Becca felt free to talk about her insecurities and fears because she knew she could trust Joy.

In my years of counseling, I have seen the effect that honesty, or dishonesty, can have on a relationship. Whether two people need to be honest about small preferences, hurt feelings, or something as significant as an extramarital affair, if honesty is missing from their relationship, they will not grow in authentic love.

Of course we can't make someone be honest with us. But when we live and speak truth, we free *ourselves* to love well and create the space for someone else to love us. Without honesty, all the other traits of a loving person are incomplete.

~ Am I Trustworthy?

One of the things we'll look at in this chapter is how individuals have different opinions about what constitutes lying. To find where you fall on this spectrum of opinion, answer the following questions on a scale from zero to five, zero being "never" and five being "usually."

1. Telling small lies to protect myself or other people is okay.

2. It doesn't matter if I believe what I say as long as I appear to believe it.

3. If my boss knows everyone is stretching the rules a little, it's all right if I do it too.

4. I find it difficult to take a stand for what I believe because I don't know for sure if I'm right.

5. If I tell someone the truth and she gets upset, I just assume that's her problem.

Count up your answers. If your score is five or less, you clearly have a desire to be a loving truth teller. If it's higher, this chapter might challenge you to rethink the importance of truth. It's surprising how significant honesty becomes when we are determined to love authentically.

The Characteristics of Love

As I was doing the research for this book, I asked numerous people to give me the name of someone they considered a loving person. Then I followed up with these questions: *Why? What about that person leads you to conclude that he or she is a loving person?*

Most of the answers I received fell within the characteristics of love that we have already discussed in this book. The loving person was said to be kind, patient, forgiving, humble, courteous, and giving. But a significant number of my respondents also indicated that the person was loving because he or she would tell the truth even when the other person didn't want to hear it. A casual acquaintance may tell you what you want to hear, but a true friend will tell you what you need to hear.

Mark wrote that his wife always gives him honest answers when he's discouraged. "She'll listen to me and then tell me her thoughts on the situation—even if that means pointing out a weakness on my part that I need to apologize for. But she tells me the truth in such a caring way that I know she really wants to help."

Anne in Minnesota said of her friend Angie, "She always thinks of others first and makes everyone feel special. When I first came to the company, she often walked over to my desk to say good morning or good-bye. Later, when we got to know each other better, she suggested a hairstyle change for me in a really nice way. Instead of telling me how boring I looked, she told me how great I could look. She sees potential in everything." Talking about hairstyles might seem minor, but giving opinions with gentleness and respect reflects a freedom of relationship that can only come from authentic love.

Another question I asked was: What are the characteristics of a truly loving person? Here are some of the answers I received:

- "A loving person is always honest with the people he loves and will tell them the truth in a tactful manner."
- "A loving person is someone who is truthful yet nonjudgmental."
- "A loving person is willing to help you in tough decisions, comfort you when you are hurting, love you when you are needy, celebrate with you when you have accomplished something little or big. She will be honest with you when she sees things in your life that need to be changed."
- "A loving person is willing to give advice and be critical when necessary in order to help you be a better person. He is honest and yet sensitive."

Honesty was a common response to a variety of questions about what it means to love, whether I was asking men or women, young or old. We all are eager to know people whose words and actions are consistent with each other and reflect a desire to make love a way of life.

> HONESTY: A loving consistency in speech, thought, and action.

The late Fred Rogers, beloved host of the *Mister Rogers' Neighborhood* television show, wrote many beautiful songs for children that hold great truths for adults as well. In "I Like to Be Told," he writes of every child's desire to be told "if it's going to hurt," if a parent is going away, or if something will be new or difficult, because "I will trust you more and more" each time these things come true.

We never outgrow our desire to be told the truth. A fellow writer told me the story of waking up one morning when she was a child and being told she wouldn't be going to kindergarten that day but to the hospital for eye surgery. Her suitcase was already packed. She was old enough to understand that this meant her parents had withheld information from her. The memory of being betrayed is more painful than the memory of the surgery itself.

Compare this with a young boy who recently faced heart surgery. He asked his grandfather if it was going to hurt. His grandfather answered with honesty that engendered hope: "Yes, for a while. But every day the pain should get less and less, and it means you'll be getting better and stronger."

Dishonesty is like plaque that builds up in a friendship, marriage, family, or work relationship. If we are to be loving people, we must speak and act out of the truth. Only then are we free to love others for who they really are. This is why honesty is so crucial to loving relationships.

SPEAKING TRUTH IN LOVE

Just as we've seen in previous chapters, as we strive to be honest in our relationships, we need to speak *truth* and speak it in *love*. When these two elements are a part of our relationships, we are on our way to developing a habit of honesty. Speaking truth in love means keeping every other character trait of a loving person in mind.

- *Kindness.* Allen and Lucy enjoyed having local college students over for dinner every Sunday evening. Over the school year they got to know and enjoy these young adults, and the students got to know them as surrogate parents on campus. But Thomas, a sophomore, was more difficult to like. From the time he stepped into their house, he rarely stopped talking about himself. It was difficult for anyone else to tell a story because Thomas always had a story to top it. He never asked questions or listened when others tried to start a different conversation.

  One evening Allen invited Thomas to go for a walk. As they started walking through the neighborhood, Allen asked, "Thomas do you want to know why people don't like you?"

  Thomas's answer came as a surprise: "Yes, I do. And no one will tell me."

  Allen then suggested how Thomas could listen more and

improve his social skills. Thomas was eager to hear the kindness of an honest answer.

Loving someone honestly has to do with the inner attitude with which we approach the person as well as the words we say. Allen spoke the truth because he loved Thomas, not because he enjoyed critiquing him. When we remember that kindness calls us to put others before ourselves, we are honest because we want to build a relationship up, not tear it down.

- *Patience.* There are two ways to speak the truth: as bullets or as seeds. Use the truth as a bullet, and you will kill relationships. Plant the truth as a seed, and it will take root and grow, influencing the person in whose heart it was planted. Love has the patience to plant seeds.

  In some relationships, particularly marriage, patient honesty might mean telling the other person your feelings even though you'd rather he figured them out himself. Honesty calls you to be patient with the fact that the other person isn't as aware of you as you want him to be. You put the relationship before your desire to be noticed and speak the truth so your anger doesn't fester.

- *Forgiveness.* The purpose in speaking the truth is not to condemn but to restore. Sometimes honesty calls us to point out an error committed by someone we love. If we approach the conversation with the desire to forgive the other person and restore the relationship, we are showing a loving honesty.

- *Courtesy.* When the customer in front of us in line drops a twenty-dollar bill and doesn't notice, it might be tempting to pocket the bill and move on. It's unlikely we would do the same thing if that customer were a close friend. When we act honestly out of a courteous spirit, we treat everyone as if she were a friend. We have many opportunities to do this every day, whether we are confronting a loved one, meeting with an employee for his annual review, or filling out insurance papers. The person we're relating to might be a friend, an enemy, or a stranger, but authentic love calls us to be honest because it is the courteous thing to do.

- *Humility.* A young man named Daniel told me, "The hardest thing I have ever done was to confront my brother when I knew he was being unfaithful to his wife. I started by saying, 'I find it hard to bring this up because I know that I could well be in your shoes. I hope that if it were me, you would do what I'm trying to do. I love you too much to be silent.' Then I told him what I knew and urged him to talk with a counselor. He did, and in time he and his wife were reconciled. I am so glad that I had the courage to confront him in love."

  If Daniel had approached his brother with an attitude of superiority, his brother might not have listened. Instead, Daniel humbled himself to acknowledge that he was not above similar wrongdoing. He put himself in his brother's place and used words that spoke love and humility.

- *Generosity.* The wife who wants to give honest feedback to her husband about how he is relating to their teenage daughter could tell him her thoughts with sharp words or while she was in the middle of another task. Honesty in the context of authentic love calls her to give all her attention to her husband for that conversation and offer her suggestions with gentleness and respect.

  When we have a spirit of generosity, we realize that our time, money, and abilities were gifts to us in the first place. We don't hold so tightly to them that we lie about finances or become too busy to give our time to strengthen a relationship through honest conversation.

What Does Honesty Look Like?

To be honest about honesty, we have to admit that it's not always easy to know what honesty looks like in the context of authentic love.

According to a survey about honesty conducted by *Reader's Digest*, 71 percent of respondents had lied to friends or family members about the others' appearances in order to avoid hurting their feelings. In addition, 50 percent had kept money that didn't belong to them when they were undercharged or received too much change, while 28 percent had lied to a spouse or partner to cover up an illicit romantic relationship.[1]

It's obvious from this poll that most of us have decided that at times lying is of greater value than telling the truth. We might even do this without realizing it; by nature, we seek truth in others and twist truth for ourselves. That's why parents do not have to teach children to lie. The false self tends to lie when doing so has personal benefits.

The same *Reader's Digest* poll showed that while men and women lie at about the same rate, they tend to do their lying in different ways. Men's dishonesty generally has to do more with impersonal objects, such as taking office supplies or fudging on tax returns. Women meanwhile are more likely to lie in order to avoid conflict (such as fibbing to a boyfriend or husband about the cost of a purchase) or to spare another person's feelings (such as saying, "No, you don't look fat at all!").[2]

This raises interesting questions: Is it ever all right to be dishonest? What if we lie to protect someone else? Whether we are conscious of it or not, we ask these questions every day. *Is it all right to tell my wife she looks nice in that outfit when she doesn't? Should I tell my dad that the doctor said the cancer has spread? Do I need to tell my husband about kissing that guy on the business trip when it really was nothing?*

The best standard for answering these questions is to ask yourself: *Do my words and actions right now encompass all the traits of a loving person? Will speaking truth in this situation show kindness, patience, forgiveness, courtesy, humility, and generosity? If not, what could be said that is truth-filled and still loving?*

HABITS TO ACQUIRE
When you are not sure whether to say something, ask yourself, *Do my words reflect every trait of a loving person?*

These questions help us become aware of what truth telling is *not.* Truth telling does not mean . . .

- *Telling everything we know.* By truth telling, I do not mean that we are to be totally transparent about ourselves or others.

Telling everything we know would ruin the reputation of many good men and women who have abandoned their unloving practices of the past and have gone on to be upright and productive citizens. This is where all the traits of a loving person come in. Love chooses to forgive and refuses to speak of something that would be detrimental to the reputation of someone else.

- *Verbalizing all our emotions.* Emotions are our unsolicited responses to the events that happen throughout the day. We are emotional creatures, and our emotions fluctuate easily. If someone speaks to you harshly, you are likely to have negative feelings. If he speaks to you kindly, you are more likely to have positive feelings. To give a daily report of all your negative emotions is not only unnecessary but destructive. Far better to recognize that negative emotions indicate that the relationship needs attention. Make positive changes in your words and actions, and your friend, spouse, or colleague is likely to reciprocate. When his behavior becomes more favorable, your negative emotions will fall by the wayside.

- *Making an excuse to be unloving.* When you allow your emotions to control your behavior and then express them under the guise of honesty, you stimulate additional negative emotions in the other person's mind. Those negative emotions become a barrier indicating that something is amiss in the relationship.[3]

- *Telling secrets for personal gain.* Truth telling should not be used as an excuse to tell the secrets of your business operations to a competitor for personal gain or to break the trust of a coworker so you can look good with your supervisor. Jean Giraudoux's well-known statement summarizes this perspective of truth: "The secret of success is sincerity. If you can fake that, you've got it made." Giraudoux was neither the first nor the last to sacrifice truth on the altar of personal success.

- *Jeopardizing justice.* Truth telling does not mean giving away information when doing so would put someone else at risk of being unfairly treated. We see this illustrated in the families of those who hid Jewish citizens in their homes to protect them from Nazi deportation during World War II. Oskar Schindler, Raoul Wallenberg, Corrie ten Boom, and Chiune Sugihara are just a few of the individuals who risked their lives to save others, even if it meant holding back the truth at times. The small Dutch village of Nieuwlande unanimously decided in 1942 and 1943 that every home in the village would house one Jewish individual or household. Dozens of people were saved because neighbors protected their refugees as well as one another. Men and women of integrity will not tell everything they know when to do so would be detrimental to the cause of justice.

With all these things in mind, why is truth telling so important? Because even though we are inclined to distort the truth, deep within every one of us is an awareness of a *difference* between truth and false-hood. I remember the five-year-old boy who answered the phone and said his mother wasn't there. Then he paused and said, "Actually, she *is* here, but she's in the bathtub." We constantly struggle with our false self, yet something inside us wants us to be known as people who speak truth. We lose respect for the person who chooses falsehood continu-ously, and likewise we respect the person who speaks honestly. No mat-ter what our behavior is right now, something in us knows that falsehood destroys and love builds.

Inside and Out

Becoming an authentically loving person calls for putting off the prac-tice of lying and putting on the practice of truth telling. But honesty goes beyond what we say to who we *are*. When we speak truthfully, we are being honest. When we live truthfully, we are being authentic. We are being people of integrity.

We often refer to the integrity of a leader or a politician. In other words, we're looking for the leader's words to match her actions. We overlook a lot of faults when we believe that at least the person is be-ing truthful. In personal relationships, others will be aware of our love for them when we act with integrity in even the smallest circumstance.

True honesty goes beyond what we say to who we are.

Living with integrity means . . .

- *Being open about our weaknesses.* When Carl took the job as president of a small exercise equipment manufacturer, he knew he was stepping into a difficult situation. The previous president had departed in a cloud of financial controversy, leaving behind bitter employees and a spirit of disillusionment in every department of the company. The board hired Carl because he had experience turning companies around, although he had never worked in this particular industry. He was also known as a man of integrity. Even so, he could tell as he shook hands with his wary employees at the first staff meeting that it would take time to build an atmosphere of trust again.

  "The first thing I'd like to do," he told the staff, "is spend a day in each department. I have a lot to learn from all of you."

  And so for his first week of work, Carl spent time in sales, production, promotion, legal, and development, asking questions about how the company worked and the strengths and weaknesses of its product.

  "This is not the kind of contract I'm used to," he admitted easily to a middle manager. "Could we go through each paragraph?"

  It didn't take long for Carl's employees to see he was a trustworthy man. As he got to know the company, he never compromised his leadership or apologized for his authority. He simply admitted that he still had a lot to learn before becoming the best president possible.

  Integrity means being who we are, not who we want to appear to be. Trying to act smarter, braver, stronger, or more experienced than we are takes a lot of energy. When integrity becomes part of our daily speech and actions, we are free to show our weaknesses, knowing that even our vulnerability can be a way of loving others.

• *Recognizing the importance of truth.* The person with integrity recognizes that his behavior always has an impact on others. If we do something loving, it has a positive impact. If we do something deceitful, it has a negative impact. The seeds we plant will eventually grow up and bring a blessing or a curse to others.

How many times have I sat in my office and watched a parent weep, knowing that his own deceitful living had negatively affected the character of his child? We do not determine our children's behavior, but we do greatly influence it.

By contrast, the person of integrity sets a model to be emulated. I remember the young man who came to me after his father's funeral and said, "I realized as I reflected on the life of my father that he was a man of integrity. I am not. In thirty-five years I have managed to make a mess of my life. I need to make some radical changes, and I am asking you to help me." The life of a truth teller continues to influence others even after death.

• *Being consistent in behavior, words, tone, and meaning.* The pediatrician Diane Komp writes about a painting that she received years ago from a twelve-year-old girl named Korey. Korey was preparing for surgery for bone cancer and wanted her parents to give Komp the painting. It concerned Korey that she would be in the operating room under anesthesia when the doctor first saw it.

"When Dr. Komp opens the package, look at her eyes. She may say that she likes it, but I want to know what she really thinks," Korey told her parents.

Korey's request disturbed Komp. "Was it doctors specifically or adults in general that she didn't trust to always speak the truth with their lips? . . . When listening for the truth, most of the world counts on both lips and eyes to say the same thing. . . . We can't have 'no, no' on our lips and 'yes, yes,' in our eyes and tell the truth."[4]

We sometimes hear of the "integrity" of a building. If a building has integrity, it is structurally sound, through and through. When we have integrity, our eyes, voices, words, and actions are structurally sound, all reflecting the same truth.

• *Taking risks for the sake of truth.* Lynn saw her father frequently after she graduated from college, so she noticed when his behavior started changing. He often asked her more than once about upcoming plans or forgot important appointments. Once he drove to work but took the bus home. Lynn was not sure what to do; her father had always been so alert to details. She knew he took great pride in his job and relationships, and she hated to cause him any pain.

After a few months of his odd behavior, Lynn felt she was living dishonestly as she made excuses for him to others and even lied to him about things he had forgotten in order to protect him. One weekend evening she sat down with him and explained some of the things she had observed in recent weeks.

Her dad took off his glasses and rubbed his tired eyes. "Lynn," he said, "I'm so glad you said something. I just haven't felt myself, but no one has seemed to notice."

Because Lynn took the risk of being honest, her father underwent tests that determined he was facing early-onset Alzheimer's. Lynn's confrontation allowed him to receive early treatment and spend more time with his family before his health declined.

If you are an emotionally sensitive person, confronting someone with hard truth may be difficult. But it might also make you just the right person to speak. A person of integrity does not relish exposing the drug use of a spouse or telling a friend there are signs of abuse in her marriage. But love is behind both the struggle to confront and the desire to confront. Integrity calls us to take the risk of loving others by telling them the truth when it is needed.

• *Keeping promises.* When you promise to get ice cream for a child and then forget your promise, don't excuse yourself by saying, "It's too late now. You've got to go to bed." Far better to find an ice-cream shop that is open till midnight, let the child stay up later than normal, and keep your promise. When you promise an employee a raise or a spouse a birthday dinner, be sure to keep that promise. It takes only one broken promise left unacknowledged for someone to question your integrity.

> ## ~ A Person of Integrity
>
> The American Psychological Association offers several statements that a person of integrity would endorse. The following list is taken from the book *Character Strengths and Virtues* by Christopher Peterson and Martin E. P. Seligman.
>
> - It is more important to be myself than to be popular.
> - When people keep telling the truth, things work out.
> - I would never lie just to get something I wanted from someone.
> - My life is guided and given meaning by my code of values.
> - It is important to me to be open and honest about my feelings.
> - I always follow through on my commitments even when it costs me.[5]

Honesty at Work

We all are familiar with a lack of integrity in the workplace. In recent years public scandals have exposed Enron's accounting fraud, the securities fraud of WorldCom, and the ways that a Tyco executive allegedly used company money as his own. If we don't think such behavior harms relationships, just consider the losses such lack of integrity have meant to employees, small investors, and the credibility of our corporate world.

Closer to home, we all have probably experienced deceit in our own places of business, whether it's the coworker who cheats on her expense account, the employee who says a project is done when it isn't started yet, the boss who fudges numbers on the profit-and-loss statement, or the corporate office that promises more in its shiny brochures than it can deliver.

In fact the *Reader's Digest* survey I mentioned earlier revealed that lying is very common in the workplace. Cheating the company, however, seems to be more commonplace than lying to a fellow employee. While only 13 percent of respondents admitted shifting blame to a coworker for something they did, 63 percent said they've taken sick days when they were feeling just fine. Also, 91 percent of men and 61 percent of women admitted to pilfering office supplies.[6]

It's ironic that other surveys have shown that most of us value honesty above all else in our employees and supervisors. Terry Bacon, the author of *What People Want: A Manager's Guide to Building Relationships That Work*, has found in his research that honesty is "the top desired trait" in a supervisor. We also want others to trust us. In fact "the No. 1 thing people want from a boss is to feel trusted."[7]

We may imagine that lying about paperwork or office supplies does not affect our relationships, but every choice we make to act outside the characteristics of love has potential to harm those close to us. If a coworker can't trust us to follow through on a report, how will she trust us when we make personal promises?

The Darkness of the White Lie

One of the conclusions of another recent survey on honesty is that "The point at which a white lie becomes a fully fledged lie is different for each individual."[8] This tells us something about how blind we are to the dangers of those "little white lies" that come so easily.

I once was acquainted with a businesswoman who frequently told small lies for convenience, such as when she wanted to end a conversation or if she hadn't had a chance to prepare for a meeting. She often claimed she'd been told a different time for lunch rather than admit she was running late, and she sometimes had her assistant fabricate an "urgent" phone call at just the right time when she didn't want to admit that she needed to go. Those who worked with her on a regular basis came to expect these falsehoods—to the point that when she *did* have an urgent phone call, everyone went along with it but assumed it wasn't true. In other ways, she was delightful and well respected; lying was simply part of how she lived.

We were chatting one day when she mentioned a recent opportunity she had to teach her teenage daughter about relationships. Apparently a friend from school called and the daughter didn't want to talk with her, so she asked her mom to say she was out.

"I told her, 'You can't make up lies like that to your friends! You can either talk with her now or I'll just say you don't want to talk.' " She laughed and shook her head.

It was obvious to me why this girl wanted to lie to her friend: She'd learned from her mother that dishonesty in that kind of situation was all right. I realized then that this woman had gotten so used to living on the edge of truth that she didn't even realize she did it. She could see dishonesty in other people, but her desire for self-protection was so strong that she was oblivious of the destructive choices she was making herself. Her employees enjoyed her, but they didn't trust her to make the best decisions about their salaries. Her supervisors respected her, but they weren't planning to put her in charge of large contracts. And no coworker would confide a personal matter to her since everyone could see she betrayed confidences.

Small lies destroy relationships. Every time we slip into falsehood, we put distance between ourselves and the people we want to build relationships with.

HABITS TO ACQUIRE
Make it a practice not to tell even small lies at work or with your friends and family.

I know of a garbage company that named its street Reliable Circle. The owners of the company obviously want to communicate one thing above all else: You can count on us. That's speaking of a relationship between a garbage company and its customers! But isn't this what we want to communicate to everyone we relate to? *You can trust me to be true, inside and out.* When we are honest in small ways, we are building a foundation for positive relationships to grow.

As we've already discussed, honesty must encompass all the traits of love. When we are aware of loving intentionally, it will become natural to discern what is true and what is not. We will *want* to speak and act truthfully because that is the only way to build relationships. Then the traits of a loving person help us determine how to speak truth in love.

Force of Habit

Once, in the presence of his fiancée, Kelly, Derrick joked about watching pornographic videos and was stunned to see the look of dismay on her face. He had no idea that she would care about his occasionally looking at porn, but that day Kelly made it very clear to him that she *did* care and that if he was going to marry her, he was going to have to give up porn. Derrick promised. He meant that promise too. But some months into their marriage he discovered several Internet porn sites. At first he took a peek now and then when Kelly wasn't around, but soon he was planning ahead to get online whenever he knew she would be out for a length of time. Before he knew it, he was hooked on porn.

One night he was so caught up in checking out Web sites that he didn't hear his wife come home. The first thing he noticed was the sound of her crying from the office doorway. Their argument went long into the night, with Derrick in the end promising once again to give up porn.

But he couldn't—or at least didn't—give it up for long. He became skilled at hiding his activities, often lying about needing to stay late at work or to send "important" e-mails at home. Kelly suspected what was going on. When Derrick denied that he was still into porn, the lying hurt Kelly as much as his addiction did. The couple even began discussing divorce. After several months of counseling, Derrick admitted his problem and began to make progress in purging his life of porn. But rebuilding trust with Kelly took years.

As we've seen in every trait of a loving person, we love or fail to love because of habit. Lying is especially habit-forming. Each lie requires another in order to cover the deception. That's why dishonesty, perhaps more than any other unloving trait, is an easy pattern to ignore in our own lives. I have counseled people who have so wrapped themselves in falsehood that they have come to believe their own lies. If they continue to live out of their false selves, they will forever live pseudo-lives.

Frank W. Abagnale made a career of lying and wound up in prison because of it. Between the ages of sixteen and twenty-one, he was one of the most successful con artists in the world. He cashed $2.5 million in fraudulent checks in fifty states and twenty-six countries. His lies led him to play the parts of an attorney, an airline pilot, a college professor, and a pediatrician before being captured by the French police. Fortunately, in Abagnale's case, good habits have replaced destructive ones. Today he is respected as an expert on embezzlement, forgery, and document falsification.

The 2002 movie *Catch Me If You Can* portrayed the life Abagnale built by stacking one lie on top of another. It also showed Abagnale's character slowly losing trust in others, leading him to a life of isolation and broken relationships. George Bernard Shaw once said, "The liar's punishment is not in the least that he is not believed, but that he cannot believe anyone else." One of the hidden dangers behind the habit of lying is that the less trustworthy we become, the less trustworthy we assume others are. As a result, the habit of lying damages relationships in more ways than we first imagined.

We love or fail to love out of habit.

The good news is that truth telling is also habit-forming. When we are aware of cultivating honesty in everyday life, the dishonest words that slip from our mouths will begin to stand out. We will begin to dislike them because we see how they hurt our relationships.

The more we tell the truth, the better we feel. To be authentic is liberating, psychologically and relationally. We need not think, *What did I tell the last person?* because we know that we are giving the same story to everyone.

Rebuilding Trust

The first step toward becoming a person of integrity is to acknowledge personal failure. Confessing the lies of the past is the pathway to gaining self-respect. My observation is that the person who chooses to walk the path of confession will find people genuinely willing to forgive. Something in the human soul likes to see others do what is right. The courage to confess indicates a desire to walk a different path in the future. This is the process of putting off the false self and putting on the true self.

CONFESSING IMMEDIATELY

In any relationship, you do not have to be perfect in order to rebuild trust. But if you have deceived a spouse, friend, or coworker, then in the future you must immediately confess and seek forgiveness. Otherwise, you will fall back into the pattern of deception, and trust will never be restored.

ACCEPTING RESPONSIBILITY

Truth telling means that we accept responsibility for our own behavior. When a supervisor asks, "Who forgot to reserve the conference room?" the truth teller says, "I did," if he is guilty. When a roommate asks a hard question about a discrepancy in household expenses, a person who seeks integrity responds with the truth. Many marriages and friendships that have fallen apart could have been saved if the individuals had decided early on to tell the truth at all times.

BECOMING TRUSTWORTHY

I am often asked in the counseling office, "How do I rebuild my spouse's trust in me? I've deceived him for so long. Now the truth is out. I want to change my behavior, and he is willing to forgive. But I don't know how to make him trust me again after all I've done." There is only one road to the rebuilding of trust. The person who has violated trust must become trustworthy. If she speaks truth from the point of confession, eventually trust will be reborn.

Because of this, I advise someone who has been unfaithful in marriage to give her spouse complete access to her computer, her cell phone, and her financial records. The message is: "My life is an open book. I have nothing to hide from this point on. I've finished with deception. I am a truth teller. I give you the freedom to examine my life as thoroughly as you wish." With this attitude and the commitment to be a truth teller, the unfaithful spouse has taken the first step in rebuilding trust in the marriage.

Trust is like a tender plant. When someone violates trust, it is as if she were stepping on the plant and pushing it into the mud. Truth telling is the water that restores it to life again.

REMEMBERING THE TRUE SELF

When we apologize, we are saying, "I know the difference between right and wrong, and this time I did wrong. I know that my actions and my behavior have hurt you, so I want to make it right. What can I do to make it possible for you to forgive me?" The quicker and more thorough the apology, the more likely the apologizer is to receive genuine forgiveness and restoration of the relationship. People of integrity make every effort to restore relationships by apologizing and requesting forgiveness. Our false selves may exert their influence from time to time and pull us into lying, but because of love, we apologize, seek forgiveness, and recommit ourselves to telling the truth.

Competitor to Honesty: Self-Defense

If someone were to wield a baseball bat in your face, your first instinct would probably be to cover your head with your arms and turn away. Likewise, if someone were to accuse you of cheating on a test or forgetting a date, your first instinct would probably be to lie and say that you didn't do it or that it wasn't your fault. Our false selves come through loud and clear when it comes to honesty. Every one of us has a natural inclination to protect ourselves, even if it means lying to do so.

When we lie, we forget that in the process of protecting ourselves, we are leaving our relationships open for destruction. We are preserving how we want to appear, not who we really are.

Choosing to be a truth teller is one of the most freeing choices we can make. The opinions of others matter to us only as they relate to how we are loving the other person. When we nurture the habit of honesty, we naturally want to preserve our integrity above all else, not because of how it looks, but because acting with integrity is a way of loving others.

Standing on the Side of Truth

Living honestly means standing up for truth even when it goes against popular opinion. When William Wilberforce took his first public stand against human slavery in England in 1789, he was taking the side of truth and justice even though it was a very unpopular stance. But because of his effort in the face of opposition, that dark chapter in history was closed, and British slave trade was declared illegal in 1807.

When Aleksandr Solzhenitzyn trumpeted in his Nobel speech, "One word of truth outweighs the entire world," he was speaking of what he had experienced. In 1966, when asked to give a public reading at the Soviet Union's Lasarev Institute, instead of just reading from his novels, he spoke against censorship and the KGB. The response was far greater than he had expected. Later he recalled, "Almost every sentence scorched the air like gunpowder! How those people must have yearned for truth! Oh, God, how badly they wanted to hear the truth!"[9] The author Os Guinness writes that Solzhenitzyn and the leaders of the Velvet Revolution knew "there were only two ways to bring down the might of Soviet tyranny. One was to trump Soviet force physically, which was impossible for a tiny handful of dissidents in a day of SS-20 missiles and the KGB. The other was to counter physical force with moral, staking their stand on the conviction that truth would outweigh lies and the whole machinery of propaganda, deception, and terror. They chose the latter and the unthinkable happened. They won."[10]

The ebb and flow of history are filled with illustrations of people like Wilberforce and Solzhenitzyn who stood on the side of truth when the majority of their culture believed the lie. It was the truth that resonated with the hearts of the oppressed.

On the other side of history are those who perpetrated a lie and the thousands who stood by in silence while the lie took its toll. Hitler and the Holocaust are monuments to this tragic reality. In 1980 the Polish government reconstructed the design of the concentration camp at Auschwitz, where more than 1.5 million people died during World War II. Engraved on a plaque in the Italian section are these words: "Visitor, observe the remains of this camp and consider: whatever country you come from, you are not a stranger. Act so that your journey is not useless, and our deaths not useless. For you and your sons, the ashes of Auschwitz hold a message. Act so that the fruit of hatred, whose traces you have seen here, bears no more seed, either tomorrow or forever after."[11]

Standing for the truth does not imply that we are without error. It does mean that we take no delight in evil but rejoice greatly with every expression of honesty.

In daily life, standing for the truth might mean investing time and energy in protesting a political stance you believe is wrong. It might mean confronting your boss's supervisor about sexual harassment in your department, even at the risk of losing your job. It might be something as simple as heading home after a movie when your friends decide to sneak into another show without paying for it.

Standing for truth also means speaking the truth to ourselves. We hear scores of messages each day—on television, in magazines and newspapers, and on numerous Web sites. We must filter through the messages of our day and ask: *Is this right?* When we choose to live by the truth, we are loving ourselves and loving others. We are reminded that though at times truth seems eclipsed by the darkness of the world, it is never extinguished.

The Price of Dishonesty

Former president Richard Nixon is known as a man of great determination. He is also known as a man who knew many people yet formed no close relationships. Dozens of biographies have addressed why this was the case, exploring Nixon's relationship with his parents, times when he was bullied as a child, and incidents of betrayal in his political career. The historian Stephen Ambrose offers a different explanation: Nixon cultivated no close friendships because he lacked the character trait of integrity.

Ambrose contrasts Nixon with President Dwight Eisenhower, who "played no roles, only himself."[12] Eisenhower's consistent leadership comes through clearly in his military career, such as the time he chastised General George Patton for abusing a wounded World War II soldier. Although Eisenhower needed Patton desperately in the war, his integrity would not allow him to ignore Patton's actions. He wrote Patton to say that he could not excuse such behavior, concluding: "No letter that I have been called upon to write in my military career has caused me the mental anguish of this one, not only because of my long and deep personal friendship for you but because of my admiration for your military qualities. But I assure you that conduct such as described . . . will *not* be tolerated."[13] In large part because of the consistency of his words and actions, Eisenhower enjoyed throughout his military and political careers the friendships of many, including that of General Patton.

By contrast, Nixon took on different personas for different situations. His speechwriter once said that Nixon could "don a personality by opening a door."[14] Nixon's lack of integrity in everyday interchanges slid into the deceit of the Watergate scandal. After his resignation he told an aide that when a person gets to the top, "you can't stop playing the game the way you've always played it. . . . So you are lean and mean and resourceful and you continue to walk on the edge."[15]

Nixon was known for being guarded and unable to trust others, perhaps because he himself was untrustworthy. He admired people such as Charles de Gaulle, who "acted a part, playing a role he himself created."[16] He once told an associate, "The minute you start getting familiar with people, they start taking advantage of you."[17]

Asked about his lack of close relationships, Nixon pointed to the loneliness of leadership: "In my job you can't enjoy the luxury of intimate personal friendships. You can't confide absolutely in anyone. You can't talk too much about your personal plans, your personal feelings."[18] His words contradict the lives of many of history's great leaders, such as Eisenhower, who cultivated honest, candid friendships with a close group of people.

As he played the parts he thought were expected of him, Nixon was never honest enough to let someone know his true self. As a result, few people stood by him in the end; the inconsistency of his words, actions, and values cost him not just friendship but the presidency.

The freedom of living honestly makes room for rich relationships. When we hide our words, our feelings, and our beliefs, even in small ways, we are hindering our attempts to love authentically. The only way others will receive the love we want to give is when they can trust us—not just for what we say but for who we are.

What would your relationships be like if you . . .

- Were always aware of whether your outside self was matching your inside self?
- Made it a habit to speak the truth in love to others?
- Stopped telling white lies even when they seemed like no big deal?
- Apologized for your failures rather than tried to hide them by deceit?
- Chose to stand on the side of truth even when to do so was unpopular?

Making It Personal

QUESTIONS FOR DISCUSSION AND REFLECTION

1. Give some examples of leaders, athletes, or business owners caught in the web of a lie. How did those public lies affect personal relationships?
2. Do you believe little white lies are wrong? Why or why not?
3. Who are some of the people who have spoken the truth in love to you through the years? How did you respond?
4. Have you had an occasion to speak the truth in love to someone who was on the wrong path? How did the situation turn out?
5. Think of one small lie you have told recently. Did those words stand out to you at the time as a lie?
6. When has taking a stand for truth cost you something?

OPTIONS FOR APPLICATION

1. Does lying come easily to you? If so, what first step could you take to become a truth teller?
2. When are you most likely to stretch the truth out of a desire for self-preservation? What do you need to remember in those situations in order to act with integrity?
3. For one day, write down everything you say that isn't quite true. Ask yourself if those statements deceived anyone. If the answer is yes, what is the first thing you need to do to restore that relationship?
4. Think of a time when you spoke honest words. Now consider the

characteristics of a loving person in addition to honesty: kindness, patience, forgiveness, courtesy, humility, and generosity. Did your words and actions in that instance reflect these traits? Which traits do you need to cultivate more in your expressions of honesty?

Part Three

MAKING LOVE A WAY OF LIFE

CHAPTER NINE

Making Love a Way of Life in Marriage

A successful marriage is an edifice that must be rebuilt every day.
—ANDRÉ MAUROIS

Charlotte and John dated throughout grad school before getting married near Charlotte's parents' home in Chicago.

"The first two years were heavenly," Charlotte told me in my office, glancing at John. "We lived in this tiny apartment in Bloomington; we each had two jobs and barely enough money to pay off our school debt, but we were happy. We went to a local coffee shop every Saturday morning and sat and read the paper together." She smiled a little. "John always brought me my favorite, a cinnamon scone, while I sat at the table with my coffee. Whenever we had vacation days, we biked or went antiquing.

"Then John's mom became ill, and the year before she died, things got harder. The pace of John's full-time job picked up while mine slowed down. Most weekends John felt he needed to visit his parents. A month before his mom died, we found out we were expecting a baby. We got so annoyed at people telling us how much our lives would change with a child. But it's true that everything changed when Caitlin was born. It seemed like the only time we spent talking was when we were passing off child care and had to give an update on how much she had slept or eaten that day.

"I got pregnant with Jackson sooner than we expected, and I had to quit my job. Financially, that was okay, because John's job was going so well. But I didn't really feel it was fair that I had to put my career on hold. The kids are in school now, and I'm working part-time, and I still feel as if John and I never really see each other. I tell him all the time that I want to go out on a date, but he doesn't seem to care. We pay the bills and help with homework and have company over, but it's as if we're business partners, not lovers."

Charlotte's eyes grew teary at this last statement. I looked at John, who was staring hard at the floor.

"How would you describe your relationship?" I asked him.

John cleared his throat. "Well, it's true that we used to spend more time together. We didn't argue much. But it's not as if things were perfect then. We were always worried about paying the rent. I thought I could lose my job at any time if I didn't work hard enough. Sure, we would go out for coffee sometimes, but at least now we have a nice house, two cars, and the kids. She makes it sound as if we don't even love our kids."

"You know I didn't mean it like that," Charlotte said sharply.

"Don't interrupt me," John said before turning back to me. "She was the one who volunteered to stay home after Jackson was born. A lot of days I wished I were the one who got to nap in the afternoon instead of having to work ten hours and then come home and change diapers.

"Now we're trying to make things work with two jobs. The other day I had to leave work to pick the kids up from school because she had a meeting. She said she would be home by dinner, but it turns out she decided to go out with some friends after the meeting. She called about seven to let me know. I ended up feeding the kids, helping them finish their homework, and getting them to bed before she waltzes in at nine as if it's no big deal. I had a big meeting myself the next day, and I hadn't been planning on giving up six hours of prep time because she decided to party." He hesitated. "I'm the one making most of our money anyway."

Charlotte looked at him. "I *did* call earlier. I called when the kids got home from school to make sure everything went all right. You said things were fine and I should take my time. So I did. And does it ever occur to you that I'm bringing in money for this family too? I schedule my whole day around the kids. Every once in a while I'd like to make my own decisions about when I get home."

"I thought you were on your way when you called. I meant for you to take your time driving *home*." John looked at me and continued. "As far as going out on dates? That would be great except for the fact that we can barely keep up with life as it is. And I wouldn't mind if she tried a little harder to keep up with things around the house. I can't do it all. I don't know when she's going to realize that."

"We're here," Charlotte said to me, "because I'm tired of living like this. I feel as if we're always on the brink of an argument. I feel as if John is always mad at me and I'm always alone. Honestly, I'm not sure if we're going to make it."

Then they both looked at me with the question in their eyes that I have seen so many times in my office: *Can you make us be in love again?*

Falling in Love and Hitting the Earth

Over the years I have spent many hours listening to couples share their struggles. Invariably, each blames the other for their poor relationship. Each individual desperately wants to be loved by the spouse, but each waits for the other to take the initiative. Long before they come to my office, they have complained to each other. Their complaints have often been wrapped in condemnation because each believes the other person is acting unfairly. She reasons: If only he would do what he promised: "to love and to cherish so long as we both shall live"! Seldom does she understand that he has the same thoughts and feelings about her. The astounding divorce rate in this country stands as evidence that thousands of individuals never discover freedom from this addictive thinking.

These couples live with the wrong assumption. As we have seen in earlier chapters, love is not a feeling beyond our control. Many couples remember the euphoric feelings of their dating experience, when they longed to be together every waking moment. But sometime after the wedding the emotions subsided. Their differences are now obvious, and they find themselves arguing. Arguments lead to harsh words, which lead to negative feelings, and eventually the couple brings out the worst in each other. Add the stresses of parenting and work, and sometimes divorce seems like the only thing that will make life better.

As I look back on my own life, I realize that when I got married, I was "in love" but knew nothing of true love. The "in love" experience is emotionally based. We are swept along by high emotions. We see the best in the other person, and the relationship stimulates the best in us. Indeed, we will do and say things that appear to be genuinely altruistic. We give gifts we cannot afford, make promises we can never keep, and do things for each other that make us believe that we are truly lovers.

Social scientists tell us the average life span of this "in love" phenomenon is two years.[1] Then we come down off the emotional high, all the euphoria evaporates, and we discover that we are not in fact lovers. We are two self-centered people who have made promises to each other that we are incapable of keeping. Euphoria is replaced with hurt, anger, disappointment, and fear.

> **The average life span of the "in love" feeling is two years.**

Understanding the truth about love is the only thing that will open the doorway to a lifelong loving relationship. Love is an attitude that leads to a change in behavior. Love seeks the well-being of another and finds meaningful ways to express it. These expressions of love stimulate warm emotional feelings inside the other person. When our spouse reciprocates, we also feel warmly toward her or him. The emotions are the results of love; they are not love itself.

◁ Am I a Good Lover?

On a scale from zero to ten, with ten being the highest, rank yourself on how well you've shown the following characteristics of love in your marriage (or engaged relationship) in the last seven days. Keep your strengths and weaknesses in mind as you read the rest of the chapter.

____ Kindness
____ Patience
____ Forgiveness

____ Courtesy

____ Humility

____ Giving

____ Honesty

When Love Is a Way of Life

When love becomes a way of life in marriage, the seven characteristics of love discussed in this book flow freely between the husband and the wife. Let's look at what Charlotte and John's marriage would look like if love became a way of life for them.

KINDNESS

Every trait of a loving person is important in marriage, but if I could pick just one to emphasize, it would be kindness. Putting your spouse before yourself is crucial to making marriage work.

It was clear early in my conversation with John and Charlotte that they had stopped being kind to each other. Maybe one or both of them had tried to be kind to the other when their children were young but had grown discouraged because the other person didn't seem to reciprocate. Maybe they came to believe that nothing they did would make a difference, so they gave up.

It's not an overstatement to say that small kindnesses in daily life can save a marriage. Kindness shows that we value the other person. We recognize his needs and want to put those needs before our own. That means being alert to the way a spouse receives love. John was showing love by bringing in a good paycheck every two weeks, and Charlotte wanted him to show love by taking her out on dates. When alert to the call to be kind, John would decide to take Charlotte out even if he thought it was a poor use of time. He would show love to her in this way because he deliberately put her needs first.

Equally, kindness calls Charlotte to see that John was working hard to provide for their family. She could appreciate his work and tell him so, even if it wasn't the primary way she wanted to be loved. Kindness would call Charlotte to sacrifice time with her friends, if needed, just as John sacrificed time at work that day. Kindness would say thank you—without implying "It's about time"—as a way of recognizing that John's time was valuable.

When love becomes a way of life in marriage, someone cooks meals, washes dishes, vacuums floors, cleans toilets, walks the dog, trims the shrubs, pays the bills, and dresses the kids—all with a positive attitude. He may not use these words, but his attitude says "It is my pleasure to cook this meal for you" and "I am delighted to take the trash outside."

Charlotte and John were in the attack mode with each other. Their pride was not ready to concede that the other person could do something loving. In marriages marked by kindness, the spouses talk to each other with respect. They speak up when they are hurt or angry, but their words always affirm each other's value.

The more we practice kindness, the more our spouse practices kindness. And remarkably, the more we are kind to a person, the warmer we feel toward her.

PATIENCE

The more we talked, the more I could see that both Charlotte and John believed they were demonstrating extreme patience in their relationship. Charlotte patiently waited to restart her career after the children were born. She patiently waited to go out on a date with her husband. She patiently got the kids ready for bed most evenings. John believed he was showing patience every time he helped with the kids when he really wanted to work or watch television at the end of the day. He was patient with what he saw as Charlotte's failings to keep the house orderly. He patiently waited for Charlotte to get home the evening she went out with her friends.

Every marriage relationship involves waiting, whether we wait years for a spouse to develop a certain character trait or twenty minutes while she tries on jeans at the store. But waiting is not the same as having a patient attitude. When love becomes a way of life in marriage, one spouse does not pace the floor, saying to the other, "I don't know why it takes you so long to get ready." Patience may request change, but patience never demands change. If change is not forthcoming, patience accepts the imperfections of the spouse.

One husband told me, "I wish my wife would close the dresser drawers when she gets what she needs. But after two years I finally realized she doesn't have a drawer-closing gene. After that, I accepted closing the drawers as my responsibility." What a contrast with John and Charlotte's attitude of "The house [or kids or work] is his/her responsibility. If I do it, I will be giving in when I'm not the cause of the problem in the first place."

Patience bears with the imperfections of others. It's understandable that John would be angry or worried when Charlotte didn't come home at the time she said she would. A patient attitude would be ready to hear Charlotte's explanation and be open to her perspective. Patience doesn't make excuses for people, but it reminds us that it's unreasonable to expect someone to be perfect.

Charlotte and John could make positive changes in how they relate to each other and turn their marriage around. Marriage is a constant process of growth. Every couple has behavioral traits that annoy each other, as well as blatant weaknesses that hurt each other. Patience shares frustration and requests change. When a spouse still does not change, a loving spouse learns to compensate rather than condemn. We wait with the hope and desire for someone to change, but our love is not dependent on that change.

Love is not dependent on whether or not our spouse makes positive changes.

FORGIVENESS

If love were a way of life in John and Charlotte's marriage, Charlotte would be quick to apologize for staying out later than she intended, and John would accept the apology and not hold it over her in the future. True love would also help John see how his own weaknesses contributed to the situation. It was the first time that school year, in fact, that he had picked up the kids and seen them through their afternoon routine, and he'd only agreed to do so begrudgingly. A spirit of forgiveness and confession would allow John to see that selfishness on his part contributed to Charlotte's desperate need to relax with friends.

It was obvious to me that the incident John described was just one of a string of incidents over the years in which one person felt he or she had been wronged. Both John and Charlotte spoke with resentment about the stress in their marriage, hours spent at work, and even each other's attitude toward their children.

If love became a way of life in their marriage, this couple would not allow bitterness to grow between them. They would still offend each other at times, intentionally or unintentionally. But the offender would be quick to apologize, and the offended would stand ready to forgive, remembering that there can be no long-term positive relationships without apologies and forgiveness.

COURTESY

It's a reflection on our culture's view of marriage that we don't often think of courtesy as part of a marriage relationship. What does holding the door open for someone or getting her a glass of water have to do with lifelong commitment? But since courtesy means acknowledging someone's potential as a friend, when we are courteous to our spouse, we are communicating that we want to build a friendship with her. This is important because one of the keys to a successful marriage is not just loving each other but liking each other. The happiest married couples are good friends, not just lovers or roommates.

A lack of courtesy in marriage in fact is one of the signs that love is not a way of life for a couple. I saw this quickly in John and Charlotte. They came into my office with an air of anger, a spirit of "every man to himself." During our conversation they interrupted each other, spoke sharply to each other, accused each other freely, and rarely made eye contact.

The story they told me reflected the deterioration of common courtesy in their marriage. The courteous thing for Charlotte to have done before going out with her friends would have been to call John to check in with him. Perhaps she could have thanked him for picking up the kids that day. This is what she would have done if a neighbor had picked them up. Instead, she made assumptions based on his words almost as if she had wanted to make him angry, rather than go out of her way to be clear in an effort to maintain the relationship.

If John had been doing a favor for a friend, he would have cared for the children with a more positive attitude. Remember the cinnamon scones he used to bring Charlotte? His unwillingness a few years later to acknowledge some of his wife's deeper needs probably started with neglecting her smaller needs.

When love becomes a way of life in marriage, a husband and wife will ask questions to make sure they understand what the other person is saying. Yelling will not be a lifestyle for them. If the husband discovers that his wife appreciates his opening the car door for her, then he will do it. On the other hand, if he discovers that it is not one of her desires, he does not impose his concept of courtesy on her. You will often hear courteous couples making positive comments about each other in the presence of others. They will say thank you to the other for performing small tasks. Whatever the couple consider common courtesies will be reflected in their everyday actions.

Just as leaks in a dam reflect the potential of larger problems, giving up on courtesy in marriage reflects the bigger issue of not valuing each other. The consequences of forgetting "small" actions remind us of how big those actions were in the first place.

The consequences of forgetting "small" acts of love remind us how big those actions really are.

HUMILITY

When they were first married, it's likely John and Charlotte made many sacrifices for each other. They lived with little income so that each could pursue a chosen career. They took extra jobs so that the other one didn't have to work more hours than necessary. They visited each other's families even when they would rather be doing something else. Each of them did these things because they valued the other person. They were so secure in their love for each other that they were willing to step aside for the benefit of the other. Now they sat in my office unwilling even to clean the house for the other person. What had happened?

When Charlotte told me she didn't know why she had had to put her career on hold and John told me she had seemed glad to do it at the time, I believed both of them. Charlotte probably had been willing to step aside and let John take the career lead. However, she might have been waiting for recognition from him that her sacrifice had value. When she didn't receive that affirmation in words, her resentment grew. Resentment can also grow in retrospect: Charlotte may have acted humbly earlier in their marriage because she thought it was good for their relationship, and now she wonders if it was worth it.

Earlier we defined *humility* as "a peacefulness of heart that allows you to stand aside in order to affirm the value of someone else." When we truly value our spouses, one of our greatest desires is to see them succeed in life. A humble spirit gives us a peacefulness of heart because we don't see "their" success as damaging to "our" success.

It's true that putting your husband's career before your own, letting your wife tell a great story to a group when you wanted to, or encouraging your spouse to take that speaking engagement out of town may affect your professional success. But remember that authentic love changes the meaning of the word *successful*. True success comes from the desire to affirm the value of others while strengthening relationships—even at the risk of sacrifice.

GENEROSITY

"What would you like most from John right now?" I asked Charlotte.

"I'd like for him to kiss me when we see each other at the end of the day. I'd like to talk a little before bed—about something other than the kids. I'd like him to take the initiative to call a babysitter every once in a while so we can go out for dinner."

I asked John what he would like most from Charlotte.

"I'd like for her to see that I'm doing the best I can for our family. I'd like for her to give me some space on weekends to be by myself a little. I'd like for her to clean up the kitchen more often instead of always expecting me to do it. And I'd like for her to stop talking about all the things that are wrong with our marriage as if it's all my fault."

What Charlotte wanted most from John was time. He thought he was already being generous with his time by devoting himself to work all day and helping around the house. Charlotte had trouble recognizing his love because she wanted him to sit and talk with her. He perceived that as an even greater sacrifice because it meant leaving other things undone.

On the other hand, John believed he was being shortchanged. Early in their marriage Charlotte often helped around the house and always seemed pleased when John got a promotion or a raise. Now it seemed anything she did for him she did with resentment.

When love becomes a way of life in marriage, both the husband and wife will look for ways to enhance the life of the other. First, they give each other time. Twenty minutes on the couch looking, listening, and interacting may not have been John's concept of love when he married. But when he discovered this was important to his wife, authentic love called him to give.

The loving couple also shares abilities with each other. Cooking meals, repairing lawn mowers, ironing clothes, and refinishing furniture all are abilities that can be used as expressions of love.

In a loving marriage, the attitude of giving will also influence how the couple handles their money. They will openly discuss their finances and make decisions together that will honor and value each other. They will not view money as "my money" and "your money" but rather as "our money." Unlike Charlotte and John, who argued over who was sacrificing the most to make the most money, a truly loving couple view themselves as a team. Whether one spouse is bringing in more money than the other doesn't matter; the couple are working together to make life work and so anything that comes to them is a result of both their efforts.

One thing John and Charlotte rarely talked about as I got to know them was being generous to others outside their family. Generosity inside a family promotes generosity outside a family, and the reverse is also true. Giving generously to others helps us keep our own problems in perspective. John and Charlotte had become so self-focused that their biggest priority, other than caring for their children, was getting what they wanted out of the day.

HONESTY

When love becomes a way of life in marriage, neither spouse allows resentment to build in the relationship. Love says, "Maybe I'm seeing this the wrong way, but here is what I'm feeling. . . . Can we find a better way to do this?" Again, love is not making demands but is seeking a path on which both people feel respected as individuals.

Charlotte and John had lost many opportunities to be honest with each other. If Charlotte had expressed her need for John's affirmation when she left her job, her resentment might not have built over time. Instead, she waited years for him to "figure it out."

John had never told Charlotte the financial burden he felt in his job. He was embarrassed for her to know that he worried about not doing well in his career. This reluctance to share his thoughts and feelings was also seen in other areas of life. When Charlotte called before dinner that evening, for instance, he could have said kindly but honestly that he was concerned she wouldn't be home in time to help the children with their homework.

The need to clarify details and feelings with a spouse is not a sign of defeat. The most loving couples I know don't assume that the other spouse can read minds. As one friend told me recently, "I like it when my wife tells me what she's feeling. I don't have to worry that she is sitting around brooding about something." Over the course of years, brooding can cause major damage in a marriage. Authenticity calls us to speak the truth with every trait of love in mind.

Small acts of dishonesty, or the withholding of information, lead not only to resentment but to bolder lies. John and Charlotte made an important step when they acknowledged they needed help for their marriage. Doing so kept them from falling into the habit of practicing true deception because of self-centered interests.

Real Satisfaction

Without the seven traits of a loving person, our self-centered nature will take over when the excitement of dating fades. When we learn to love authentically, we have the opportunity to experience a depth of relationship that's more satisfying than any temporary euphoria.

I believe marriage was designed to give husbands and wives the opportunity to serve each other in meaningful expressions of love, with freedom to develop their independent interests and skills. When we feel secure in each other's love, we can serve others from a strong foundation at home.

Marriage was never designed to make people miserable. It was designed to be an institution of love, service, and great joy. Marriage can also help you grow as a loving person in a way you might not have otherwise. When love becomes a way of life, marriage reaches its highest potential.

Making It Personal

FOR PERSONAL REFLECTION

1. Think of a recent argument you had with your spouse. Was your initial response to blame him or her for the disagreement? If so, how did you show that?
2. Think of a time when you showed love to your spouse even though he or she did not reciprocate that love. How did you handle the lack of response?
3. What characteristic of love comes least naturally to you in your marriage? What is one thing you could do this week to demonstrate that loving characteristic toward your spouse?

FOR COUPLES TO DISCUSS

1. How would you rate the level of sacrifice in your relationship?
2. If you could change one thing in the way you relate to each other, what would it be?
3. Most couples say they argue about the same thing over and over. Consider something you frequently argue about, or consider a recent argument—even if it was about something "small." What would it look like if each of you responded with each of the seven loving traits in that situation? Go through the traits one by one as we did with John and Charlotte, and see how being more aware of those characteristics might change the way you act in the future.

CHAPTER TEN

Making Love a Way of Life in Parenting

Whatever you would have your children become,
strive to exhibit in your own lives and conversations.
—LYDIA H. SIGOURNEY

Jonathan and Erika were sitting in my office. They had been married two years. I knew them, but not well, and when I saw their names on my schedule, the thought that ran through my mind was: *Oh, no. I hope they are not having marital problems.* I was pleasantly surprised when Jonathan said, "We just found out that Erika is pregnant and we realized that we don't know anything about being parents. I grew up in a rather dysfunctional home, and so did Erika. We don't want our child to grow up in a home like either one of us had, so we thought you could give us some guidance on how to learn to be good parents."

I affirmed Jonathan and Erika for trying to learn something about parenting before the baby arrived. Then I told them, "The most fundamental thing that parents can do for children is to love them and to teach the child to love others. If a child feels loved, he or she will also feel secure and will be emotionally open to learn from the parents. If the child does not feel loved by the parents, he or she is far more likely to resist their teaching and discipline."

"I think we know about that," Jonathan said, "because neither of us felt much love from our parents. My father left my mother when I was five years old. It's still hard for me to think about it. Erika's father never left, but he was very harsh with her mother and very critical of her and her sister. I think that's why we are so concerned. We don't want our children to grow up with the feelings that we have toward our parents."

"You can certainly break that pattern," I said. "It begins by making sure that the two of you are loving each other." I focused the rest of our conversation on loving children because I believe it is the most fundamental of all parenting skills.

Every parent thinks at some point *I wanted to travel [or take this job, or spend more time outdoors . . .], but now I have a child, and I cannot.* Such thoughts are natural, but when we allow that self-focused attitude to overtake a loving attitude, our child will know it. On the other hand, when we concentrate on building satisfying relationships in our home, the child becomes the recipient of that love.

If you are a parent, you know that parenting brings out our selfish natures more readily than we would like. It can also bring out authentic love as nothing else can—and lead to one of the most fulfilling relationships of our lives.

> **Loving your child with the seven traits of love is the most fundamental parenting skill you will ever learn.**

What Are My Parenting Strengths?

On a scale from zero to ten, with ten being the highest, rank yourself on how well you've shown the following characteristics of love to your child(ren) in the last seven days: Keep your strengths and weaknesses in mind as you read the rest of the chapter.

_____ Kindness

_____ Patience

_____ Forgiveness

_____ Courtesy

_____ Humility

_____ Giving

_____ Truthfulness

A Musical Story

A young mother, Julie, told me of a recent incident with her seven-year-old son that provides a great way to look at the traits of love through the lens of parenting.

For weeks Julie's son, Caleb, chattered about his second-grade school musical. He was thrilled that he would be playing the drums in the final song. As the afternoon of the performance grew closer, Julie realized that she just couldn't take time off from work that day. She told Caleb that she would be attending the rehearsal the day before and that his dad would attend the actual performance. Caleb seemed fine with that plan.

The day of the rehearsal Julie watched as the music teacher, Mrs. Horner, slowly lost control of the room full of second graders. Instruments came in at the wrong time, children stared straight ahead instead of singing, and the noise of kids laughing and talking grew louder and louder. Julie could tell Mrs. Horner was frustrated. She could also tell that sensitive Caleb was barely containing his distress at the chaos in the room and the anger in the teacher's voice.

"I need everyone to sit down where you are right *now!*" Mrs. Horner finally yelled above the din.

At this, Caleb ran out of the gym.

Julie followed. She found him crying at the water fountain. She knelt to meet his eyes and said, "There was a lot going on in there, wasn't there?"

"I hate it! I hate Mrs. Horner! I hate the drums! I hate people yelling at me! I'm not going back in there!" Caleb yelled through angry tears.

Julie cringed at the level of his voice and had to keep herself from telling him he was overreacting. In the same instant she wanted to whisk him back home, where he would be safe. *It's our fault he's so sensitive*, she thought. *I should have done something to prepare him for this kind of thing.*

Instead, she said, "Caleb, I understand why you're upset, but we don't yell like that. You don't need to use hurtful words when you're mad." Julie spent several minutes talking to Caleb about what was happening back in the gym and explaining that other people were probably frustrated too. "But we need to go back in there. Mrs. Horner has worked so hard with all of you, and you're doing a great job."

Eventually Julie was able to lead her teary son back into the gym, past the curious eyes of teachers and a handful of other parents. *He's been sick; that's why today is harder than other days,* Julie wanted to explain. *He has such a big heart. . . .* But she kept quiet, nodded encouragement to Caleb, and sat silently in one of the folding chairs for the rest of the rehearsal.

Caleb made it through the day, but that evening he and Julie played out the whole scenario again.

"I'm *not* going!" Caleb yelled while systematically throwing his stuffed animals across the room. Julie saw a potential battle ahead. She sat down on the floor in his room and waited until Caleb had gotten out some of his frustration.

"Today was a frustrating day, but I know you can do it, Caleb. Remember how excited you were about playing the drums? The musical may not go just like you want it to, but I really think you'll feel better if you go."

"But I don't *want* to go anymore. And you're not even going to be there! You always make me do things I don't want to do!" He paused and glanced at Julie before adding, "I hate you!"

Julie tried to keep her voice steady. "I'm sorry you feel that way about me. That's not how I feel about you. Did you know that words like that hurt my feelings even though I'm a mommy? I'd like you to apologize before we talk more."

Caleb seemed surprised by his own outburst. "I'm sorry," he grunted. When Julie didn't say anything, he looked up and said more clearly, "I'm sorry."

"Thank you. I was going to tell you, Caleb, that I made a choice today because I really want to be at your musical tomorrow. I told Mr. Cates that I needed to miss that meeting. Whether or not I'm there, I think it's important that you keep the promise to Mrs. Horner that you would be in the musical. That's the kind thing to do."

Caleb eyed his mother suspiciously. After several more minutes of discussion he agreed to participate in the musical the next day.

"Caleb, we need to talk about one more thing," Julie said before she left the room. "You just agreed to participate in the musical, and

I'm proud of you for making that decision. If you whine about it anymore or have a bad attitude tomorrow, I will take away your computer privileges for a week. Got it?"

Caleb nodded solemnly.

Julie sighed with relief when Caleb prepared for school the next morning. He had a grim face but was not complaining. She was tempted to tell him he didn't have to go. But as he bounded over to his parents after the performance that afternoon, she was glad she'd stuck with her original decision. Caleb's face radiated pride and satisfaction in doing his best at a job he didn't want to do at all.

KINDNESS

Let's examine the qualities of love we have discussed in this book to see how Julie showed love as a way of life in parenting. First of all, she spoke kindly to Caleb even when his frustration level was high. When someone is yelling, our instinct is to yell back. One simple thing we can do in everyday parenting is to respond to our children with a soft voice. Screaming at a child is permissible if he or she is about to run into the street in front of a car. But screaming is never to be a pattern of life for the loving parent. It's an easy habit to fall into, but yelling stimulates resentment in the heart of a child.

Julie also showed kindness by validating Caleb's feelings. She didn't tell him, "Shape up or else!" She recognized that his needs went deeper than the surface situation and honored him by taking the time to talk with him. She also modeled kindness for Caleb by speaking well of Mrs. Horner, even though the situation was largely a result of the teacher's impatience.

If we want our children to treat others kindly, we must model it. The father who does something as simple as kindly helping his daughter put on her coat is teaching her how to help others. Harsh treatment and cutting words kill the spirit of a child, while tender touch and kind words enrich it.

PATIENCE

Patience is the cardinal virtue of the parent. Whether we are waiting for a two-year-old to put on her own socks or trying to get through to a seventeen-year-old who hasn't really spoken to us in days, parenting reminds us again and again that just like us, our kids are in process.

Many parents find it easier to be patient when a child is young. When a child is learning to walk, for instance, we get two feet away and say, "Come on. You can walk. Come on." The child takes half a step and falls. What do we say? We don't say, "You dumb kid. Can't you walk?" We say, "Yea! Good try!" What happens next? The child gets up and tries again.

We often forget the power of patience by the time a child reaches Caleb's age. Like Caleb, our children deal with the same problems again and again. When will they learn? Is it our fault? How often do we need to have the same conversation?

Patience in parenting takes time. We assign responsibility, praise the child for effort, and teach the child how to move to the next level of maturity. Julie showed this in how she instructed Caleb to keep the commitment he made, recognized his efforts, and encouraged him to do something that was difficult for him. She also gave him time to express his feelings.

Children learn bit by bit that good behavior brings benefits and poor behavior makes life more difficult. The parent who is patient with the process is expressing love.

FORGIVENESS

Within a few hours Caleb had embarrassed Julie in front of other parents, yelled at her, and told her that he hated her. Julie showed her desire to forgive him by telling him she was hurt and by explaining why his behavior was wrong. Then she asked him to apologize. When Caleb expressed regret, she accepted his apology and moved on.

Forgiveness does not mean that a parent will not discipline a child. Just as in adult relationships, forgiveness does not always remove the consequences of what we did or said. The child must learn that unloving behavior always has negative fallout. Forgiveness allows the relationship to continue and to grow in the future.

For loving parents, forgiveness is a two-way street. We will forgive the child when he apologizes, and we will apologize when we have treated the child unfairly. Some parents are reluctant to apologize to children, fearing that a child will not respect them if they apologize.

The opposite is true. A child will respect a parent more when the parent apologizes and will better understand that all relationships require apologies and forgiveness in order to grow.

COURTESY

Julie showed simple courtesies to Caleb by saying please and thank you even when tensions were high. Most important, she showed him respect by honoring his sensitive temperament.

Common courtesies are taught; they don't simply appear as the child gets older. Loving parents treat their children with the respect they have for a friend. Julie never compromised her authority with Caleb, but she showed that he was a person of value and that his feelings were important. That attitude of courtesy helped her communicate love in a difficult situation.

HUMILITY

Humility is not a word you find in most books on parenting. We typically think of parents as being the authority, and humility does not seem to fit with that image. But true humility and loving authority always go together. In order for us to help a child grow, we must sometimes be willing to put our own needs for affirmation or approval aside.

For example, Julie got down on Caleb's level physically and relationally when he needed help. In truth his behavior was hurting her pride. She felt defensive in front of the other parents, but she decided that it didn't matter what other people thought. What mattered was Caleb's personal growth and the way he treated himself and other people.

Humility also calls us to avoid one of the easiest traps of parenthood, guilt. If you wonder whether you are being a perfect parent, I'll tell you the answer: You're not. But if you remain preoccupied with all your weaknesses, you will be distracted from loving your child.

If Julie had spent too much time thinking about all the things she did wrong as a parent, she would not have been able to offer Caleb authentic love. Instead, in humility she concentrated on what Caleb needed in that moment. After the musical, Julie may have reflected on ways she could better prepare Caleb to deal with other people's anger. Humility means being willing to improve our parenting skills while not assuming all responsibility for our child's misbehavior.

> Humility acknowledges our weaknesses as parents
> but does not dwell on them.

GENEROSITY

Giving begins the day your child comes into your home and continues throughout a lifetime. When love is a way of life, giving is one of the most common actions in the home.

Julie gave Caleb the time he needed to talk about his feelings and make a good decision. She also showed him that sometimes we need to sacrifice something important for the sake of others; she sacrificed her meeting on the day of the musical, and Caleb sacrificed by doing something he didn't want to do.

Generosity does not mean that we give children everything they want. Julie could have been "generous" in giving Caleb a day off from school, but such giving would have been a selfish choice.

In daily life, it is difficult to know when to say no to a child. It helps to ask yourself, *Am I saying no for my own benefit, or am I speaking out of the seven traits of a loving person?*

HONESTY

Children don't want truth sugarcoated. Julie was tempted to tell Caleb, "I know you'll have a great time," or, "Mrs. Horner told me she was sad you were thinking of missing the musical." Those white lies might have gotten Julie and Caleb through that particular conversation more quickly, but they would not have served to build their relationship or taught Caleb the importance of the truth. The truth was, he might *not* have had a good time at the musical, and Mrs. Horner probably hadn't been thinking about anything but getting through the next day. Caleb needed to know that even though things weren't just as he wanted them, he would probably feel better if he followed through on his commitment. Julie was also honest when Caleb hurt her feelings. He needed to know that his words had the power to harm.

If you forget about attending a piano recital and tell your child that you were caught in traffic, or if you are tired of playing ball and falsely tell your child that you have to make a phone call, you are subtly teaching your child that it is all right to fudge the truth to protect yourself. You are the first person in the world your child trusts. A healthy parent-child relationship cannot be built on lies.

George Bernard Shaw once wrote, "The best brought-up children are those who have seen their parents as they are. Hypocrisy is not the parents' first duty." Loving parents do not lie to cover up blunders or to get out of sticky situations with their kids. Their words, actions, and attitude inside and outside the home are consistent with one another.

A Powerful Love

The author Elizabeth Stone writes that having a child is like having "your heart go walking around outside your body." Children know just what annoys us, pleases us, and melts us. Every day they can bring out the best or the worst of our nature, or rather, we can "let" them bring out the best or the worst. As with any relationship, we do not rely on our child's actions to determine how we show love. With love as a way of life, we seek to parent for the benefit of our children and for the satisfaction of seeing what love can do in another person's heart.[1]

Making It Personal

QUESTIONS FOR DISCUSSION AND REFLECTION

1. How do you think your childhood experiences affect how you parent?
2. What is one of your favorite ways to express love to your child? Why?
3. When is it most difficult for you to show authentic love to your child?
4. What is your usual reaction when you are feeling guilty for something you did or said to your child?

OPTIONS FOR APPLICATION

1. Think of a common conflict you have with your child. What would it look like to respond with each of the seven loving traits in that situation? Go through the traits one by one as we did

above, and see how focusing on those characteristics might change the way you react in the future.

2. Would you be willing to ask the following questions to your child and take his or her answers seriously? (I suggest you ask one question per week.)

    a. What can I do to help you?

    b. What is one idea you have for how I can be a better mother/father?

    c. This month what would you like for me to teach you?

    d. What do I do that you wish I would stop?

CHAPTER ELEVEN

Making Love a Way
of Life in the Workplace

*Small kindnesses, small courtesies, small considerations
habitually practiced . . . give a greater charm to the character
than the display of great talents and accomplishments.*
—MARY ANN KELTY

Ramona stared at the e-mail in front of her. "We are excited to an-nounce the launch party of the new Tomkins monitor. The party will be next Wednesday at 10 A.M. in the conference room." The e-mail from Jeff was written to the marketing, design, and production depart-ments. "In preparation for our midyear trade show, we will demonstrate the product and brainstorm new ways to implement our marketing strategies based on the product's unique design. (You'll note that the design department took us in a slightly different direction from that originally planned.) Then we will celebrate the arrival of this exciting new instrument that has been so long in coming." He signed off with a few more positive statements.

Ramona was livid, and her anger ran deep. Her history with Jeff was loaded with land mines: He had unrealistic expectations. He pushed his own ideas without listening to others. He made comments that sounded cheerful but put down others. In her better moments Ramona knew that Jeff was good at his job and trying to do his best. This was not one of her better moments. She picked up the phone. She put it down again. She stood up and sat down. Then she got up, stormed into Tim's office across the hallway, and shut the door. Tim turned around in his chair with a knowing look. "I know, I just read it."

"That e-mail is just one more example of Jeff's not listening. I told him last week that we would not be ready for a launch meeting for at least a month. And did you see the digs about our changing direction?

He just doesn't get it. Maybe if he had paid attention to the test trials, he would see why we had to change in midstream. I'm so tired of his telling us we're running late all the time. Just to make himself look good, he makes it appear that everything is our fault. I don't see *him* at the office at eight o'clock at night when I'm here working."

"I know," Tim said. "He's always giving us a hard time when he doesn't even know what it's like to be on our side of the process. If we demonstrate the monitor this season, we'll never have a chance to fix the battery issue before we start getting orders."

They looked up when their supervisor, Meghan, knocked on the door and stepped in. "Just wanted to get this back to you," she said as she handed Tim a manila folder.

"Thanks. Hey, did you see Jeff's e-mail?"

"Yeah, I'm going to go talk with him about it now. I really don't think we'll be ready by next Wednesday, do you?"

Tim and Ramona glanced at each other with satisfaction. "We were just talking about that," Ramona said. "Jeff has a problem with details, doesn't he? Or maybe it's just that he doesn't listen."

"Well, I'll let you know what I hear." Meghan closed the door behind her.

"I've had enough of this," Ramona said after Meghan left. "I think we need to talk with Meghan about why Jeff shouldn't be in that position." Tim and Ramona commiserated for several more minutes, often lowering their voices to loud whispers as they discussed the faults of their brash coworker. Soon Meghan knocked on the door again.

"Just wanted you to know I talked to Jeff. We're going to move the launch to next month. That will give us a little more time to get our act together, and Mark will be in town then, so he can join us. I told Jeff we were still aiming for the trade show, but we do want to make sure we have the best product possible."

"Jeff didn't even know Mark would be out of town?"

Meghan raised her eyebrows. "Jeff had actually scheduled the meeting early because he knew you wanted Mark to be there, and he'd heard that Mark was available. I haven't seen Jeff this excited about a project in a long time. He's itching to get it out there."

"I guess he didn't know the production department still needs to work on the battery issue." Ramona tried to sound gracious toward Jeff's oversight as well as production's inefficiency.

"He knows there's an issue, but he thought we would have enough to go on. He said you guys talked about that last week."

Ramona hesitated. She wasn't about to make a concession to Jeff at this point. "We talked about how it would be *possible* to meet early but that it would be better to schedule the meeting later."

"Well, that's not what he heard. Anyway, we're set now. He's going to send out another e-mail in a few minutes." Meghan had started to leave when Ramona called her back.

"We were actually just talking about how this kind of thing comes up too often with Jeff," Ramona whispered. "Don't you think so?"

"Oh, not necessarily. I know Jeff says things without thinking sometimes. When he gets focused on one thing, it's hard for him to hear anything else. But he does a great job. In many ways, our sales increases last quarter are because of him." Meghan smiled and walked out, this time leaving the door open.

Ramona was deflated. Apparently Jeff wasn't going anywhere in the near future. "I guess that's it," she said to Tim. "I'd better get back to work." When she returned to her office, she read Jeff's e-mail again. The problem with the meeting might be resolved, but she knew she would never like Jeff. Maybe the next time something like this came up he wouldn't get off so easily. She shook her head and clicked the e-mail off the screen.

How Loving Am I at Work?

On a scale from zero to ten, with ten being the highest, rank yourself on how well you've shown the following characteristics of love to your coworkers in the last week. (You might keep just one person in mind for this self-test, either the person you work most closely with or one you disagree with most often.) Keep your strengths and weaknesses in mind as you read the rest of the chapter.

_____ Kindness
_____ Patience
_____ Forgiveness

_____ Courtesy

_____ Humility

_____ Giving

_____ Honesty

The Call to True Success

Relationships in the workplace can challenge our best intentions to live out the seven traits of a loving person. Most, if not all, of our colleagues are not people we would choose to spend eight (or ten or eleven . . .) hours a day with. Yet many of us spend more time with them than we do with our families.

Work relationships have great potential to stretch our capacity to love because they call on us to see the value of people who have different priorities, unique personalities, deep personal needs, and sometimes driven agendas. Meanwhile, we're under stress as we deal with demanding supervisors, impatient customers, and deadlines. We might not think of work as a place to show love, but when we want to build strong relationships with our colleagues, we find the motivation to make each of the seven traits of love a habit.

KINDNESS

We have been trained to try to get ahead at work rather than to look out for others. Professional ambition is not wrong in itself. Wanting to do well in front of the boss, cringing when someone puts down our great idea, and looking for opportunities to show our strengths all are natural parts of our workday. But it's easy to use the failures of others to highlight our accomplishments, to take credit for something someone else did, and to act as if someone working on a lower level doesn't matter.

Succeeding in a career yet failing at relationships is a poor trade-off. The temporary rush of self-centered moments is not worth devaluing other people or destroying relationships that could bring professional benefits down the road.

One of the best ways to develop an attitude of kindness in the workplace is to *assume the best* of the people with whom we work. Instead of taking Jeff's e-mail at face value, Ramona took it as a personal attack. She read into his words all the negative things she knew about him, rather than give him the benefit of the doubt or look at things from his point of view. In other words, she was on the lookout for what Jeff did wrong.

Ramona seemed unaware that being kind to others can actually promote professional success. When we act out of love, coworkers are more likely to respond in love. If you wish your supervisor were more attentive to the department's needs, act as if he were. If you wish your fellow clerk were more confident in her actions, act as if she were handling her responsibility well. Jeff is much more likely to respect Meghan in the future because she respected him. Kindness calls us to retrain our minds to understand that professional success and personal success can exist together.

Relational success often promotes professional success.

PATIENCE

It takes patience to put aside anger while waiting to hear someone else's perspective. Meghan modeled for Tim and Ramona how to handle a potential conflict situation. In the end, gathering information, going to the person involved, and moving on take a lot less time than stewing about someone's weaknesses.

Small matters of conflict lead to angry explosions, hurt feelings, and inefficiency. This was not the first or last time Ramona would disagree with Jeff's choices. He had a strong personality and, by nature of his position, was much more aware of the bottom line than Ramona's creative sensibilities allowed. Ramona justified talking with Tim because Jeff had gone behind her back too many times for her to be patient with him now.

"Patience" isn't "patience" if it has a limit. Jeff had faults and quirks. He could say the same thing about Ramona. Until Ramona gives Jeff the freedom to be *in process,* she will always find reasons to get angry with him.

FORGIVENESS

Put more than one personality and opinion in a room, and you have an opportunity for conflict. Put four, five, or twenty-five in a department, and you are guaranteed to have disagreements. When we have an attitude of negotiating irritations and forgiving wrongs, we are able to differentiate between wrong behavior and simple disagreements.

A forgiving attitude would prompt Ramona to distinguish that difference in her relationship with Jeff. If she decided that he had done something to wrong her, authentic love would lead her to go to him, explain her perspective, and be ready to receive his apology. Love would also prompt her to apologize for ways she miscommunicated or worsened the situation.

Apologizing in a work situation is difficult because it puts us in a vulnerable position. What if the boss finds out we made a mistake? What if the person we apologize to never lets us forget it? We need to use our best judgment when it comes to reconciliation with difficult or untrustworthy coworkers. The most important thing is whether we are communicating that the other person has value.

If you get angry every afternoon because you have to fill in for a coworker who arrives late, your anger is going to get in the way of your relationship with him, and it will probably spill over into how you relate to customers that afternoon as well. Authentic love calls on us to confront someone when doing so would create a more productive and healthy working environment.

COURTESY

The list of common courtesies in the workplace is as long as similar lists for the home. Courtesy means not talking loudly on your cell phone—or not even letting it play its tango ring tone—while the person in the cubicle next to you is trying to work. It means showing up to work on time so the person on the same shift doesn't have to carry your workload. As Meghan showed, courtesy means knocking before entering an office, respecting an employee's privacy, and honoring someone's intention to do well. When you need to give someone bad news or make suggestions about his work, do so with respect.

Perhaps one of the most important ways to show courtesy in the workplace is to avoid falling into a common trap, gossip. The writer

Walter Wangerin, Jr., says, "Gossip is . . . guerrilla warfare: it hits and quickly disappears before there can be genuine engagement." Small comments can plant seeds of destruction. Commenting to a coworker, "Paul's been in Dean's office a long time. Hope everything is all right. I know that last sales trip didn't go too well," might sound like small talk, but it's really gossip that has the power to hurt others and destroy relationships.

Ramona probably would have called her conversation with Tim venting or, to put an even better face on it, trying to figure out how to respond. We all need to talk about our jobs sometimes, especially when they are not going well. Ideally, we talk to the person with whom we have the grievance. If you simply want to vent, the best thing to do is talk to someone who cares about you and doesn't work where you work. Whomever you talk to, the questions to ask are, *Is talking about this person helping me love her more? Is it helping the person I'm talking with to think better of her or worse?*

Of course at times we need to talk with coworkers or supervisors about another employee. Courtesy calls on us to talk about that person as if she were a friend, rather than look for ways to show our superiority. Friends want other friends to succeed. When it's especially difficult to speak well of someone, do your best to communicate needed information and nothing more. Meghan could have joined in the conversation about Jeff, but instead, she simply stated facts.

If you want to practice being courteous at work, compliment coworkers behind their backs. Start (true) rumors about something they did well. Make it a habit to act as if the person who makes you the maddest at work were a friend. Step back and see what a difference it makes.

HUMILITY

Disagreements in the workplace challenge our pride more pointedly than do most family and friend situations. Even if we don't see ourselves staying in the same positions or industries for long, most of us want to do well at our work. We want affirmation, raises, and the personal satisfaction of doing our jobs well. This makes it difficult to applaud when someone else receives praise, money, the better desk, or the promotion we wanted. When we're feeling insecure at work, we are even more likely to jump at the opportunity to look good.

Ramona had several chances to show humility in her conversation with Meghan about Jeff, even in the context of expressing her frustration. She could have acknowledged that since they were behind on the product, they needed an extension beyond the original plans. She could have expressed appreciation that Jeff had planned the launch. She could have spoken well of the things he was doing and admitted that she sometimes overreacted to his attitude. She could have even acknowledged to herself that she wanted to look good and that Jeff wasn't helping by pushing the project too fast. Humility called her to put herself in Jeff's position rather than judge him from her own position. Instead, her end goal was to show her power and superiority by getting Jeff fired.

Meghan, by contrast, acted in humility even though she was the one in the situation who actually did have power. She respected Jeff by going to him directly and not talking about him behind his back. She chose not to flaunt her position or suggest that her department worked harder or better than his.

The radical love of humility calls us to value success, even if it is not our own, and to build up others rather than tear them down to look good ourselves. If that sounds difficult, it is. That's why we need to practice.

GENEROSITY

When we go to work with a generous attitude, we are ready to share our time, abilities, and attention to bring out the best in others. Some combination of phones, faxes, e-mails, patients, customers, beepers, or the PA system distract us every day. Many of these things are essential to our job, but they also have the potential to keep us from the person who needs our attention.

Meghan did not chat about Jeff with other people or call him from her office while she checked her e-mail. She took the time to talk with him directly. Not only was this a loving choice because it showed respect for another person, it was an efficient choice. Taking five minutes to clear up a situation might not feed our self-centered desire to get angry about it, but it takes a lot less time and energy.

Being generous at work also means being careful not to hoard knowledge unnecessarily. Ramona was ready to blame Jeff for something as minor as not knowing about another coworker's business trip.

Her tiny bit of knowledge about someone gave her a one-up on Jeff's knowledge. At times we are responsible for classified information, and we need to keep those facts private. But it's all too easy in an ambitious environment to hold on to facts that give us power and then share them when power is needed. A generous spirit communicates in ways that helps others be their best.

Being generous means doing our jobs well as we give all we can. Acting efficiently, appropriately, and wisely at work is a way of loving others.

It takes time and energy to have an enemy at work.

HONESTY

Unless we are conscious of making the seven characteristics of love a habit, lying will come easily in work situations. Until Ramona was prompted, she never mentioned that she and Jeff had talked about the possibility of an earlier meeting. It probably didn't occur to her because she was so determined to point out Jeff's inappropriate behavior, behavior it would be easier to complain about if she didn't mention their earlier conversation. True honesty means not telling lies about others, not making up inaccurate information to cover up a mistake, and not stretching the truth for one's own benefit.

Being honest at work also means not flattering someone falsely to get ahead. When we are intent on living consistently in word, action, and thought, we will speak affirming words in good conscience. This kind of affirmation has the ring of truth to it and is most helpful to the other person.

The Heart of the Job

Many people count a coworker as one of their closest friends. And when rivals in the office come to appreciate and enjoy each other over time, the satisfaction of relationship is particularly rich.

No matter how much technology sits on our desks, relationships are still at the heart of the job. If you need a reason to show authentic love in the workplace, consider this: Choosing to value people in everyday life leads to better employee and customer relations, higher productivity, and less turnover. When the seven characteristics of love become habits of our day, we build the relationships that will bring true professional satisfaction. We find enjoyment not just in what others do but also in who they are.

Making It Personal

QUESTIONS FOR DISCUSSION AND REFLECTION

1. Which of the seven character traits of love do you think is most absent from the workplace? Why do you think that is?
2. Which of the seven character traits is most difficult for you to demonstrate at work? Why?

OPTIONS FOR APPLICATION

1. Is there someone you harbor anger toward at work? What would releasing that anger look like? Are you willing to do that? Why or why not?
2. Is there someone you need to apologize to at work? What are your greatest fears about apologizing?
3. When was the last time you gossiped about someone at work? What can you do to break the habit?
4. Think of a recent conflict you had with someone at work. What would it have looked like for you to demonstrate each of the seven traits of a loving person in the midst of that conflict?
5. Think of three people with whom you work closely. What do you enjoy most about them? How can you tell them that this week?

CHAPTER TWELVE

The Motivation to Love

You will find as you look back on your life that the moments that stand out above everything else are the moments when you have done things in a spirit of love.

—HENRY DRUMMOND

It was a cold, rainy November night as I made my way into the hospice care center to visit Joe and Carolyn. Six months earlier they had made an appointment with me to discuss Joe's funeral. Since they were friends of mine, and since they knew I am an ordained minister, they had asked me to conduct Joe's funeral.

"I've got this cancer," he had said on that earlier occasion. "I'm going to fight it with everything I have, but I know there is the possibility that I may not make it. While I'm feeling good, I want to make arrangements for my funeral. I want to make it as easy on Carolyn as possible when the time comes."

Now, after months of treatments, it appeared that the time for Joe's going was near. I had come to discuss the details of the funeral and say good-bye. A smile broke on Joe's face as I entered the room. He said, "I'm so glad you came."

A little later he told me, "I am a blessed man. Carolyn and I have had forty-seven years together. They haven't been perfect, but they have been good. We have five children plus our daughter who died at the age of four. We have thirteen grandchildren, of whom we are very proud. I've had good jobs through the years. We have moved a number of times to different cities and have made friends everywhere we have gone. I could not ask for more. I've told the children not to worry about me. I'm ready to go. We've been working over the final details of my funeral, and I think you can help us."

For the next twenty minutes I listened, took notes, and answered questions. At the end of our time I suggested we pray together. "I'd like that," Joe said. He reached out to me with his left hand and reached out to Carolyn with his right hand. I joined hands with Carolyn across the bed. We prayed. At the end of the prayer he released my hand but held on to Carolyn's. Pulling her hand to his face, he kissed it, smiled, and then released her.

Looking for Love

As I left the room and walked back to my car, the thought kept running through my mind: *I wish all couples could end the journey with such love and support.* I believe that the missing ingredient in failed marriages, or in any failed relationship, is the kind of authentic love that we've explored in this book. Why do siblings lose touch? Why do friendships fade? Why do athletes on the same team want to improve their personal stats more than they want to help the team win? Why do workers in the same work group turn to crawling over one another to get ahead in the company? In every case, it's because the individuals involved put the false self of self-focused living before the true self of serving. They fail to pursue the traits that make up real love.

In the preceding chapters we have looked at the qualities of love. We have talked about what these qualities look like when we make love a way of life. Now I wish to focus on a fundamental question behind these loving characteristics: What makes our motivation to love greater than our motivation to look out for ourselves? As I asked at the beginning of the book: Is love realistic? Is it possible to love consistently in daily life, given our tendency toward selfish living? Or to put it another way, if we want to be as successful in any of our relationships as Joe and Carolyn were in their marriage, where do we find the ability to overcome our selfish natures?

A Higher Power

Thousands of alcoholics have found freedom from chemical dependence by taking steps one and two of the Alcoholics Anonymous program. These steps say, "We admitted we were powerless over alcohol—that our lives had become unmanageable. [We] came to believe that a Power greater than ourselves could restore us to sanity."[1]

Self-centered living is not a chemical dependence, but it is an addiction, one in which we focus on getting what we want. It views every transaction and relationship through the lens of "What will this mean for me?" In this kind of living, even what appear to be acts of love are motivated by selfish desire and so become manipulation, not love at all.

Over and over again I hear the refrain of the person who says, "I would be willing to make changes if she would meet me halfway." Such a statement sounds reasonable, but it has nothing to do with love. The I-will-if-you-will approach to life is based on a contract mentality designed to get something one desires.

This egocentric bondage runs deep in the human soul and is not easily healed. After three decades of working closely with people in my counseling office, I have concluded that those who are most successful at making love a way of life are those who recognize their need for outside help. Each of us, if we were being honest and self-aware, would have to admit, "I cannot truly become a lover in my own power."

Self-effort alone will not break the chains of our egoism. This is true for any relationship. In my own life I saw its reality most clearly in my relationship with my wife. I'd like to share that story with you.

Self-centered living is an addictive cycle that can be broken.

The Journey to Love

I held undergraduate and graduate degrees in anthropology and had completed one year of graduate theological studies before I got married. I was madly in love with Karolyn and could hardly wait to be as happy as I was sure I was going to be after marriage.

I had visions in my mind of what it would be like. I could see myself coming home in the afternoon after a hard day of classes and finding a wife who would meet me at the door with hugs and kisses and usher me to the couch, where I would rest while she finished preparing dinner. While eating, we would gaze into each other's eyes as we shared the events of the day. After dinner I would help her with the dishes, and then we would have a quiet evening. I would sit at the table preparing my academic assignments while she sat on the couch and read a book of her choosing. At ten-thirty each evening we would go to bed together and make love. Life would be beautiful.

If you are married, I can imagine that you are now smiling because you see yourself in what I have written. Or maybe you are angry because you see my naive and blatant egotism. Little did I know that in my wife's mind were dancing very different visions of what life would look like after marriage.

I quickly discovered that my wife had no interest in sitting on the couch and reading a book while I completed my studies of the day. She much preferred going to the mall or attending a social function where she could interact with people. In her mind, 10:30 P.M. was not the time to go to bed but the time to unwind by reading a book or watching television. When I saw her on the couch reading, I would think, *Why didn't you read your book while I read my book? Then we could go to bed together.* I soon learned that going to bed together was not one of her objectives. What I considered "making love" was not her idea of a perfect ending to a wonderful day.

Our conflicts emerged early in our marriage. We both were taken by surprise at the depth of our feelings of hurt and anger toward each other. How could the love feelings we had while dating have evaporated so quickly after the wedding? We had no skills in conflict resolution because in our minds, we weren't supposed to have conflicts. Thus we had many arguments but few resolutions, and in time I began to be plagued with the thought that I had married the wrong person. I do not wish to convey that we had no pleasant times together; we did. Just beneath the surface, however, lay all these unresolved conflicts that created great emotional distance between the two of us.

All the while I was continuing my theological studies in preparation to be a minister. But the chasm between my vocational objective and the nature of our marital relationship was ever widening. I was having difficulty imagining how I could offer hope to others when I felt so hopeless in my own marriage. There were days and weeks in which I was able to throw myself into my studies and assume that after graduation things would be different. But in my heart I knew that was an illusion.

As the day drew nearer when I would complete my graduate studies and be forced to leave the ivory tower of academia and enter the real world, I became more and more frustrated. In my frustration I lashed out at God and blamed him for getting me into an unworkable marriage. After all, hadn't I prayed and asked for his guidance before I got married? And why had I felt so certain that I was doing the right thing when I got married and so frustrated afterward? And had I not been praying all along that he would help us find a way to resolve our differences? All those prayers seemed to make no difference at all. I was mad at God and didn't know how I could ever be one of his ministers.

A SERVING LOVE

For a while after that day when I got angry at God, things seemed to get a little better in our marriage. Karolyn and I had some pleasant conversations and found areas of agreement on a few of our conflicts. The apparent change was short-lived, however, and within a few weeks we went back to arguing or suffering in silence. I remember the day several weeks later when I said to God, "I don't know what else to do. I've done everything I know to do, and things aren't getting any better. In fact they seem to be getting worse. I don't know how I can ever help others when I am so helpless to change my own marriage." I ended my prayer with the same refrain with which I had begun: "I don't know what else to do."

When I finished the prayer, there came to my mind a visual image from a story in the Bible. This story tells of the night before Jesus was hung on the cross, when he was celebrating the Jewish festival of Passover with his closest followers. At one point Jesus shocked the men at the table by getting up, pouring water into a basin, and washing each of their feet in turn. This act of service was usually reserved for the lowliest slaves, since it was such an unpleasant task. (Would you like to wash the feet of men who have been walking dusty roads in sandals?) Yet Jesus, the leader of the group and their Lord, deliberately performed this humble, loving act of servanthood for his friends.

With that image filling my mind, in my heart I knew I was hearing God's answer to my prayer: "That is the problem in your marriage. You don't have the attitude of Christ toward your wife." I understood the message clearly because I remembered what Jesus said to his followers when he arose from the basin and laid aside the towel. "Do you understand what I was doing? You call me 'Teacher' and 'Lord,' and you are right, because that's what I am. And since I, your Lord and Teacher, have washed your feet, you ought to wash each other's feet. I have given you an example to follow." On another occasion Jesus had said something similar to them: "Among you, those who are the greatest should take the lowest rank, and the leader should be like a servant."[2]

This encounter with God moved me deeply because I knew I had found the answer. I had not been following the teachings of Jesus. My attitude in the early years of our marriage could be encapsulated by the words I had been repeatedly saying in one form or another to my wife: "Look, I know how to have a good marriage. If you will listen to me, we will have one." Karolyn would not "listen to me," and I blamed her for our poor marriage. But that day I heard a different message. The problem was not Karolyn, the problem was my attitude. So I said to God, "Please forgive me. With all my study of Greek, Hebrew, and theology, I missed the whole thing. Please forgive me." Then I prayed: "Give me the attitude of Christ toward my wife. Teach me how to serve her as Jesus served his followers."

THREE QUESTIONS THAT CHANGED MY LIFE

In retrospect, that was the greatest prayer I ever prayed about my marriage because God changed my heart. A whole new vista opened in my mind, and I saw myself playing a totally different role in our marriage. I was no longer to be the king, barking out orders to my wife and announcing my expectations of her. Instead, I would give myself to acts of love and kindness designed to enrich her life and encourage her to become the person she was designed to be.

Three questions made all this practical for me. When I was willing to ask these three questions, our marriage radically changed. They are simple questions, but they gave me the information I needed to become a lover toward my wife:

1. What can I do to help you today?
2. How can I make your life easier?
3. How can I be a better husband to you?

When I was willing to ask those questions, my wife was willing to give me answers. In fact I found no reluctance on her part to answer these questions. And when I allowed her answers to teach me how to express love to her in meaningful ways, our marriage changed dramatically. It did not happen overnight, but within a month I saw a change in Karolyn's countenance and her attitude toward me. Within three months she was beginning to ask me those three questions in return. I was amazed at the changes I saw in her attitude and behavior. I had not anticipated that our relationship could take such a positive turn so quickly.

I did not know then what I know now after so many years in the counseling office. Love always stimulates love. Because people so desperately need love, when they receive it, they are drawn to the lover.

**To be a better lover, ask those you care about:
How can I serve you better?**

Taking the Journey of Love to the End

My wife and I have been walking the road of love for more than forty years, and we have an incredible relationship. I said to her not long ago, "If every woman in the world were like you, there would never be a divorce." Why would a man leave a woman who is doing everything she can to help him? And my goal through all these years has been to love my wife so well that no other man could treat her as well as I do.

I have shared my personal journey toward love not with a view toward establishing myself as the epitome of a lover or with the view that everyone must duplicate my experience. It is my hope that my vulnerability might help some discover the true source of love and that with God's help we can find the motivation and the power to change our attitudes and behavior. My selfish tendencies had motivated me to put my needs first. When I saw how this was destroying my marriage, I turned to God, who motivated me to want to *serve* Karolyn. Serving became a deliberate habit.

I have focused on marriage in this chapter because that is the area in which I have experienced and observed the most change. But many can testify to the power of God-given help to rescue friendships, business partnerships, and other relationships that previously seemed doomed. When we ask God for the motivation to love someone else, we always receive an answer.

I am convinced that most of us need outside help to turn the tide toward love in our relationships with others, whether in the workplace, the grocery store, or the home. We are not by nature lovers, and two self-centered people will never create a loving relationship. Until we are touched at the core of our beings with a power greater than ourselves, we will continue to live with the perspective "What's in it for me?," and making the seven traits of a loving person a way of life will prove too difficult.

I am not suggesting that nonreligious people cannot become lovers. All humans have the capacity to love. However, for most of us, the desire for self-preservation overpowers our desire to help others. Human history stands as a witness to this reality. As for me, I am fully willing to admit that I need divine help in order to make love a way of life.

Overcoming our natural selfishness in relationships is a lifelong endeavor. My relationship with Karolyn was revolutionized when I realized that I was not loving her. In the decades since, I have had to continue to learn what it means to serve her. Believe me, I have not always achieved it, but I keep working at it.

When we make serving others a habit, we are aware when we fall out of that habit. Over time this practice of servanthood leads to the sweet enjoyment of kind, loving, intimate relationships.

I want to finish strong. I want to keep practicing authentic love and enjoying the relationships that love produces. And at the end of the journey of life, if I am the one to go first, I plan to look at Karolyn, smile, and take her hand in mine to kiss it.

Making It Personal

QUESTIONS FOR DISCUSSION AND REFLECTION

1. How would you say common views of love, such as our culture's focus on being "in love," differs from authentic love?
2. What motivates you to love others?
3. How have you seen self-centeredness hurt your relationships?
4. Is loving others hard for you? If so, when and why?

5. What do you think about the idea that victory over our self-centeredness in relationships requires us to turn to God for help?

6. How has your attitude toward love and relationships changed since you started reading this book?

OPTIONS FOR APPLICATION

1. Which of your relationships do you most want to enrich with authentic love?

2. Which of the seven traits of a loving person do you think you need to work on the most? Why?

3. Would you be willing to ask for divine help in strengthening that characteristic in your relationships? Why or why not?

Epilogue

A few years ago I was walking across the campus of the University of Virginia, where I was scheduled to speak. As I passed the Cabell Hall Auditorium, I paused to read the following words engraved over one of the entrance doors: "You are here to enrich the world, and you impoverish yourself if you forget the errand" (Woodrow Wilson). Those words capture the essence of the worldview I have tried to share with you in these pages.

My purpose in writing this book is to help you focus attention on the greatest thing in the world, giving love to others. Nothing will bring greater satisfaction to your life, in time and eternity, than giving and receiving authentic love.

In the early years of the twenty-first century, we face the threat of global terrorism and despotic leaders who kill thousands every year and push hundreds of thousands into refugee camps. Drug-related crimes and pandemic diseases destroy the lives of many of this generation's finest youth. The instability of marriage and family relationships has left millions with emotional scars. Extreme poverty is the norm for many countries.

Some would conclude that with each passing day, the world becomes darker. But I would remind you that the greater the darkness, the greater the need for the light of a life of love. If the people in our world can rediscover the power of love in their everyday interactions, we can replace the darkness with light, the sickness with healing, the poverty with sustenance, and the brokenness with reconciliation. It is not just wishful thinking to say that love can win.

I believe that Albert Schweitzer was correct when he said, "One thing I know: the only ones among you who will be really happy are those who will have sought and found how to serve." It is my sincere desire that this book will help you discover your identity as an authentic lover and leave your corner of the world better than you found it.

Notes

Please note that all Internet addresses were active and appropriate at the time of the writing of this book. I regret that I cannot guarantee their availability or content beyond that time.

CHAPTER ONE: THE SATISFACTION OF A LOVING LIFE

1. Gary Chapman, *The Five Love Languages* (Chicago: Northfield, 1992, 1995).
2. Catherine Skipp and Arian Campo-Flores, "Beyond the Call," *Newsweek* (July 10, 2006), 71.
3. Quoted in Timothy George and John Woodbridge, *The Mark of Jesus* (Chicago: Moody Publishers, 2005), 47–48.

CHAPTER TWO: KINDNESS:
DISCOVERING THE JOY OF HELPING OTHERS

1. Inaugural address of George H. W. Bush, January 20, 1989, www.yale.edu/ lawweb/avalon/president/.navy/bush.htm.
2. See www.pointsoflight.org.
3. Jackson Diehl, "Guantanamo Interrogators Succeed with Kindness," McCall, July 25, 2007, http://www.mcall.com/news/opinion/anotherview/all-diehl7-25 .5962177jul25,0,5058959.story.
4. David Wilkerson with John and Elizabeth Sherrill, *The Cross and the Switchblade* (New York: Random House, 1963), 72.
5. Heard October 10, 2006, at the Benton Convention Center in Winston-Salem, North Carolina.
6. Many studies show the mental, physical, and emotional benefits of kindness. This particular list is compiled from Allan Luks, *The Healing Power of Doing Good: The Health and Spiritual Benefits of Helping Others* (New York: iUniverse.com, 2001). The Niagara Wellness Council in Niagara Falls, New York, compiled this list from Luks's book and posted the compilation on Health Benefits of Kindness, http://www.actsofkindness.org/inspiration/health/ detail.asp?id=2.

7. Benjamin Franklin, "Benjamin Franklin to Benjamin Webb," http://en
.wikisource.org/wiki/Franklin_to_Benjamin_Webb.

8. Jeff Leeland, "Our Story—The Power of One," Sparrow Clubs, http://www.spar-
rowclubs.org/About_Us/Our_Story/default.aspx. For more information about
Michael's story and Sparrow Clubs, USA, see also Jeff Leeland, *One Small Sparrow* (Sisters, Ore.: Multnomah, 2000).

CHAPTER THREE: PATIENCE:
ACCEPTING THE IMPERFECTIONS OF OTHERS

1. Greg Risling, "California Highway Closed Due to Road Rage," *Chicago Tribune*
Web Edition, July 21, 2007, http://www.chicagotribune.com/news/nationworld/
chi-roadrage_sat1jul21,0,1552580.story.

2. Numerous translations of Aesop's fables exist. This version of "The North Wind
and the Sun" is found at Page by Page Books, http://www.pagebypagebooks.com/
Aesop/Aesops_Fables/The_Wind_and_the_Sun_p1.html.

3. Andrew Hill and John Wooden, *Be Quick—But Don't Hurry!* (New York: Simon & Schuster, 2001), 71–72.

4. Erich Fromm, *The Art of Loving* (New York: Harper & Row, 1956), 96.

5. Proverbs 30:32–33.

6. Proverbs 15:1.

CHAPTER FOUR: FORGIVENESS:
FINDING FREEDOM FROM THE GRIP OF ANGER

1. Jay Evensen, "Forgiveness Has Power to Change Future," *Deseret Morning News*,
October 3, 2005, http://deseretnews.com/dn/view/0,1249,600157066,00.html.

2. Ibid.

3. Leah Ingram, "Victoria Ruvolo, Compassionate Victim," beliefnet, http://www
.beliefnet.com/story/179/story_17937_1.html.

4. "Forgiveness in the Court," Good News Blog, August 22, 2005,
http://www.goodnewsblog.com/2005/08/22/forgiveness-in-the-court.

5. For more information on how to apologize effectively, see Gary Chapman and
Jennifer Thomas, *The Five Languages of Apology* (Chicago: Northfield Publishers, 2006).

6. Quoted in "Getting Angry Won't Correct the Past," The Forgiveness Project,
http://www.theforgivenessproject.com/stories/michael-watson.

CHAPTER FIVE: COURTESY: TREATING OTHERS AS FRIENDS

1. Andrew J. Horner, *By Chance or by Design?* (Wheaton, Ill.: Harold Shaw, 1995),
58.

2. Ibid.

3. Quoted in Lynne Truss, *Talk to the Hand* (New York: Penguin, 2005), 44.

4. Malcolm Gladwell, *The Tipping Point* (Boston: Back Bay Books, 2002), 8.

5. David Haskin, " 'Butt Dialing' and the Nine New Deadly Sins of Cell Phone
Use," *Computer World*, June 22, 2007, http://www.computerworld.com/action/
article.do?command=viewArticleBasic&articleId=9025358.

6. George Sweeting, *Who Said That?* (Chicago: Moody Press, 1994), 128.

7. Ibid., 209.

8. Herbert V. Prochnow and Herbert V. Prochnow, Jr., *5100 Quotations for Speakers and Writers* (Grand Rapids, Mich.: Baker, 1992), 335.

9. Keith Benman, "Is U.S. a Fast, Crude Nation?," nwi.com, July 8, 2007, http://nwitimes.com/articles/2007/07/08/news/top_news/docb9a1489cab90ee7e8 6257312000195f1.txt.

10. Deborah Tannen, *The Argument Culture: Stopping America's War of Words* (New York: Ballantine Books, 1998), 1–3.

11. Gene Weingarten, "Pearls Before Breakfast," Washingtonpost.com, April 8, 2007, http://www.washingtonpost.com/wp-dyn/content/article/2007/04/04/AR2007040401721.html.

12. Peter Hay, *Movie Anecdotes* (New York: Oxford University Press, 1990), 274.

13. Evelyn Underhill, *The Spiritual Life* (Harrisburg, Penn.: Morehouse Publishing, 1937), 93.

CHAPTER SIX: HUMILITY:
STEPPING DOWN SO SOMEONE ELSE CAN STEP UP

1. Jim Collins, *Good to Great: Why Some Companies Make the Leap . . . and Others Don't* (New York: HarperBusiness, 2001), 12–13.

2. Ibid., 27.

3. Susan Cheever, *My Name Is Bill: Bill Wilson—His Life and the Creation of Alcoholics Anonymous* (New York: Simon & Schuster, 2004), 190.

4. Quoted ibid., 188, 190.

5. Ibid., 190.

6. Ibid., 191.

7. Quoted ibid., 182.

8. John H. Rhodehamel, ed., *American Revolution: Writings from the War of Independence* (New York: Library of America, 2001).

9. Joy Jordan-Lake, *Working Families* (Colorado Springs: WaterBrook Press, 2007), 158.

10. Roger Ebert, "I Ain't a Pretty Boy No More," *Chicago Sun-Times*, April 24, 2007, http://www.suntimes.com/news/metro/355049,cst-nws-ebert24.article.

11. Henri Nouwen, *In the Name of Jesus: Reflections on Christian Leadership* (New York: Crossroad, 1989), 10–11.

12. Quoted in Raymond McHenry, *The Best of In Other Words* (Houston: Raymond McHenry, 1996), 135.

13. Quoted in James S. Hewett, ed., *Illustrations Unlimited* (Wheaton, Ill.: Tyndale, 1988), 298.

14. Jacquelyn Berrill, *Albert Schweitzer: Man of Mercy* (New York: Dodd, Mead, 1956), 5.

15. Ibid., 127.

16. Stephen E. Ambrose, *Comrades* (New York: Simon & Schuster, 1999), 100–101.

17. Quoted ibid., 102.

CHAPTER SEVEN: GENEROSITY: GIVING YOURSELF TO OTHERS

1. John Kasich, *Courage Is Contagious* (New York: Doubleday, 1998), 63–64.

2. Tony Bartelme, "Jack McConnell, M.D.: 'What Have You Done for Someone Today?,' " originally published in *Physician Executive* (November–December 2004), http://findarticles.com/p/articles/mi_m0843/is_6_30/ai_n8563545.

3. Ibid.
4. "Jack McConnell, M.D.: Curing a Clinic Shortage," *AARP* (January 2008). http://www.aarpmagazine.org/people/impact_awards_2007_ mcconnell.html.
5. Kasich, 63.
6. James Vollbracht, *Stopping at Every Lemonade Stand* (New York: Penguin, 2001), 86.
7. Annie Dillard, *The Writing Life* (New York: Harper Perennial, 1990), 32.
8. This provocative quote has been attributed to a number of people, including J. P. Morgan, John D. Rockefeller, and Winston Churchill.
9. Robertson McQuilkin, *A Promise Kept: The Story of an Unforgettable Love* (Carol Stream, Ill.: Tyndale House Publishers, 2006), 22.
10. David Bach, *The Automatic Millionaire* (New York: Broadway, 2004), 214.
11. C. S. Lewis, *Mere Christianity* (New York: Macmillan, 1952), 81–82.
12. 1 Corinthians 13:3, New International Version.
13. Frederick T. Gates, in 1906, quoted in the PBS documentary *American Experience*, "The Rockefellers, Part One."
14. Sheldon Vanauken, *A Severe Mercy* (New York: HarperCollins, 1977), 33.
15. For more information, visit www.joniandfriends.org.
16. Jack Canfield et al., *Chicken Soup for the Volunteer's Soul* (Deerfield Beach, Fla.: Health Communications, 2002), 60–63.
17. Mother Teresa, *Words to Live By* (Notre Dame, Ind.: Ave Maria Press, 1983), 79.
18. Quoted in Vollbracht, op. cit., 95.
19. Gary Tuchman, "The Kindness of Others . . ." Anderson Cooper Blog 360°, August 6, 2007, http://www.cnn.com/CNN/Programs/anderson.cooper.360/blog/archives/2007_08_05_ac360_archive.html.
20. Personal conversation, August 14, 2007. For more about Barbara's story, see www.barbaracurtis.com.
21. Anna Quindlen, *A Short Guide to a Happy Life* (New York: Random House, 2000), 16, 23.

CHAPTER EIGHT: HONESTY: REVEALING WHO YOU REALLY ARE

1. Nancy Kalish, "Honesty Survey: Discover How Honest You Are Compared to Others Across the Country," *Reader's Digest* (January 2004; results updated July 24, 2006), http://www.rd.com/content/do-you-lie/.
2. Cynthia Dermody, "Battle of the Sexes: Do Men and Women Lie Differently?" *Reader's Digest* (January 2004, results updated July 24, 2006), http://www.rd.com/content/are-men-or-women-more-honest/.
3. For further help in processing emotions in your relationships, see Dr. Chapman's books *The Five Love Languages* (1995) and *The Five Languages of Apology* (2006), published by Northfield Publishers.
4. Diane Komp, *The Anatomy of a Lie* (Grand Rapids, Mich.: Zondervan, 1998), 141–42.
5. Christopher Peterson and Martin E. P. Seligman, *Character Strengths and Virtues* (New York: Oxford University Press, 2004), 250.
6. Nancy Kalish, "How Honest Are You? Nearly 3,000 People Took This Survey. Their Answers Surprised Even Themselves," *Reader's Digest* (January 2004; results updated July 24, 2006), http://www.rd.com/content/how-honest-are-you/.
7. Quoted in Dana Knight, "What Workers Want," *Indianapolis Star*, August 5,

2007, http://www.gazette.com/articles/boss_25703_article.html/looks
_workers.html.

8. Paul Nicholson quoted in Nick McDermott, "Two Thirds Admit to Being Dishonest—and the Rest Are Probably Lying," *Daily Mail*, http://www.dailymail.co
.uk/pages/text/article.html?in_article_id=472709&in_page_id=1770&in_main
_section=News&in_sub_section=&in_chn_id=1469. See also Royal & SunAlliance, "UK Honesty Test Reveals a Nation of Liars," news release, March 8,
2007, http://www.royalsunalliance.com/royalsun/media/showpressitem.jsp?type=
press&ref=411&link=4&sub=56.

9. Quoted in Os Guinness, *Time for Truth* (Grand Rapids, Mich.: Baker, 2000), 10.

10. Ibid., 10–11.

11. Quoted ibid., 71–72.

12. Ambrose, op. cit., 67.

13. Quoted ibid., 59.

14. Quoted ibid., 67.

15. Quoted ibid., 68.

16. Ibid., 71.

17. Quoted ibid., 72.

18. Quoted ibid., 72–73.

CHAPTER NINE: MAKING LOVE A WAY OF LIFE IN MARRIAGE

1. Dorothy Tennov, *Love and Limerence: The Experience of Being in Love* (New York: Stein & Day, 1979), 142.

CHAPTER TEN: MAKING LOVE A WAY OF LIFE IN PARENTING

1. If you'd like further help in making love a way of life in parenting, you might read a book I wrote a number of years ago: Gary Chapman and Ross Campbell, *The Five Love Languages of Children* (Chicago: Northfield Publishers, 1997). If your children are grown, you may wish to read Ross Campbell and Gary Chapman, *Parenting Your Adult Child* (Chicago: Northfield Publishers, 1999).

CHAPTER TWELVE: THE MOTIVATION TO LOVE

1. Bill W., *Alcoholics Anonymous: The Story of How Many Thousands of Men and Women Have Recovered from Alcoholism* (New York: Alcoholics Anonymous World Services, 1976), 59.

2. John 13:12–15; Luke 22:26.

Readers' Guide

The questions and discussion topics that follow are intended to en-hance your reading of Dr. Gary Chapman's *Love as a Way of Life*. We hope they will enrich your experience of this exhilarating book. To find other great choices for reading groups, visit http://www.randomhouse .com/doubleday/readers/.

QUESTIONS AND TOPICS FOR DISCUSSION

1. In the introduction to *Love as a Way of Life*, Dr. Chapman describes the two responses he received when trying to trade seats on an air-plane. How easy is it for you to be a "friend in disguise"? How did this book change your beliefs about love and human nature?

2. Did you hesitate in signing the commitment at the end of Chapter One? Discuss the obstacles as well as the goals that played a part in your decision to embark on Dr. Chapman's journey to love.

3. What did you discover about your habits as you worked through the initial self-test on kindness? What are the most striking examples of kindness that you encountered once you began consciously looking for it in the world around you—at home, at work, with friends and family, and in other settings?

4. How does your approach to life compare to the results of the "marsh-mallow test" described in Chapter Three? What roles do patience and pride play in your daily interactions? Which one is more often rewarded in contemporary American culture?

5. What new insight did you gain from the stories of forgiveness in Chapter Four? What elements of Dr. Chapman's discussion, including trust, anger, and self-forgiveness, play roles in these scenarios, and in your life?

6. How did you feel about your score on the "Am I Courteous?" quiz? What opportunities exist for you to let courtesy flourish in your home and workplace, and in the ordinary places you visit frequently—from the grocery store to the ballpark?

7. Did the portrait of leadership offered at the beginning of Chapter Six surprise you? What is the greatest challenge you face in finding genuine humility within yourself, or within your community? What is the best way to recognize and perform acts of true humility, not ones based on the hope of praise or other rewards?

8. Throughout your life, how have you set your priorities regarding time and money? Which people, activities, and purchases have typically ranked the highest for you? What gifts of talent, time, and financial support are you ready to offer now? Which individuals do you most want to serve?

9. Have email and the Information Age made it harder to be dishonest, or does dishonesty spread more rapidly than ever before? Discuss the temptation of dishonesty as it has affected all levels of your life, from being honest with yourself and your loved ones to the issue of integrity in the world.

10. Though romantic relationships and marriage are most often associated with love, Dr. Chapman writes candidly about the difficulty in maintaining truly loving behavior even in these interactions. How does the concept of "servanthood" change the way you view dating and marriage?

11. Did you grow up in a family that demonstrated authentic love? As a parent or the member of an extended family, what can you do today to spark the habit of authentic love in future generations? How would Dr. Chapman's recommendations serve the children in your life?

12. Do your coworkers perceive the workplace as an opportunity for love? How does the concept of loving behavior change the way you think about work and livelihoods?

13. In your opinion, what are the most important philosophies of love presented by Dr. Chapman? Which of these will have the most lasting impact on your future?

14. Which of the personal stories presented in *Love as a Way of Life* resonated the most with your personal experiences? What does the range of examples—from the apologies of Lee Atwater in the political sphere to the strained marriage of Charlotte and John—indicate about the power of love to transform humanity?

15. Written for the twenty-first century, how does *Love as a Way of Life* build on the foundations established in Dr. Chapman's previous books?

ABOUT THE AUTHOR

GARY CHAPMAN is an ordained minister and marriage counselor. He is the author of the bestselling *The Five Love Languages*, which has sold more than 4 million copies and was the first in a popular series of love-language books. The host of a national radio program and a popular conference speaker, he lives in Winston-Salem, North Carolina.